CHANGING CHANNELS

The logos of some of the broadcast services for which Peter Grant
helped to obtain regulatory approval.

PETER S. GRANT

CHANGING CHANNELS

CONFESSIONS

OF A CANADIAN

COMMUNICATIONS

LAWYER

To Bill

Peter Grant

The Porcupine's Quill

Library and Archives Canada Cataloguing in Publication

Grant, Peter S., 1941–, author
    Changing channels : confessions of a Canadian communications
lawyer / Peter S. Grant.

Includes bibliographical references and index.

ISBN 978-0-88984-366-0 (pbk.)

    1. Grant, Peter S., 1941–. 2. Lawyers—Canada—Biography.
3. Telecommunication—Law and legislation—Canada. 4. McCarthy
& McCarthy— Biography. 5. Canadian Radio-Television and
Telecommunications Commission—Biography. I. Title.

KE2560.G726 2013   343.7109'94   C2013-906331-5

1   2   3   4   •   15   14   13

Published by The Porcupine's Quill, 68 Main Street, PO Box 160,
Erin, Ontario NOB 1TO. http://porcupinesquill.ca

Edited for the press by Chandra Wohleber.

Represented in Canada by Canadian Manda Group.
Trade orders are available from University of Toronto Press.

We acknowledge the support of the Ontario Arts Council and the Canada
Council for the Arts for our publishing program. The financial support of the
Government of Canada through the Canada Book Fund and the Government of
Ontario through the Ontario Media Development Corporation is also gratefully
acknowledged.

Canada

Ontario
Ontario Media Development
Corporation

Canada Council   Conseil des Arts
for the Arts   du Canada

ONTARIO ARTS COUNCIL
CONSEIL DES ARTS DE L'ONTARIO

To Grace, Kristin, Tom, Rory and Robbie

Table of Contents

8. BRANCHING OUT

9. CHANGING CHANNELS

A Showdown in Paris

It was a crisp fall day in Paris. Tourists lined up as usual to ascend the elevators to the top of the Eiffel Tower. From there, only a few blocks away they could see the UNESCO headquarters. Built in 1958 at the Place de Fontenoy, the UNESCO complex is easy to recognize. The main building is a Y-shaped structure which has won many architectural awards. The conference venue is a large accordion-shaped building with fluted concrete walls and a copper-plated fluted roof. And in its largest conference room, delegates from over 150 countries were engaged on that day—October 20, 2005—in the final day of arguments concerning a proposed new international treaty.

This was no ordinary debate, for this was no ordinary treaty. It was a treaty first suggested by a blue-ribbon trade advisory panel in Canada five and a half years earlier. It dealt with the delicate subject of cultural expression, as seen in books, magazines, music, film and television. The long and rather convoluted name of the treaty was the UNESCO Convention on the Protection and Promotion of the Diversity of Cultural Expressions. The treaty had thirty-five articles and it sought to enshrine the idea that countries were entitled to support space and choice for their local cultural expression without prohibiting foreign expression, and without fear of trade retaliation.

The convention was highly controversial. The United States, having re-joined UNESCO after a twelve-year absence, was trying feverishly to dilute the treaty or kill it. A few weeks earlier, it had played a last frantic card, a personal letter from Secretary of State Condoleezza Rice to all the UNESCO member country ambassadors. The letter criticized the draft convention, complained of the process and darkly hinted that the US might reconsider its support for UNESCO if member states agreed with the draft.

The Canadian delegation sat nervously in the crowded room. The fate of the draft treaty was out of its hands. Each country was now entitled to speak in support or in opposition to the treaty and then to exercise its vote. The US had risen a number of times to attack the draft treaty and to propose amendments to dilute it, but all had been voted down. Now as each country made its final statement, the Canadians watched with amazement as their lobbying efforts paid off. Through La Francophonie, Canada had enlisted Senegal and Benin to support the treaty, and other African countries then joined the chorus. Latin America's support was led by Brazil, as China and India led the Asian continent in support. But now the US turned hopefully to the United Kingdom, its ally in so many other venues. This year, the UK was the spokesperson for the European Community as well as for itself, and as its representative stood to speak, the room hushed. He started by commending UNESCO for initiating the process. But then, calmly and forcefully, he dismantled each of the US arguments in opposition to the treaty. The actual wording did not support any of these criticisms, he said. In fact, the treaty was very well balanced and should be strongly supported.

The voting then started. As the Canadians watched in surprised delight, country after country rose to endorse the document. The final vote was overwhelming: 148 in favour, 2 opposed (the US and Israel) and 4 abstaining.

On March 18, 2007, three months after at least thirty countries had ratified the treaty, it came into force. But it was widely understood that the Convention would not be seen to have broad applicability unless a significant number of countries—say fifty or sixty—ratified it. Soon enough this also occurred. In fact, by the middle of 2013, the Convention had been ratified by one hundred and twenty-eight countries around the world, including large and small players from every part of the globe. The international support for the Convention and the speed with which it was ratified were almost unprecedented. Even Australia, which had abstained from voting in 2005, had a change of government and ended up ratifying the treaty in 2009.

The result was a stunning victory for those who felt that the rules of international trade needed to defer to the desire for cultural diversity. At the same time, the debate revealed what appears to be an unbridgeable chasm between the position of the US and that of the rest of the world.

On October 20, 2005, at the time the vote on the Convention took place in Paris, I was back in Toronto. I was practising communications law with the law firm of McCarthy Tétrault LLP. But I had a special reason for savouring the UNESCO victory. For I had been a member of that blue-ribbon trade advisory panel in Canada and in fact I was the one who first suggested the idea of an international treaty to support cultural diversity. Later, after the Canadian government had endorsed the idea and efforts had begun to convince other countries around the world to support it, I had co-written a book supporting the idea of such a treaty.

As I celebrated the UNESCO vote, I had occasion to reflect on my somewhat curious career. As a Canadian lawyer, I was practising in the area of communications and cultural policy. Of course, when I was called to the bar in 1969, there was no such thing as a 'communications lawyer' in Canada. In that regard, I can immodestly take some credit for pioneering this field. At the same time, my experiences were at the centre of Canada's coming of age in this area.

We are now in an era when the communications industry is 'converged' to an unprecedented degree. Two decades ago, the big news was the entry of the telephone companies into broadcast distribution and the entry of the cable companies into telephony. But in the last decade, these same companies have acquired most of Canada's radio and television programming services as well. This degree of consolidation is frankly unprecedented around the world.

My career exhibited the same convergence between content and carriage. My initial interest was in how the Canadian content rules applied to Canadian television. But I rapidly became interested in how the telephone companies were regulated, and I spent a number of years fighting Bell Canada for fun and profit. Later on, as my career developed, I also found myself attracted to the Canadian cultural industries—including book and magazine publishing, sound recording, and film and television production. This turned out to be highly prescient, since communications and cultural policies in this country are deeply intertwined.

My journey as a communications lawyer reflected Canada's journey towards a distinctive place in the world of popular culture. In particular, I ended up being involved in the following stories:

• How a number of popular Canadian television channels—including The Movie Network, Family Channel, Showcase, W Network, Business News Network and History Television—got their broadcast licences
• How and why a number of Canadian-owned cultural industries, including Canadian book publishers and record companies, broke free from the multinational companies that dominate the field

• How cable companies and telecom carriers took over the Canadian broadcasting industry and discovered the curious economics of Canadian content

• The rise of the independent-television-production industry in Canada and how it survives despite the dominance of Hollywood films and TV shows

• The real story behind the Chapters/Indigo merger and how it has affected the creation and distribution of Canadian books

• What happened when *Sports Illustrated* attempted to sell Canadian ads in its US magazine and how Canada lost a battle at the World Trade Organization but ultimately won the war

• How the lessons of the past played out as Canada's content creators sought to maintain their voices in the face of new technology

All of these events involve Canada's cultural industries and the government policies that support them.

It may be surprising that someone coming from small-town Canada could be involved in all of these happenings. Before I became a communications lawyer, in fact, I nourished the idea that I might become a composer and arranger of popular music. Obviously I got sidetracked: as I disclose in this memoir, my whole career as a lawyer focusing on Canadian content and communications law was based on a paper I wrote in second-year law school.

But more about that later. In the meantime, how did it all get started?

1. Kapuskasing

ABOUT MY FATHER

My father, Norman Stewart Grant, was born in 1899. He was the only child of Alexander Grant and Margaret McLachlan. Alexander Grant was born in 1874 and spent some time working in Western Canada before he moved back east, married and bought a farm in the Brussels area in southwestern Ontario.

By all accounts, farm life was hardscrabble in those days. But the Grant homestead valued literacy, and my grandfather subscribed to newsletters issued by the Ontario Agricultural College in Guelph. One issue predicted the imminent arrival of potato blight and recommended that farmers treat their potato seeds with a chemical solution before planting. My grandfather told me of a Sunday dinner in his home later that year, to which the neighbouring farmers had been invited. His wife brought out a dish heaping full of delicious potatoes. 'Where did you get those potatoes?' his neighbours asked incredulously. 'Why, right out there in the field behind the farmhouse,' he replied. Of course the neighbours couldn't believe it since all their potatoes had been hit with the blight. So they scrambled out to the back forty in their Sunday best and dug up potatoes with their hands. Sure enough, all his potatoes had been spared because he had treated the potato eyes with the recommended solution before planting them. I always loved this story and so did my children when I recounted it to them years later.

My father went to a one-room public school in Brussels, Ontario, and then to high school in Stratford. He was the only student from his one-room school to go to university. He went into chemical engineering because it was the least expensive course he could take at the University of Toronto.

He had been too young to serve in the war, but at university found himself in classes with returning veterans. He had a strong baritone voice and became the head of the Hart House Music Committee. He also went out with Margaret Stevenson, a Stratford girl who was studying at the Toronto Conservatory of Music.

My father, Norman Grant, as mayor of Kapuskasing.

Once he graduated, my father pursued a career in the pulp and paper industry. He worked as a chemical engineer in mills in various Ontario towns: Fort Frances, Kenora, Fort William and finally, Kapuskasing, where he was the technical director of Spruce Falls Power & Paper Company Ltd. In the meantime, his father, Alex Grant, had sold the farm and moved to Stratford after his wife died in 1937. There, he became a much-loved janitor at Hamlet Public School. After he retired from that, he moved in with our family, living with us in Fort William and then Kapuskasing until 1954, when he was moved to a nursing home in Stratford a year before his death.

My father had an excellent speaking voice and instilled confidence in everyone he met. He knew how to run a meeting. He was calm, confident and a man of integrity and character. He could have been a great lawyer. As it was, he plunged into local politics wherever he lived. He was on the school board in Fort William, and in Kapuskasing he became an alderman, then served as mayor from 1957 until he retired in 1965. When he was elected mayor of Kap in 1957, he garnered 73.6 percent of the vote, the highest percentage of votes achieved by anyone in a town over 5,000 in Ontario that year. Thereafter he ran unopposed and was elected by acclamation.

During his tenure as mayor, he organized the repaving of all the streets, the amalgamation of the town with adjoining built-up areas and the takeover of the Community Club and its conversion to a municipal centre. He was also active in lobbying the provincial government to improve the roads throughout northeastern Ontario.

In 1960, he joined the board of governors of Huntingdon University, which was part of the federated universities in Laurentian University just being launched in Sudbury.

In January 1963, my father was involved in the Reesor Siding incident, which attracted national attention. That month, the woodcutters of Spruce Falls had gone out on strike, seeking higher wages. However, independent local farmer-settlers were also suppliers of pulpwood to the mill and they continued to stack piles of wood along railroad sidings for the company. Tensions between the strikers and the settlers heightened. As the mayor of Kap, my father was quoted in the *Globe and Mail* saying, 'These settlers are getting so desperate they are going to go into the bush with guns and shoot anyone who tries to interfere with their cutting.' He also sent a telegram to the attorney general of Ontario asking for police reinforcements. There was no response. But my father's warning proved prophetic.

On February 10, 1963, a shipment of six hundred cords of pulpwood was scheduled to be loaded onto waiting railcars at Reesor Siding, about halfway between Kap and Hearst along Highway 11. At midnight four hundred unarmed union members showed up to disrupt the shipment. Twenty settlers were on hand to protect the pulpwood. Police had erected a chain line to keep the groups apart, but as the union members advanced, the settlers began shooting, killing three union members and wounding eight others.

Following this deadly confrontation, an additional two hundred OPP officers were sent to Kapuskasing. Within a week, the strike was settled. The union members were charged with illegal assembly and fined. All the settlers were charged with non-capital murder but the charges were dismissed because of lack of evidence, although they were fined for firearms violations. The Reesor Siding incident has been seen as one of the defining labour conflicts in Canadian history.

My father was a heavy smoker and had a weak heart. Early in 1965 he announced that he would not stand for re-election in the fall and for health reasons would be moving to Toronto. The *Timmins Daily Press* devoted a full-page editorial to him on March 13, 1965: 'Great Loss for Kapuskasing.' The editorial went on:

It would be hard to find another community in the North, and perhaps across all of Ontario, where a mayor's post was held with more dignity and ability. An educated man, Mayor Grant brought to his office the assets of sound reasoning and logic that are too often lacking in elected municipal officialdom.

In September 1965, my father moved with my mother to an apartment on Alexander Street in the midtown area of Toronto. The *Toronto Daily Star* (its name later shortened to the *Toronto Star*) noted this in a front-page story with the title: 'He's coming here ... for the sun!'[1] The story quoted him as saying that his decision to live in Toronto was the result of a heart condition: 'The cold air shortens my breath, something that isn't good for my health.'

Two days later, Gary Lautens, the humour columnist for the *Toronto Daily Star*, devoted a full column to his arrival.[2] Some excerpts:

Toronto got a terrific boost the other day. Mayor Norman S. Grant of Kapuskasing … confesses that he can no longer endure those cold Northern Ontario winters and plans to retire to a more moderate paradise.

Where? To Toronto, of course.

Apparently he intends to buy a small orange grove in Scarboro or, perhaps, a sugar plantation in Don Mills and spend the rest of his days basking in the tropic sunshine of Metro …

There's no reason why we can't grab a big piece of the winter tourist trade. If Toronto is considered a regular Honolulu by people in Kapuskasing, you can imagine our image up in Yellowknife or at Moose Factory.

My father was tremendously amused by this attention. But his health declined further. After suffering a stroke, he passed away in late 1966.

ABOUT MY MOTHER

My mother, Margaret Glenn Stevenson, was the second of four children of a well-off family in Stratford. Her father, John Stevenson, had dropped out of school to go into real estate and insurance and did very well at it. He also served a stint as the mayor of Stratford. His wife, Catherine Robertson, was the youngest of seven children, six of them boys.

My mother was a remarkable woman. Born in 1903, she went to Stratford schools but studied piano with Cora Ahrens before going to the Toronto Conservatory of Music (which became the Royal Conservatory of Music in 1947). There she studied under the Danish pianist Viggo Kihl. He was a tough taskmaster and she frequently broke into tears at his lessons. However, she ended up getting her licentiate diploma in 1922 with the highest marks in the country. Years later, Viggo Kihl toured across the country and gave a piano recital in Fort William. My mother was delighted to invite him to her home, where he regaled my parents with anecdotes about life as a concert pianist.

But my mother was not cut out to be a concert pianist herself. Instead, she returned to Stratford where she opened a studio and began

My mother, Margaret Stevenson Grant, as adjudicator
of the Kiwanis Music Festival in Toronto.

giving piano and vocal lessons. There she found her real métier. She was a superb piano teacher and later became a distinguished adjudicator.

In 1928, my mother married my father in Knox Presbyterian Church in Stratford. Right after the wedding, they went over to the Stratford hospital to visit my mother's favourite uncle, Uncle Pete. His full name was Peter Stewart Robertson and he had been unable to attend the wedding because he had sustained a leg injury while riding a sulky. My mother came into the hospital room dressed in her bridal outfit. She was very close to her uncle because he had lost his only son in the war. As she left the hospital room, he looked up from his bed and said, 'You know, Margaret, Peter's a nice name for a son ...' She never forgot this and when I was born in 1941 she named me after him.

My mother moved with my father to Fort Frances in 1928, to Kenora in 1930, to Fort William in 1932 and to Kapuskasing in 1946. They stayed in Kap until 1965, when they moved to Toronto. She became the centre of musical life in all the Northern Ontario communities in which she lived. When she arrived in Kapuskasing, her first step was to create a Girls' Glee Club, which was active until the local high school hired a music director and a school choir was formed. My mother not only taught piano to a number of students, but also gave pointers to all the piano teachers in the area, including a nun who was teaching piano in Smooth Rock Falls, a community about 60 kilometres east of Kap. She would bring her whole class to our house and my mother would assess each student and then give the nun new ideas on how to proceed with their instruction.

In 1959, she was asked to adjudicate piano classes in the Toronto Kiwanis Festival, the largest music festival in the Commonwealth. She did extraordinarily well at this task, and was asked back to adjudicate for a number of years. In 1976, she wrote a book called *Your Child and the Piano: How to Enrich and Share in Your Child's Musical Experience*.[3] The book reflected much more than her years of experience as a music teacher; it also reflected her warmth and humanity. Included with the musical insights were little nuggets like these:

• I am well aware that, in the average home, some weeks are disorganized and nothing goes right.
• I have been a parent, a teacher and an adjudicator. Of the three, being a parent is the worst.
• No one gains by humiliation and no child should be put in a position of

having to accept his or her own performance with shame or resignation.
• Avoid being too critical of experiments. If your small child gives you a cookie with a grubby hand, are you not still pleased and grateful?
• Start fresh! Without that credo, many of us would have gotten nowhere.

Well into her eighties, my mother continued to teach piano to a number of adult students, working out of the apartment on Alexander Street in Toronto. She passed away in 1995 at the age of ninety-one.

MY EARLY YEARS IN KAPUSKASING

I was born and raised in small-town Canada. My birthdate was November 26, 1941, eleven days before the Japanese attack on Pearl Harbor. I was born in the hospital in Port Arthur, Ontario, right next door to Fort William. (Years later, in 1970, Port Arthur and Fort William merged to become Thunder Bay.) In 1946, when I was four, the family moved from Fort William to the town of Kapuskasing, where I lived until I went off to university in 1960.

Kapuskasing is 825 kilometres north of Toronto. It lies at the western end of the Great Clay Belt, a band of fertile soil sitting on the Canadian Shield just south of the Hudson Bay Lowlands. In 1910, an astute surveyor for the National Transcontinental Railway (later the CNR) noted that the point where the railway would cross the Kapuskasing River would make an ideal location for a town. Unlike the areas farther south, where the Canadian Shield was covered only by poorly drained muskeg, the rich clay soil in the Kap area looked like it might support farming. A few years later, an experimental farm was set up at the site and operated for many years.

In the end, the short growing season proved to be a daunting problem for would-be farmer-settlers. But that was not the end of the matter. All around the Kap area was a treasure trove of black spruce, a species that was somewhat small for lumber, but perfect for pulpwood, the key ingredient of newsprint. And the Kapuskasing River flowed north to join the Matagami, where it could be harnessed for hydro power at a place called Smoky Falls. Astute promoters acquired the rights to the timber limits and it all came together in the 1920s, when Kimberly-Clark and the *New York Times* financed the creation of a pulp-and-paper mill on the south side of the railway that crossed the Kap River. The company was called Spruce Falls Power & Paper, and eventually it produced both newsprint and creped wadding (from which tissue paper was made).

When Kap was created in 1927, it benefited from having a specially designed townsite following the principles of the Garden City movement in England. The town slogan was 'Model Town of the North' and there was an extensive riverside park, and central public spaces with radiating avenues. A prominent feature was the main shopping area, a small 'Circle' where the stores surrounded a fountain. The company also built some imposing brick buildings designed in the neo-Tudor style, including Diamond Jubilee Public School, Sensenbrenner Hospital, the Kapuskasing

My brother, John, and I are pictured here with Mother.
We hated the short pants.

At the Kapuskasing Winter Carnival in 1946.
Somehow I managed to stay on my skates
without falling.

Inn and the Community Club. This last building was a large, multipurpose recreational facility with an auditorium, library, bowling alley, meeting rooms and soda bar. All these elements gave Kap a quite distinctive look compared with other towns in Northern Ontario.

The school system in Kap was first-rate, a feature that was researched by my parents before my father decided to take the job of technical director at Spruce Falls in 1946. We lived on Riverside Drive, only a block from the Circle, and right across from the tennis courts in the riverside park.

My brother, John, was three and a half years older so when I was in public school he was in high school; when I reached high school he was off to university. Accordingly, we were 'out of sync.' I had relatively little interaction with my brother and we had quite different circles of friends.

I have few memories from my early years but I do vaguely recall an incident that is immortalized in a hilarious photo of me at age five, on wobbly skates, dressed in top hat and tails, and being held up by two girls my age. As part of the annual Winter Carnival, I had been chosen to be propelled on the ice in this garb. I circled the arena on my wobbly skates without falling and got a warm round of applause for doing so. There is a tendency in our life today to deride this sort of event as being typical of what passes for amusement in small-town Canada on a winter night. But there is a kind of sweetness to it that I find very appealing.

There was no kindergarten in the public school in Kap, so my parents decided to enrol me in a kindergarten at the Immaculate Conception Catholic school. My brother helpfully told me that the nuns whipped the kids regularly, so on opening day, I had to be carried into the kindergarten bodily by my mother, screaming and yelling. However, I got acclimated within a few minutes as the nuns gently showed me the toy house at the back of the schoolroom.

My time at Immaculate Conception only lasted a few weeks, though. Even at that age, the nuns were intent on drilling the children in the Catholic catechism. I apparently arrived home mouthing large extracts from it, and my mother felt that life was guilt-ridden enough without having this added to my burdens. So I was pulled out of kindergarten.

Grade 1 at Diamond Jubilee Public School was a different story. I not only welcomed going to grade 1 but in advance of arriving, I practised bowing gravely to the teacher and saying, 'How do you *do*, Miss Middlemiss?' to the vast amusement of my parents.

An incident that my mother frequently mentioned to me was my encounter with Charles Atlas. Or, as I then pronounced it, 'Char-less Atlas.' Yes, this was the famous Charles Atlas who according to the pictures in the ads had sand kicked in his face when he was a ninety-seven-pound scrawny weakling and later developed into a muscular man. When I was seven years old, dismayed with my puny rib cage, I filled out the coupon requesting information on his unique Dynamic Tension lessons.

Of course what followed was a series of letters exhorting me to buy the lessons. The letters got more and more threatening. I became annoyed and wrote a strong letter of protest, which included the accusation: 'CHARLES ATLAS: YOU ARE A FAKE!'

My mother kept the letter for her private amusement and sent a more formal letter simply pointing out that the Peter S. Grant they were haranguing in Kapuskasing was only seven, and please don't bother him again. So the letters stopped.

We had a cocker spaniel named Bunty, and I spent endless hours playing with Bunty and my friends at the river's edge, either in the park or in the wooded area farther along the river where it was possible to build 'forts' in the woods. It was also possible to climb onto rocky outcroppings in the river, where you could skip flat stones on the water. One time I was playing with some boys on a little peninsula and as I leaned down to pick up a likely flat stone, one of my friends who was on the main shore skipped a rock across the water. As it hit the water, it skimmed upwards and struck my left temple, just in front of my ear. Blood started gushing. For some reason I felt nothing except for a bit of throbbing. I walked back home and rang the doorbell. My mother, who was having tea with some of her friends, came to the door and looked down at me. I was standing there with my T-shirt drenched in blood. My mother was aghast but she calmly and quickly drove me to the Sensenbrenner Hospital, six blocks away, where Dr McTavish closed the wound with six stitches. To this day I have a slight scar just below the hairline on my left temple.

By the time I was in grade 7, my parents had acquired a Webcor-Chicago tape recorder and this added a whole new element to my life. I began writing radio plays with my friends and me doing the voices and sound effects. In grade 8, I wrote a short play based on the famous scene in *The Adventures of Tom Sawyer* where he persuades his chums to whitewash the fence. It was performed in front of the school auditorium.

The CBC radio network played American radio drama like *Boston*

Blackie and *The Lone Ranger*. It also featured *Wayne and Shuster* every Saturday, followed by *The Happy Gang*. I was a devoted follower of *Wayne and Shuster*. Once, during a trip to Toronto, my mother called up the CBC and wangled an invitation for me to attend a live-to-air taping of the radio show in its studio at Yonge and Summerhill, where I heard Eric Christmas portraying Madame Humperdinck. Like any boy of that age, I was fascinated by how they did sound effects on radio drama.

In aid of civics, each fall the public school would replicate the municipal elections with its own mock election. Once the candidates for local office had been nominated, the school would choose students to represent each candidate and they would each speak to the assembly in a mock public meeting. Ballots would be prepared for the mock election and the students would vote; the results would be announced a week before the real election.

During this period, my father was first a councillor, and then was elected mayor. So, of course, I was invited to speak in his name at the assembly. All I can recall is that my speech ended up with a few couplets:

Norm Grant, he is a hardy Scot—
He'll save the pennies that you've got.

He'll work to keep the taxes down,
And still make Kap a better town!

As I recall, I also gave the valedictory address in rhyming couplets.

By grade 6, I had been offered the chance to skip a grade. However, my parents were opposed. My brother had skipped a grade and he had paid a social price in classes where everyone was bigger and taller. The school argued that if I wasn't accelerated, I would be bored with school and become 'lazy.' But my mother resolved to keep me busy with extracurricular activities.

The first of these activities was music. I studied piano, ostensibly with one of the local teachers, but I was really under the guidance of my mother. She was a superb piano teacher and I was a star pupil. For two summers, when I was twelve and thirteen, I attended the National Music Camp in Interlochen, Michigan, one of only twelve Canadians in a camp of eight hundred. But my mother did not want me to learn piano at Interlochen since she felt she could teach me anything in that area. Instead, I went as a cornet player.

Now in fact I was a mediocre cornet player. The only teacher in town was Omer Poulin, the town's fire chief, whose repertoire focused on 'The Last Post' and 'Taps'. However, after working my way through the 'E-Z Method' for trumpet and cornet, I was sent off to Interlochen to play in the intermediate band. In a concert band with twenty-two players in the trumpet section, I ended up in twenty-second place, which correctly reflected my ability on the cornet.

Back home, my mother entered me in the various music festivals that were a feature of Northern Ontario life: the Cochrane Music Festival, where I won the Rose Bowl, and the Porcupine Music Festival in Timmins, where I competed in the boy-soprano class, the piano class and the trumpet/cornet class. For good measure, in high school I was also the piano accompanist for one of my mother's vocal students, Roberta Ross, a fine singer who was competing in a girl-soprano class.

The test piece was a tricky song with a complex piano accompaniment but Roberta and I worked it up and travelled to Timmins for the competition. Upon arrival at the hall, I discovered to my horror that I had forgotten to bring the music! I was too afraid to mention this to either my mother or Roberta. In due course our turn was called and I walked out and sat down at the piano. Roberta stood in front of the piano. The adjudicator nodded at us to proceed and I began the piece, playing it entirely from memory. Roberta sang well, not aware that I had no music.

We completed the song and I am happy to say Roberta won the class. The adjudicator went out of his way to commend the accompanist (me) for having memorized the music. I then confessed to both Roberta and my mother that I had misplaced the music and had no choice but to play without it. They looked at me with a mixture of horror, amazement and admiration.

In October 1951, when I was nine, Princess Elizabeth and her husband, Prince Philip, visited Kapuskasing. Presumably they chose Kap to be part of their first visit to Canada because it was the 'Model Town of the North,' but I think a more important feature was the fact that its airport was served by Trans-Canada Air Lines (later Air Canada), so the royal couple could arrive and leave by air.

The town spruced itself up for the occasion and visitors came in from all the nearby communities. The prince and princess stayed overnight at the Kap Inn. The royal couple's motorcade passed right in front of our house four times, so that even my grandfather could see the princess clearly from his second-floor bedroom window. I prepared a large cedar-framed sign to put on our property, facing the street. It read: WILL YE NO COME BACK AGAIN? My brother was in the high school cadets and they were lined up in front of the Kap Inn as Princess Elizabeth entered the building. My parents attended a gathering at the Community Club where they were presented to the royal couple.

My father later told me a memorable story about the newspaper coverage of the trip. Of course all the Toronto papers sent their reporters to cover the royal visit. They all filed their stories at the CN Telegraph Office at the railway station, where they had to wait to get their stories out. The *New York Times* sent Clifton Daniel, one of its top reporters, to Kap to cover the trip. I suppose that since the *Times* owned 50 percent of the local pulp-and-paper mill, they thought the visit was worth covering. (Daniel later covered the queen's coronation in London.) However, the *Times* reporter did not need to go to the Telegraph Office to file his story. Instead, all he had to do was walk into the shipping room at the mill, where there was a direct communications line to the press room of the *New York Times* in New York City. Normally, it was used for shipping purposes since half of the newsprint for the *Times* came from the Kap mill. But on this day, the line served double duty and, to my dad's amusement, gave the *Times* an advantage over all the other reporters.

For many years after, the Kap Inn displayed the registration journal from the royal visit in a glass case in its lobby, where the signatures *Elizabeth R* and *Philip* could be seen in large flowing script. It also named its cocktail lounge the Princess Lounge. Years later, after going through various owners, the Kap Inn closed in 2002, and the building burned down in 2007. The OPP built its area headquarters on the site.

A few small towns in Canada like to elevate themselves by referring to celebrities who were born or raised there. For example, Timmins, Ontario, claims Shania Twain as its own, and Stratford, Ontario, has a road sign on the way into town honouring local boy and hockey star Howie Morenz. But Kap has generally escaped notoriety on this ground. Perhaps its closest claim to fame came on August 14, 1954, when James Cameron, later to be the world-famous director of *Titanic* and *Avatar*, was born in Kap. His father was an electrical engineer with the Spruce Falls company until the family moved to Chippewa, Ontario, in 1958, when James Cameron was four and I was sixteen. As a result, I have no memory whatever of him and I expect that he has little if any memory of his days in Kap.

HIGH SCHOOL

By the time I reached Kapuskasing District High School in the fall of 1955, my piano skills had improved and I was increasingly attracted to popular music. My mother did not discourage this. She never thought I should try to be a professional musician, but felt that music would be a wonderful hobby for me if I reached a level where I could be a 'triple threat' on the piano—able to sight-read, to improvise by ear and to play technically challenging pieces in the classical repertoire.

My mother had a unique way of teaching sight-reading. She would bring out the United Church hymnary and open it at a random hymn. Then, sitting at the piano, I would be challenged to sight-read the hymns as fast as I could, for five minutes. The hymns were typically set to four voices (soprano, alto, tenor, bass), and a hymn in one key and time signature would be followed by a hymn in an entirely different key or time signature. My mother, keeping track of the five-minute limit in the kitchen, would call, 'STOP!' when the time was up. We would count the number of chords I'd played successfully and deduct five points for each error. (My mother could easily detect errors, even listening from another room.) The score would then be entered on a graph. After a year of this, I could sight-read any hymn fairly accurately 'at speed.'

Then I graduated to sight-reading Gilbert and Sullivan scores, which often meant negotiating a right-hand arpeggio against an *um-pa-pa* left hand. To sight-read these at speed, you have to quickly form a *gestalt* of the chord involved and then play a version of it, devil take the hind-most. I turned out to be a voracious sight-reader. To this day, I am an excellent sight-reader at the piano, which has come in very handy at times. I am eternally grateful to my mother's foresight in emphasizing this part of my musical training.

Playing the classical repertoire, I worked my way up to an AMus diploma at the Western Conservatory of Music, in London, Ontario, achieved in the summer of 1959 when I was seventeen. But that was the end of my classical career. I had already plunged into popular music. By

The Unknowns, 1957. From left: Butch Turcotte, Winston McIntosh, Ken Ross, Eddy Lepp; and me, at the piano.

grades 10 and 11, I was regularly accompanying the school choir in concerts, including its performance of *The Pirates of Penzance*. And I started three musical groups. One was a small dance band (piano, drums, bass, sax and clarinet) called the Downbeats. We played stock arrangements of popular standards from the 1930s at school dances. With a name like the Downbeats, it was inevitable that the group would be humorously dubbed the Deadbeats. Since I was shy with girls, I found playing in the band a convenient way not to have to ask anyone to the school dances.

My two other high school musical initiatives took the form of vocal groups. I became the pianist-arranger for a group of four boys called the Unknowns and for a group of four girls called the Emeralds.

The Unknowns were Eddy Lepp, Winston McIntosh, Ken Ross and Butch Turcotte. I wrote all the arrangements and accompanied them on the piano. They sang tunes made popular by the Kingston Trio, like 'The Lonesome Traveller' and 'The Rock Island Line'. We also invented some songs, notably one called 'Sputnik Rock', which started out with the boys following an imaginary satellite in the sky while making *beep-beep* noises. The chorus consisted of repeated lines of 'Well it's … sssss … Sputnik Rock!' against a boogie-woogie background. The Unknowns bought identical white sweaters with black flecks at Charlie's Men's Wear on the

The Emeralds. From left: Rosie Ayora, Sue Barrette, Penny Wiley, Patsy Burdett.

Circle in Kap and thought they looked quite cool. They sang at school functions but their big accomplishment was appearing on a talent show called *Focus*, on CFCL-TV, Timmins, which was seen back in Kap.

The Emeralds were Rosalyne (Rosie) Ayora, Suzanne (Sue) Barrette, Patsy Burdett and Penny Wiley. Frankly, they were better singers than the Unknowns, and I was able to write more sophisticated vocal arrangements for them. Their songs were in the tradition of the Andrews Sisters.

During my high school years in Kap, I also developed as a jazz pianist. My mother was no help there: her idea of popular music was 'Blue Moon,' with rolling chords in the left hand and octaves in the right. By contrast, I wanted to play like Erroll Garner or Oscar Peterson. I remember recording selections from Garner's best-selling album *Concert by the Sea* on our Webcor-Chicago tape recorder at a speed of 7 1/2 inches per second. Then, putting the tape recorder beside me on the piano bench, I would replay the recording at half-speed, 3 3/4 inches per second.

This would lower the pitch by an octave but make it possible to follow the rapid passages. I would stop and start the playback while I worked out bar by bar what Garner was doing at top speed in his right hand. I also taught myself to read chord symbols, and bought books showing the chord patterns used by pianists like Dave Brubeck and George Shearing. The result of all this was that by the time I arrived at university, I was a fairly competent (albeit self-taught) jazz pianist.

I generally placed second in the class, and in grade 13 I won the four-year Spruce Falls scholarship to university and a silver bowl inscribed with the words *Quisque Pro Omnibus* for being the best all-round student of my year. (My brother, John, had also won both awards before me.)

Looking back on my life in Kap, there is one feature that now strikes me as unusual. The kids came from a huge variety of ethnic groups, and I never thought twice about it. Apart from the large number of Francophones (their families made up 60 percent of the town's population), there were kids of Irish, Polish, Ukrainian, Scandinavian, Japanese, Jamaican and German extraction in my school. As well, African-American servicemen frequently came into town on leave from their duties at the Lowther USAF base, 48 kilometres west of town (this was one of the Pine Tree installations).

As I reminisce about my life in Kap, I have to say that my parents were tremendously supportive. Being raised in small-town Canada did not deprive me of a first-rate education. We had a set of *Compton's Pictured Encyclopedia* designed for school-age children as well as the university-level *Chambers's Encyclopaedia*. They subscribed to the *Saturday Review of Literature* and bought classical recordings of chamber music. Most summers, we would travel down to Stratford to visit my mother's family and attend the plays. In 1954, the Canadian Players (featuring actors drawn from the Stratford Festival) came to town and performed Shaw's *Saint Joan* at the Community Club. Afterwards, the cast was invited to our home where Douglas Campbell and his wife, Ann Casson, William Hutt, Bruno Gerussi and William Needles regaled us with theatre stories. It was a wonderful evening.

My parents also sent me and my brother to Quebec as part of an annual three-week program called Visites Interprovinciales. We were each placed with a Francophone family so we would have the opportunity to learn conversational French. In the summer of 1956, I was placed in

Ste. Rose, a community north of Montreal, in the home of a dealer in John Deere implements. In the summer of 1957, I went to St. Urbain, near Baie St. Paul and Murray Bay, Quebec, and stayed at the home of a game warden of the Laurentides Provincial Park. I would like to say that I became fluently bilingual through these visits but in fact I emerged with only a bare facility in high school French. I greatly regret not having had French immersion at an early age but it was not available as part of the educational system in those days.

SUMMER JOBS

While I had the benefit of the Spruce Falls scholarship during my years at university, I also needed a summer job. For six summers, I worked for the Spruce Falls Power & Paper Company. In successive summers, I worked as a paint scraper in the townsite department, as a statistician in the cost accounting department (keeping track of the output of the four papermaking machines in operation), and even as a landscape gardener in Smoky Falls, a tiny community 65 kilometres north of Kap that had a dam and hydro power site that provided power to the Spruce Falls operation.

In June 1961, I also worked as a census enumerator in the Kap area. I was assigned a section of Brunetville, a built-up neighbourhood just east of Kap that was later amalgamated with the town. Based on the 1956 census, this area was expected to contain relatively few houses per mile. Accordingly the per-person rate I could charge to Statistics Canada for carrying out the census was quite a bit higher than the rate set for urban areas. By 1961, however, there were many more houses along those streets. Even more important, the homes were overwhelmingly French Catholic and typically had ten to twelve children per family. So by going door to door and filling out the census form for each child, I made far more money than expected.

In the summer of 1964, apart from a three-week stint at the Eastman School of Music in Rochester, New York (more on that later), I worked as a research assistant to Dr S. D. Clark, the head of the Department of Sociology, University of Toronto, on a project in Kapuskasing being carried out for the Royal Commission on Bilingualism and Biculturalism.

As I mentioned earlier, in the fall of 1965 my father's heart condition compelled him to retire, sell the house in Kap and move the family to Toronto. In 1966, I found a summer job working for the Ontario government in its Trade and Industry Department in Toronto. And in the summer of 1967, I worked as a tour guide for Horizon Holidays, taking groups on trips across Canada. That warrants a story in itself, which I tell a little later on.

RELIGION

My parents had been married in a Presbyterian church in Stratford but when they arrived in Kapuskasing, they joined the local United Church since there was no Presbyterian church in Kap at the time.

My father became an elder in the United Church in Kap, and my mother took great pleasure in occasions when the entire family attended church together. My mother enrolled me in Sunday school and I dutifully attended. One Sunday, she had to travel to Toronto for a skin graft operation, and she took me along with her. To maintain my perfect-attendance record at Sunday school, she dropped me off at Timothy Eaton Memorial Church on St. Clair Avenue West, where I sat in with a group of boys my age. I was appalled to discover that the boys either ignored or jeered at the unfortunate Sunday school teacher. It turned out that the only reason they attended Sunday school at all was to qualify for time on the hockey rink behind the church!

While still living in Kap, I had learned to play the church organ and sometimes replaced the regular organist at Sunday services. However, by the time I left for university, I had drifted away from religious belief, even though the United Church was probably the least demanding of the religious institutions at the time.

One of the reasons for my doubts came from my musical background. It was certainly evident to me as an organist that people could gain an emotional catharsis from music played in church. But I also realized that this derived from the music itself and not from religious faith. Anyone versed in music could note that the most popular Christmas songs were written by Jewish composers, and that an anti-semitic composer like Richard Wagner could also write great music. This certainly gave me pause.

But the other point that gnawed at me was the apparent unfairness of a religion that addressed its revelations only to potential adherents in a small country in the Middle East at a certain time in the distant past, thereby consigning all other humans in the world at the time to some version of hell. I could never get over this rather unsettling problem and I soon lost any faith I may have had as a child. From university onwards, I became quite interested in topics like evolution, archaeology and higher criticism by biblical scholars, and this only reinforced my departure from religious faith.

MY RETURN TO KAP YEARS LATER

After my parents moved to Toronto in the fall of 1965, there was no reason for me to return to Kap. The house on Riverside Drive had been sold. Most of my school friends had left town to go to university and I lost touch with them.

I did not return to Kap for over twenty years. However, in 1986, the high school there had a fiftieth-anniversary reunion. Having just married my second wife I decided to go with her to see what the town was like. My first visit was to my former home on Riverside Drive and I was amused to learn that it was now occupied by nuns. The coal room in the basement had been converted into a small chapel. Over the next two days, I walked up and down the Kap streets. All the houses and distances seemed much smaller than I had imagined.

Twelve years later, I returned to Kap for a few days, this time with my wife and four young children (a girl and three boys). By this time, my old home had been resold and it was now a bed-and-breakfast called the Northern Oasis. The second floor had been torn out and replaced with three honeymoon bedrooms, each with a heart-shaped Jacuzzi tub. The chapel in the basement was now a sex boutique and each bedroom had a VCR and a selection of sex tapes on offer. My wife and I booked the entire place for my family to stay for two nights. (The sex tapes were discreetly moved to the basement.)

This trip allowed me to introduce my children to the riverside park where I had played as a kid and I showed them where I had been hit with a rock skimmed over the water. In the Circle, the town had replaced the fountain with a circle of water jets shooting up from the ground. My four kids happily jumped over and around the jets, getting thoroughly drenched.

A few years later, I returned to Kap again, this time with my three boys and two of their friends, taking a week to drive there and back in a minivan, with overnights in Sudbury and Timmins on the way north and in Temagami and Huntsville on the way back to Toronto. Again we stayed at the Northern Oasis, where the five boys enjoyed the Jacuzzi tubs. But by this time the town had really changed. The public school building was gone, leaving an empty field in its place. The hospital had been converted to a retirement home and a new medical centre had been constructed in a subdivision of the town. The high school building had been converted to a combined elementary and high school. The Strand Theatre, which had stood for years just behind our house, was now a furniture store.

In fact, Kap had come through a near-death experience. In 1991, the owners of Spruce Falls, faced with higher costs and declining demand, decided to close the mill. Tense negotiations ensued between the company and the Ontario Government, led by Premier Bob Rae. In the end, the mill was purchased by a combination of Tembec Inc. and the mill's workers in an innovative buy-out program supported by the province. The mill went through a cost-cutting exercise and emerged as a viable entity focusing only on lumber and newsprint. In 1997, Tembec bought out the shares of the workers, giving them an unexpected profit, and taking sole ownership of the mill. However, the mill was now a much different operation.

When my father had been technical director, the mill had employed 2,500 people, making creped wadding and newsprint with a groundwood mill and a sulphite mill that poured untreated sulphur liquor into the river. But the creped wadding operation and the sulphite mill closed in 1982. Newsprint was increasingly made with thermo-mechanical pulp (TMP), which could be produced with higher energy costs but many fewer workers. The woodlands operation also trimmed its workforce by 75 percent with the introduction of mechanical harvesters.

Tembec introduced a sawmill and lumber operation in the early 1990s. But even with this, the total workforce declined to only 550. As for the town itself, Kap's population declined from 13,000 in the 1950s to under 9,000. With the decline in population, the school system had to downsize and amalgamate.

Although the mill was now owned by Tembec, Kap could no longer be described as a company town. All the houses had been sold to their occupants. The Community Club had long ago been sold to the town for $1 and converted into the municipal centre, renamed the Civic Centre. The company no longer maintained the parks. The town was also functionally bilingual, having come a long way from the days when management was unilingual English and the workforce was mostly French. The river was cleaner. But the mill was still under stress. Facing lowered demand for newsprint and lumber, Tembec ordered layoffs and shutdowns. Its share price had dropped precipitously.

In 2010, I returned to Kap for a few days with my older brother. By this time, the only remaining cinema, the Royal Theatre, had ceased operations and was boarded up. The Northern Oasis had closed its doors and the house on Riverside Drive was again for sale. We stayed at a Super 8 hotel a few miles out of town. We visited the new integrated school where we had both won the *Quisque Pro Omnibus* prize in the 1950s. A few glass cases housed trophies from years past. The trip was somewhat dispiriting. But there were a number of encouraging signs. Although the Cochrane Music Festival had ceased operations many years earlier, Kap had instituted its own Festival of Music, which was held in April each year. The town was making every effort to rejuvenate.

Of more interest was the Internet, where an enterprising 'Kapster' had decided to create a blog with reminiscences about the old days. His e-mail list included most of my old school friends, and photos and stories about Kap began to be exchanged. I suddenly became interested. What had happened to the Unknowns? Where were the Emeralds? A little detective work on the Internet and a few phone calls gave me my answers.

Eddy Lepp of the Unknowns had moved to Saskatoon, where he went to the University of Saskatchewan and coached hockey. He ended up teaching high school for thirty years, including eleven years as principal of the two largest high schools in Saskatoon. He retired to BC. Winston McIntosh moved to Toronto, where he worked at Pilkington Glass and then at Thomas Lipton, handling transportation logistics. His second wife died of cancer in 1984 and he went back to school, obtaining a BA in psychology at U of T. After that he moved to Barrie, where he acts as a therapist for people with substance addiction. Ken Ross became a lawyer, articled in Toronto and then moved to Ottawa, where he practised law with small firms, doing mostly civil litigation, until 1992, when he retired. He has written several books and leads an active life travelling, skiing and running. Butch Turcotte married a Kap girl and they moved to North Bay, where he taught math at Scollard Hall, a French academy. His son, Darren Turcotte, became a professional hockey player, playing for the New York Rangers.

As for the Emeralds, Rosie Ayora moved to Toronto and adopted her middle name, Michelle. She married Jackson Chercover, a Toronto lawyer. Sue Barrette moved to Toronto and married Geoff Heathcote, an executive with Maclean Hunter. Patsy Burdett ended up living in Atlanta, Georgia, married to Alvin Holt. Penny Wiley moved to Belmont, California, and married Ron Kirkland, a director of finance at Stanford University. Like the Unknowns, all of the Emeralds ended up leaving Kap.

2. University

FIRST YEAR AT VICTORIA COLLEGE

In the fall of 1960, I followed my brother's lead and became a freshman at Victoria College at the University of Toronto, taking the poli sci and ec program. The choice of courses was driven by the fact that I had done equally well in languages and sciences in high school, and this appeared to be the only program that offered courses in both the humanities (English, history, philosophy) and the sciences (psychology, economics).

Like my brother, John, I stayed at Gate House, one of the men's residences at Burwash Hall, on Charles Street West in Toronto. The residence housed about twenty-five men. At this time, the men's residences still had hazing rituals, the chief element of which was the practice of 'dumping.' Early in the fall, at about 2 a.m. one night, the freshmen would be awoken. They would be searched and any money confiscated. They would put their clothes on under their pyjamas, and their faces would be painted with Indian war paint. Then, blindfolded, they would be bundled into cars in groups of two and dumped somewhere outside the city.

I ended up paired with Harry Greaves, a freshman from Cobourg. We were driven up Highway 48 and dumped in a field off a side road, about halfway to Lake Simcoe. We had no idea where we were but we managed to walk in the right direction to get back to Highway 48. The only traffic at 3 a.m. consisted of occasional trucks with trailers barrelling south towards Toronto. None of them was prepared to stop for two hitchhikers in Indian war paint. We walked along the highway for a few kilometres, until we came to a bungalow on a farm property. A dog began barking. Lights came on. We timorously knocked on the side door. A man sleepily came to the door. We explained who we were. He nodded, then invited us to sleep on his living room couch. He commuted every morning into North York and would give us a ride.

In the morning we woke up somewhat refreshed, washed off the war paint, and were driven to a bus stop in North York. Harry had managed to hide a $5 bill on his person (guess where) and we used that to take the TTC to the residence. We triumphantly arrived back around 10 a.m.

I took the standard courses offered in the political science and economics stream. Included in the course material for the economic history of Canada was Harold Innis's famous study of the fur trade.[1] This intrigued me, not least because in the eighteenth century the key route of the Hudson's Bay Company between Lake Superior and James Bay was along the Missinaibi River. That river crossed Highway 11 at the village of Mattice, only 65 kilometres west of Kapuskasing, my hometown. I looked up some old HBC maps at the Sigmund Samuel Library and discovered that one of the trading posts along the route was called Wapiscogamy House. It was located near the junction of the Pivabiska River with the Missinaibi River, less than 100 kilometres northwest of Kap. The post was in operation from 1776 to 1791. No current maps of Ontario showed anything at that location and there was no road of any kind in the general area.

This was interesting to me because so far as I was aware, no one in Kap had ever heard of this trading post, let alone tried to find it. The history of the Kap area did not start until 1913, when the railway line of the National Transcontinental Railway was constructed across Northern Ontario. I realized that any remains of the trading post would now be covered with 150 years of growth. But I nourished the thought that someday I might take a canoe trip down the Missinaibi River and see if there was anything left.

In the end I never took that trip. But over the years, the Missinaibi River became a sought-after destination for canoeists, since the northern segment ran all the way from Mattice to James Bay without any roads or habitation, and there were also some spectacular rapids on the river. The government of Ontario later made the area along the river a provincial park and the former site of Wapiscogamy House has been identified by archaeologists. According to a canoeist who visited the site a few years ago, only a few modest traces of the trading post are left—palisade trenches, some foundation and oven stones and a small clearing.[2]

I have to confess that while the Harold Innis book on the fur trade led me to this intriguing saga, I did not study anything else he wrote. Only after I became a communications lawyer did I discover that he had written some seminal works on communications, examining the differential impact of various media on the development and evolution of civilizations.[3] These certainly influenced the later writings of Marshall McLuhan. But they had virtually no impact on the development of Canadian communications policy, which consumed much of my later career.

To be honest, his writing style left something to be desired. Donald Creighton has described it as 'difficult, highly condensed, extremely elliptical, and not infrequently obscure.' Northrop Frye found it 'impenetrable.' In brief, as Robert Babe has noted, 'Innis is not an easy read.'[4] But his lack of impact on Canadian communications policy reflects a more fundamental problem—namely, the general disconnect between academia and the real world of Canadian media and how it is regulated.

MY MUSICAL LIFE AT UNIVERSITY

My four years at Victoria College were not distinguished academically. Based on my high school marks, I had won the Moses Henry Aikins entrance scholarship at Vic but to keep it up I had to get high marks in university, which I failed to do. My marks were particularly bad in third year, which I very nearly failed.

There was a simple explanation for this: music. Upon arrival, I joined the musicians' union and rapidly became involved in college music. There were two extracurricular musical activities at Vic. One was the Vic Music Club, which put on an annual musical—either Gilbert and Sullivan or a recycled Broadway show. The other was the Bob Revue, which annually put on an entirely original musical, written by Vic students. When I was in my first year I didn't take part in the Bob Revue—which was called *1837* and was ambitiously built around the story of the 1837 rebellion in Upper Canada. The music was written by a gifted math student in Middle House named Ed Moskal, who used Tchaikovsky's 1812 overture as the opening theme. The show also featured a barbershop quartet singing a witty song at Montgomery's Tavern.

By playing jazz piano, I soon became known for my musical talent and ended up being selected to do the music for the Bob Revue in my second and third years at Vic. For my first Bob Revue, in 1961, the book and lyrics were written by Dennis Lee, later to be known for his book of children's poetry *Alligator Pie*, and much other creative writing.[5] Dennis came up with a satirical musical comedy called *Mushroom Malady*, involving two warring societies arguing about atomic mushrooms contained in what looked like pizza boxes.

The previous spring, I had attended a concert at Hart House where I had heard Paul Hoffert playing vibraphone; I loved the sound. (Paul later became lead musician with the Canadian jazz-rock group Lighthouse.) I was already attracted by the 'George Shearing sound', featuring jazz piano with locked chords and the melody line doubled with vibes and guitar. So I approached Paul and asked him to be in my pit orchestra for the Bob Revue in the following year. He tentatively agreed. Armed with this background, I arranged the score of *Mushroom Malady* to combine a flute with the instrumentation of a jazz quintet (piano, vibes, guitar, bass, drums). However, I learned on my arrival at Vic in the fall that Paul Hoffert had gone off to Germany to do graduate work. I had no vibes player and the show was to open in late November!

I went down to Boddington's Music (then on Queen Street East near Church Street) and discovered a set of used Jenco vibes for sale. They had been owned by Freddie Grant (no relation), who played vibes at Lichee Gardens and had upgraded to a Deegan (the Rolls Royce of vibes). The used vibes were not in very good condition but I felt they were essential. I negotiated a rent-to-own deal, and Freddie Grant threw in some lessons. I learned how to play the vibes in time to use them in the show.

Working on the music for *Mushroom Malady* brought me face to face with a difficult musical problem: Hart House Theatre had no orchestra pit. As a result, the musicians had to be seated in front of the first few audience rows. If the orchestra was any size at all, the sound would obliterate the singing unless everyone onstage had mikes. The typical solution for college musicals at that time was to go with a small musical group based on piano, bass, drums and guitar. (As I recall, *1837* had actually used two pianos.) *Mushroom Malady* expanded this a bit by adding flute and vibes.

Later that year, the Vic Dramatic Society presented a modern-dress version of Shakespeare's *Cymbeline*. I was asked by its director, Fred Euringer, to write some music for 'Hark Hark the Lark', the famous song that appears in the play. I wrote a two-part duet using Shakespeare's lyrics and this was presented onstage by two players dressed as minstrels—a girl soprano and a flute player.

I also wrote the music for the 1962 Bob Revue. The book and lyrics were by Randy Howard, an older student who later became a copywriter with the Hayhurst advertising agency. The show was called *Stillwater*, and revolved around a small 'dry' Ontario town energized by a campaign to

The Bob Revue *Stillwater* production team, Victoria College, 1962.
Back row, from left: Steve Halperin, Jon Johnson, Michael Cross, Roger Nelson.
Front row, from left: Randy Howard, David Crampton, me.

allow liquor. In writing the music, I started with the same jazz quintet (piano, vibes, guitar, bass, drums) I had used in *Mushroom Malady*. But this time I added a harp and a legitimate woodwind section (French horn, two flutes, bassoon, clarinet), as well as a trumpet player.

The music from *Stillwater* is preserved on a recording made at the time. Looking back, all I can say is that the music is inventive but extremely variable. There is an innovative version of 'God Save the Queen' that I had written to start the evening off, with a fugal background on the piano. It never failed to get a round of applause. There is a nice ballad with flute and harp that is reminiscent of Ravel, a couple of choral pieces with French horn obbligato, a madrigal, a jazz dance with a background stolen from Dave Brubeck, a crowd-rouser inspired by 'Trouble' from *The Music Man*, and a song written in 5/4 time.

To say this was a learning experience is an understatement. I knew nothing about orchestration when I took this on, and I had my heart in my hands when I had the first rehearsal with the orchestra. But I survived, and immediately learned ways to improve the sound. The French horn player, a professional hired for the week-long gig, came up to me and suggested I put his obbligato against the chorus in a higher register (up about a fifth), where it would sound better. I went back to the drawing board and rewrote the chart for that piece, incorporating his suggestion.

My best orchestration was a final comic song. This had been hurriedly written only a few weeks before the opening of the show. But by this time I knew what the orchestra could do and I wrote an excellent chart that used the bassoon to good effect. (The bassoon player was Ken Bray, another professional brought in to augment the pit orchestra.)

While wrestling with these orchestrations in the fall of my third year at Vic, I touched base with some professional arrangers. One was John Fenwick, the son of G. Roy Fenwick, the adjudicator who had awarded me the Rose Bowl at the Cochrane Music Festival years before. John was the pianist and arranger for the *Spring Thaw* musicals and later directed music at the Charlottetown Festival. A second contact was Rick Wilkins, a sax player who did arrangements for *The Tommy Ambrose Show* on CBC, and later for the Boss Brass.

One day in the fall of 1962, I learned that Henry Mancini would be the guest the following week on *The Tommy Ambrose Show*. Would I like to come to the rehearsals? Would I?!

During a break in the rehearsal, I went up to Mr Mancini and introduced myself. I had bought Mancini's book *Sounds and Scores*, and wanted to study arranging further. Could he make any suggestions? Mancini was quite friendly. He said the only course on arranging for popular music that he knew of was a summer program at the Eastman School of Music in Rochester, run by Rayburn Wright, the chief orchestrator at Radio City Music Hall. Mancini suggested I apply to take that course.

I came away invigorated and promptly applied. For the next two summers (1963 and 1964), I was enrolled in the Arrangers Workshop at the Eastman School of Music. A three-week program, this course took about twelve students. All the arrangements written by the students were played and recorded by professional musicians, mostly members of the Rochester Philharmonic.

When I arrived in Rochester in the summer of 1963, I discovered that I was one of the youngest students in the program. Most of the other students were jazz musicians; one was the instructor of a college concert band. The program was exciting, but had one major drawback: there was no money for copyists. So after you wrote an arrangement, you had to laboriously copy out all the parts. I found that writing a three-minute chart might take upwards of seven hours (others wrote more quickly), and it would take another eight hours to copy out the parts. The result was that when arrangers arrived to hear their pieces sight-read by the live orchestra, they would usually be dog-tired from staying up all night writing the parts.

The program was fascinating, particularly because we all learned how to write for strings, an area that was a complete mystery for most musicians coming from a jazz background. The conductor Sir André Previn has written about the time when he was writing film scores in Hollywood in the 1950s and how invaluable it was to hear his work performed by first-rate studio musicians within days of composition. The practical insights gained as to what 'works' in a musical arrangement and what doesn't work could never be learned at a conservatory, he noted.[6] Previn was absolutely right: I learned more about arranging in three weeks of practical application than I ever could have at a music conservatory. I particularly learned that hearing music and identifying what is happening musically (i.e., what are the instruments and how are they voiced) is not something you have to be born with. You can acquire that knowledge from practice and study.

One of the exercises in the workshop was to write an orchestration of Henry Mancini's 'Moon River', using an arranging style picked from a hat. Each of the twelve students dutifully chose a style. The 'styles' included the Boston Pops, a string quartet, a woodwind ensemble, the twist, a marching band (John Philip Sousa), Lawrence Welk, the Beatles, and Stan Kenton. Picking randomly from the hat, I was assigned to write a bossa nova version, and I quickly turned out a nice arrangement with the melody doubled in flugelhorn and sax over a bossa nova rhythm background.

The student who was assigned to do a version of 'Moon River' in the style of Lawrence Welk approached Ray Wright in puzzlement. 'I've never heard Lawrence Welk's music,' he complained. 'How do you arrange in the style of Welk?' 'No problem,' replied Wright. 'Just follow ten simple rules.' And then he rhymed off a set of 'rules' for Lawrence Welk. For example: convert 4/4 to 12/8, use triplet feeling throughout, use 3rds and 6ths in the woodwinds, use cup mutes in the trombones, put pop notes at the end of every eight bars, no semitone intervals in the middle register, and so on.

The student went away and came back the next day with his arrangement. The orchestra played it through and it sounded like vintage Lawrence Welk. We all got a great kick out of this. Welk presumably took years to develop his unique style. But Ray Wright could summarize it in ten simple rules.

At the same time, the whole exercise brought home to me the industrial side of creativity. I personally abhorred the Lawrence Welk sound as being elevator music of the worst kind. But anyone seeking a career in popular arranging would certainly need to know how that sound was achieved, as well as that of any other musical genre that you might be asked to use in orchestration.

The course was invaluable in teaching how to make a small musical ensemble sound larger than it is, given the inevitable budget limitations that come with the job of arranging. I also learned the truism that sometimes your best creative efforts can be stimulated by constraints of time, budget or resources.

Speaking immodestly, I have to say that I turned out to be quite a good arranger. In my first summer at the workshop, I did an arrangement of the Bob Haggart/Johnny Burke standard 'What's New?' for male voice and muted strings that was quite pretty. (The word *pretty* is a high accolade among arrangers.) I also did an arrangement of one of the themes from Stravinsky's *Petrouchka* for concert band that worked out very well. That summer, Ray Wright gave me an A, the only one given in the course.

The workshop was financed in part by the ticket receipts from a final concert, featuring pieces written by the student arrangers in the first half, and a performance by a guest artist in the second half. In my first summer, the guest artist was Dave Brubeck, who introduced his first composition written for full orchestra: 'Elementals'.

I still remember sitting in the packed audience of the Eastman theatre in July 1963 anonymously hearing the full orchestra play my arrangement of 'What's New?', which I had rewritten, at Ray Wright's request, for trumpet, woodwinds and muted strings. There were audible sighs of delight from couples seated near me, who had no idea that I had written every note that was being played. It was an unforgettable moment for me.

* * *

By my fourth year at Vic, I was tired of the Bob Revue and, armed with the experience of my first summer at Eastman, wanted to write charts for 'big band' (later often referred to as 'stage band'). Coincidentally, I was asked to do the music for the Faculty of Engineering show, *Skule Nite*. This was also staged at Hart House but was not a 'book' show; it consisted of comic sketches intermingled with dance numbers. So I could put together a full stage band. Any numbers requiring someone to sing onstage could have the singer miked up.

I did the music for the Engineering show for two years, in the fall of 1963 (my fourth year at Vic) and in the fall of 1964 (my first year in law school). In 1963 I used a stage band (trumpets, trombones, saxes, rhythm) plus some choral singers. I also had a grand piano perched in the left wing of the stage. In the 1964 show, I used a stage band plus strings.

The theme song of the Engineers was the Lady Godiva song, done to the tune of 'John Brown's Body'. So for the 1963 show, I put together a musical extravaganza with multiple variations of the song. The highlight was a solo piano rendition played in the style of Chopin by Patricia Perrin, later (as Patricia Krueger) the staff pianist with the Toronto Symphony Orchestra, followed by a solo rendition by me dressed in a wig, in the style of Bach and Rachmaninoff. The show itself got mixed reviews. Sets: excellent (what would you expect: after all, these were the engineers). Script: mostly bad. Music: excellent (but why was this ringer from Victoria College involved?). The review of the show in the *Varsity* included the following passage:

Peter Grant's musical direction deserves praise throughout—starting with the national anthem(s). His arrangements are snappy, sparkling and often brilliant. He has the special ability of being able to write the Skule theme in Bach, Chopin and Rachmaninoff vein. At one point, Hart House goes stereophonic as he surrounds the audience with various members of the orchestra and chorus.[7]

The Engineers always included some dance numbers in their shows and enlisted girls from other faculties, notably Nursing, to participate. Posters were put up all around campus urging girls to try out. The producers also hired a lady from the CNE's Canadettes to choreograph the dance numbers.

In the two years I did the music for *Skule Nite* they had some good dancers in the cast. But the best was a young woman who was not a student but a secretary working in the computer lab at the University of Toronto. She was of Macedonian heritage and had graduated from a secretarial college. She was a very accomplished ballet and jazz dancer and had appeared not only in the Canadettes but also on some *Wayne and Shuster* specials on CBC. Her name was Gloria George.

Gloria was the best dancer by far and the producers quickly decided to have her do a solo number that became billed as 'Gloria's Number.' For the 1964 production, I worked up a jazz background with bongo solos to match the choreography and it was a highlight of the show.

In late 1963, I started going out with Gloria. Although she did not have a university degree, she was not at all daunted by this. One of my favourite moments was when I invited Gloria to be my date at the Graduation Banquet, a formal affair with a dinner at Burwash Hall. As the president of the graduating year at Victoria College, I sat with Gloria at the head table. Seated beside her was Dr Northrop Frye. She turned to him and perkily asked, 'And what do *you* do?' The great man smiled and said, 'Well, I'm working on a book or two.' She proceeded to quiz him on this with no knowledge whatever of his work or his reputation. I'm sure it made his evening!

To jump ahead, Gloria and I became engaged in 1965 and we were married in June 1966.

THE LADY GODIVA MEMORIAL BAND

In the spring of 1963, I became involved with a curious institution at the University of Toronto called the Lady Godiva Memorial Band. The LGMB was a ragtag group of musicians, mostly students at the U of T Faculty of Engineering. They would occasionally surface at Varsity football games or other venues to play the Engineering song, to the tune of 'John Brown's Body'. The LGMB's most prominent asset was a large bass drum with the image of Lady Godiva riding a horse, her nudity covered with long blond hair. Members of the student-run group would wear safari helmets or hard hats while playing pickup tunes like 'When the Saints Go Marching In,' or other tunes requiring no rehearsal.

The leader of the group at this time was an Engineering student named Don Munro, who played clarinet. After I had done the music for

Skule Nite, Don called me with an audacious idea: transform the LGMB into a real concert band and enter it in the Toronto Kiwanis Music Festival. He wanted me to be the conductor.

I was frankly dubious. What piece would they play? Don had a ready answer. They would play Franz von Suppé's *Light Cavalry Overture,* a famous warhorse piece from the classical repertoire. But Don was keen on it for another reason, namely that the middle section had a nice clarinet solo he could play. As for the instrumentation, he proposed to fill out the ragtag membership with 'ringers' so that all the parts would be covered.

I agreed to his plan and he entered the group in the Concert Band–Open class under the discreet name University of Toronto Faculty of Engineering Concert Band. We rehearsed the piece carefully under my baton and then showed up at the festival, with everyone wearing blue blazers and grey pants. The bass drum was not in view. The performance went well and the adjudicator gave the group the top mark in the class. But more strikingly, the group was chosen to play at the final concert, Stars of the Festival, to take place at Massey Hall, as the last piece in the first half of the program.

I could hardly believe our luck. We would now appear on the same stage that was used by the Toronto Symphony Orchestra! (A few years later the TSO moved into the newly constructed Roy Thomson Hall.)

On the appointed evening, our group showed up at Massey Hall. But now was the chance for the true LGMB to emerge. Instead of blue blazers, the group came out onstage wearing safari pith helmets, hard hats, Viking helmets, Engineering jackets, long scarves and the like. The bass drum with the image of Lady Godiva was prominently displayed. A roll of toilet paper hung from the tuba.

I looked nervously out to the packed audience, where there were ripples of laughter as the group entered the stage. There in the front row was Sir Ernest MacMillan, the former conductor of the TSO!

We started into the piece and I am pleased to say that the group gave an excellent rendition. We took our bows and retired in triumph. So to this day, I can claim to have conducted a major concert piece to a packed audience in Massey Hall ... and survived to tell the tale.

HIJINKS AND POLITICS AT VICTORIA COLLEGE

As I have noted, I did not have a distinguished academic record at Victoria College. But I thoroughly enjoyed myself.

Apart from my active musical life, I was also involved in a few hijinks. In my second year at Victoria College, I read that a sixty-eight-year-old man named Homer A. Tomlinson was coming to Toronto to crown himself king. He had already visited dozens of other countries to do the same, and intended to come to Queen's Park to crown himself King Homer the First, as a prelude to crowning himself King of the World in Jerusalem. Apart from this strange delusion, Tomlinson was a rather mild-mannered amiable man whose story was later written up in the *New Yorker*.[8]

Talking it over in the men's residence at Vic, my chums and I decided that we would crown our own king instead. So we dressed a student from one of the residences in royal robes (a purple carpet) and a sceptre (a converted toilet plunger), and a hundred of us paraded him on our shoulders to Queen's Park, chanting appropriate songs and distributing a list of our king's 'campaign promises'. Homer Tomlinson arrived at the appointed time in a taxi. He removed a silver-and-gold crown from a blue canvas bag and proceeded to crown himself king. Our 'king' from Victoria College came up and shook his hand and engaged in conversation. Then to our surprise and amusement, a group of students arrived in Queen's Park from Trinity College carrying a third 'king.' They had thought of the same prank as we had!

Tomlinson was unconcerned. Obviously he had run into this kind of problem before. As he left the scene in his cab, our 'king' grabbed the initiative and jumped in the cab with him. Away they sped, and we were left to distribute our leaflets to the reporters. The next day, we were delighted to see appropriate (and thoroughly amused) coverage of the event in all the papers.[9]

I was also mildly involved in campus politics. At the end of my third year, I was elected president of Gate House. This came with the rare privilege of being able to choose which room in the residence I would occupy in my fourth year. Needless to say, I chose the only room with a working fireplace!

I was also elected president of the Victoria College graduating year, although I cannot recall actually accomplishing anything as president. More memorable was my membership in the Secret Subterranean Society, a small group of Gate House students who discovered that a hidden basement door in Gate House led to the extensive network of steam tunnels that ran underground throughout the University of Toronto campus. These tunnels had a narrow runway alongside a large steam pipe, with a head clearance of only five feet. Over a number of nights, we explored the steam tunnels, trying to map where they went. Among other arcane discoveries, we found that the tunnels led to the basement of the Home Economics building at the southeast corner of Queen's Park and Bloor Street West, where there was a large empty concrete swimming pool (who knew?). Crossing Queen's Park, the tunnels went under Philosopher's Walk, the pedestrian walk to the west of the museum linking Bloor Street with Hoskin Avenue. The heat from the steam tunnels accounted for the fact that Philosopher's Walk was never covered with snow in the middle of winter. At certain points, you could climb up a ladder and lift a manhole cover to discover where you were. The steam tunnels also led to the basement of Burwash Hall, where the kitchens were located, and the basement of the girls' residence, Annesley Hall. In the dead of winter, when the temperature was way below zero above the snow-covered ground, you could run along the steam tunnels in shorts and T-shirts.

I regret to tell you that since our momentous discoveries, the university has sealed off the steam tunnels with doors and locks. So much for our enterprising efforts!

WESTWARD WE GO

Between my third and fourth years at Victoria College, my parents did something that I still think is remarkable. They loaned me their Mercedes sedan for three weeks so I could drive to Los Angeles with two of my college friends. My friends—Ron Hutcheson from Huntsville and Dave Robertson from Stratford—were both chums from Gate House and we had all turned twenty-one. So in June 1963, I drove from Kap to Huntsville where I picked up Ron, then on to Toronto, where Dave joined us.

The Mercedes had front seats that folded back flat with the back seat, allowing one to sleep fairly comfortably. So we decided to drive for two days straight, with each of us doing two hours of driving, two hours of sleeping, and two hours of sitting behind the driver. When we reached Chicago, we entered the fabled Route 66, which ran all the way from Chicago to Los Angeles, through Illinois, Missouri, Kansas, Oklahoma, Texas, New Mexico and Arizona.

As we proceeded south, we were caught in a speed trap in Texas and fined. But our first overnight stop was in Albuquerque, New Mexico, where we rented a motel room and showered. Then, at Ron's suggestion, we went to 'frat row' at the University of New Mexico. We found ourselves outside a sorority. Flashing our University of Toronto leather jackets, one thing led to another and soon we found ourselves with three girls driving up to a lover's lookout to talk and do some necking. This was all new to Dave, who was attractive and well muscled from weightlifting, but who came from a straitlaced religious family in Stratford who had banned movies and dancing. As one of the girls ran her fingers through his chest hair, she exclaimed, 'Why, Dave, you're a tiger!' Ron and I were convulsed with laughter.

The evening ended and we dropped the girls back at their sorority. Dave pleaded to stay the next week in Albuquerque, but his plea was unsuccessful and we headed farther westward.

Our next stop was Flagstaff, Arizona, and a quick trip up to the south rim of Grand Canyon. Then we drove to Hoover Dam and Las Vegas. In Vegas, we attended the Lido de Paris, the topless revue at the Stardust Hotel. The staging was of course remarkable. In particular, there was one scene where a dam burst onstage and a wall of water inundated a village while we watched. But for three twenty-one-year-old boys, the semi-nude showgirls were the real revelation!

On to LA, where we went to Disneyland in Anaheim, slept in the lane outside Dean Martin's home and hung out on Venice Beach. We then drove up to San Francisco, crossed the Golden Gate Bridge, went to a movie in Marin County (*David and Lisa*), and then went eastward to Reno over the Donner Pass. Eventually, we reached Salt Lake City, where we dropped into the Temple and, by pure happenstance, heard the Mormon Tabernacle Choir rehearsing. At a small café, we ran into some girls who told us they were Mormons. We had no idea what that meant, but in order to respond and to have fun with them, we described ourselves as Communists! Finally, we drove through to Yellowstone National Park and then homeward.

LAW SCHOOL OR MUSIC?

By the end of my four years in the Honours BA program, graduating in the spring of 1964, I had no idea what I wanted to do for a living. My brother had stood first throughout his years at Victoria College and had gone off to the London School of Economics in a blaze of glory. He eventually got a PhD, and returned to teach at U of T, after which he became the chief economist at Wood Gundy, later acquired by the CIBC.

But my marks were nothing to write home about. Graduate school was not an option. I decided to apply to law school, but also to take a few courses at the business school. I got accepted at the Faculty of Law, University of Toronto, which then had the reputation as the best law school in the country, headed by Dean Caesar Wright. It was also conveniently across the street from Victoria College.

Meantime, in the summer before I entered law school, I returned to Rochester for a second three-week stint at the Arrangers Workshop. That was the summer of 1964, when race riots tore through parts of Rochester. But those of us in residence at the Eastman School of Music felt like we were in a cocoon. Duke Ellington and his arranger Billy Strayhorn were the guest artists that year. I wrote an orchestral arrangement of 'Sally-Go-Round,' a song I had composed for the Bob Revue in 1963. The piece was performed by strings, harp, woodwinds and solo trombone at the final concert and was warmly received.

But by that time, I had learned something about my musical ability: I was slow. There were others in the course who were as good if not better than I was in arranging, but they could also write more quickly. And in the professional world of arranging, speed is just as essential as quality.

In the fall of 1964, carrying this insight, I began my first year of law school, although I did not lose interest in music. In fact, I did the music for the Engineering show that fall, using a pit orchestra consisting of a stage band plus strings.

One day, I wandered next door to the Edward Johnson Building, the home of the U of T Faculty of Music. There I ran into some girls who were playing in a classical flute quartet, set up by Professor Ezra Schabas. I heard some of their pieces and was immediately enchanted. Wouldn't it be great to write some jazz charts for these four flute players, accompanied by vibes, guitar and bass? I approached the girls and they were all enthusiastic. They had never played 'jazz' before but were keen to try.

I sat down and wrote out a number of charts, utilizing the classical skills of the quartet. Eventually we performed a well-attended concert at Hart House, a recording of which I still have. Accompanying the four girls were Dennis Jones on bass, Nelles Van Loon on guitar, and me on vibes.

In second-year law, I wrote a chart of 'At Long Last Love' for the flute quartet, which they performed, accompanied by a full stage band on the main stage of the Edward Johnson Building. Of course the flutes had to be miked up to be able to be heard over the stage band. A number of the flute players went on to greater things. Suzanne Shulman became a highly regarded flute soloist. Jadwiga Michalska-Bornyi became first flute in the Halifax Symphony. And Virginia Markson joined the flute section of the TSO. I don't know what happened to Ina Salonen. As for the sidemen, Dennis Jones dropped music and ended up a production manager in Hollywood for movies like *Back to the Future*. Nelles Van Loon taught English at Ryerson, and wrote musicals on the side.

FIRST YEAR LAW AND 'THE SPIDER'

During first year at law school I also took a few courses at the business school. But I soon found those courses to be trivial, and decided to focus only on law.

I immediately discovered that law was far more interesting. At that time, and it still applies today, the Faculty of Law at the University of Toronto was the best law school in the country. With professors like Bora Laskin and John Willis, among many others, the school was a magnet for talent. And not everyone took themselves too seriously. In first year, I took Professor James Milner's course called Contract Law, which he taught in the time-honoured Socratic method. One of the key early cases involved a dry-cleaning company. We were amused to discover that the index to his book of cases and materials included the following line:

cleaners, readers taken to the .... *passim*

In first year, I was still heavily involved with music and skipped quite a few classes, particularly those in Real Estate Transactions, a first-year course taught by Richard C.B. (Dick) Risk, then a twenty-nine-year-old assistant professor who was at the beginning of his career.

As the exam grew near, I became nervous about the classes I had missed. I approached two students who always sat at the front of the class and who took good notes—Warren Mueller and Steve Goudge.[10] I asked them whether I could borrow their notes. In return, I undertook to type them up. They agreed. So over the next few weeks, I sat at my typewriter and carefully typed up everything they had written down. To make it more interesting, I presented the notes in the voice of a mythical person called the Spider, adding wry jokes and asides to the reader from time to time. A few pages were illustrated with cobwebs and the image of a spider hanging from a thread. By the end of this exercise, I had taught myself all I needed to know and I ended up getting an acceptable mark in the subject. For their part, Warren and Steve were happy to get a copy of my typed notes, which effectively constituted a 'crib' for the course.

Soon I was approached by another student who had skipped classes—David Peterson. Could he borrow my Spider crib? I gave him a copy as well. Peterson later told me that the only way he got through the course was by using my crib. Ultimately, David decided to go into politics instead of law and he became the premier of Ontario in the late 1980s. But he never forgot the help I gave him in 1964–65 with my Spider crib.

There is an amusing follow-up to this story. Years later, when I was teaching communications law at the Faculty of Law part-time, I ran into Dick Risk in the hallway. He beckoned me to his office. He then closed the door and asked, 'Are you the Spider?' I nervously acknowledged that yes, I was. He asked me whether I knew that copies of my Spider crib were retailing at Osgoode Hall Law School for upwards of $35. He showed me a copy. The crib had been xeroxed so many times that the words were barely legible. But you could still see my sketches of the spider. I was dumb-founded. I had never made a penny from these copies! And of course, neither had Dick Risk.

During my first year in law, a few of the students went down to the courts at Osgoode Hall to watch trials. We are all interested in seeing the leaders of the Ontario bar in action—people like Walter Williston, John Arnup, and the fabled John Robinette. One day I accompanied another law student in my year, Alan Lenczner, to Osgoode Hall to attend a high-profile malpractice case. Acting for the doctor was Doug Laidlaw, a brilliant litigation lawyer at McCarthy & McCarthy. We sat discreetly at the back of the courtroom watching the case proceed. The lawyers were gowned and had the traditional tab collars. Most of the proceedings were routine. But at one point, Doug Laidlaw suddenly stood up, swung his robe around with a flourish and declared, 'My lord, this is monstrous!' The effect was stunning. Alan and I looked at each other with widened eyes.

A few minutes later a recess was called. We went out into the corridor. Alan's eyes were glowing. He said, 'You know, if sometime in my life I can say in court, "My lord, this is monstrous!" my life will be complete.' I fully agreed with him.

Later, Alan Lenczner and I articled at McCarthy & McCarthy, where both Doug Laidlaw and John Robinette practised. Doug Laidlaw later died in a tragic car accident but Alan ended up following in his footsteps and became a gifted barrister, heading his own litigation boutique. As for me, I got to know Mr Robinette quite well and he figures in some of my reminiscences to come.

Finding myself increasingly interested in law, I got involved in the biweekly student publication called the *Advocate* and eventually became its editor. The *Advocate* was not a legal journal but focused on lighter stuff. I wrote a wry piece for it on my experience working with Legal Aid and devised a crossword puzzle for law students.

But the highlight was a contribution from Hart Pomerantz, who was a law student a year ahead of me. (I had seen Hart do a comedy routine in *UC Follies;* he became a stand-up comic with Lorne Michaels, who went on to produce *Saturday Night Live*.) Hart, together with a colleague, wrote a brilliant parody court judgment titled *Regina v. Ojibway*. Purportedly a judgment of Mr Justice Blue (referred to in the judgment as Blue, J.), the decision used inspired legal arguments to conclude that a pony with a downy pillow for a saddle was in fact a 'small bird' under the law. The mock judgment has since been reproduced many times in anthologies of legal wit, and can be found in many places on the Internet.[11]

One other event from first-year law may be worth retelling. Every Sunday I was invited to have lunch at my parents' apartment. On one of these occasions, my mother told me that she had been handed a ticket for failing to stop at a stop sign. 'You're now in law school,' she said. 'Surely you should be able to get me off!'

I listened to her story. She had been stopped by a policeman on Wells Hill Avenue, a little street running south off St. Clair Avenue West, after she had failed to stop her car at the stop sign at the corner of Wells Hill Avenue and Lyndhurst Avenue. I decided to take up my mother's challenge. I went out to the location with a friend from law school, Russ McKinnon. We surveyed the scene carefully. Wells Hill was a curious road, with a major curve in it before you reached the stop sign. We looked to see if the stop sign was obscured, since that would provide an obvious defence, but no, the stop sign was in broad daylight. However, about 190 feet south of the intersection, because of the curve in the road, it was partially obscured by a tree. We combed through the Highway Traffic Act and discovered that the sign was supposed to be visible for at least 200 feet.

Armed with this fact, Russ McKinnon and I showed up to defend my mother in traffic court. I was going to use Russ as my witness, to attest to the 190-foot problem, and we had carefully rehearsed what he would say. The court was held one morning in a basement room in Old City Hall and the corridor was crowded with people. We arrived to find that my mother's name was fifth on the docket. A senior police officer was acting as the prosecutor. I introduced myself to him. My mother looked around and then said to me, 'There's the nice Constable Anderson who gave me the ticket!' She pointed to an older officer standing against the wall and made eye contact.

After a few cases were dealt with, my mother's name was called. I stood up and announced that I was acting for Margaret Grant. The prosecutor leaned towards me and whispered, 'I assume you're going to plead not guilty?' I whispered back that that was certainly my intent. I announced the plea to the court. The magistrate called on the prosecutor to present his case. The prosecutor then said in a loud voice, 'Call Constable Anderson.' No one stood up. A policeman at the courtroom door spoke into the corridor: 'Constable Anderson'. No one answered. The prosecutor turned to the court and said, 'No witness, Your Worship.' The magistrate looked down at my mother and smiled. 'Not guilty', he said. I was chagrined. 'But ... but I have a defence ...' I wanted to say. It was not necessary. I had already won my first case.

HORIZON HOLIDAYS

Following my graduation from law school in June 1967 but before I began my articles at McCarthy & McCarthy in the fall, I looked around for another interesting summer job. Many university students took the opportunity to backpack in Europe for the summer. However, I was now living with Gloria in a third-floor flat in the U of T campus area, and we felt we needed some income.

A friend at law school, Bill Charlton, had had a summer job as a tour guide for a small company named Horizon Holidays. The job involved escorting a group of people on trips to various places in Canada. This sounded like fun, particularly for the summer of 1967 when all of Canada visited Montreal for the World's Fair, Expo '67. So I applied for a summer job with Horizon. The company was owned by two young Toronto businessmen—Gordon Fairbank and Bernie Taylor—who had started the company in 1963. They typically hired law students, medical students and teachers to be the guides for their company in the summer. I got a job leading tours to the Rockies and Ontario-Quebec in the summer of 1967. First I went on each of these tours with an experienced guide to 'learn the ropes', then ran the subsequent tours by myself.

The Rockies trip started at Union Station in Toronto, and involved a train journey on sleeper cars to Calgary. After a night there, the group (usually about thirty-eight people) transferred to a bus and travelled through the Rockies to the West Coast, staying overnight at Banff, Rogers Pass, Kamloops, Vancouver and Victoria. An overnight rail leg took us up to Jasper, then back to Toronto. Along the route, I supervised the bags, the hotel check-ins, the excursions and everything else. As a result, I became an instant expert on all the tourist attractions of Western Canada.

After a ten-day trip to the Rockies and back, I would head out to guide the Ontario-Quebec tour, which included a day at Expo '67. This was a bus tour with nights in Kingston, Montreal, Estérel and Ottawa.

After that tour, I would go back and do another Rockies trip, followed by another Ontario-Quebec tour. And so it went all summer long. All in all, I had a fabulous summer. The highlight was of course Expo '67, but I also thoroughly enjoyed getting to know more about Western Canada.

* * *

Following the summer of 1967, I plunged into my law career. But that was not the end of my Horizon Holidays story. I kept in touch with the company and during summer vacations would occasionally 'do a tour' for them. And then one day after I had become a full-fledged lawyer, I received a call from Gordon and Bernie. Could I help them purchase a small hotel on Lac Brome in the Eastern Townships? I helped them find a notary in Quebec and they closed the deal.

That seemed the end of the matter, until I learned in 1975 that they had decided to offer a tour in the Eastern Arctic. No tour company had ever tried this before. I had always wanted to visit the far north. So I called them up and volunteered to be a tour guide for a few trips to the Eastern Arctic.

Horizon had a policy that no tour guide could run any tour without having gone out on the trip before. So in the summer of 1975, Gordon and Bernie took me and a second prospective guide, a teacher from Hamilton, for a dry run of the Eastern Arctic. We took a scheduled Nordair flight from Montreal to Frobisher Bay (now Iqaluit), then transferred to a chartered bush plane, a single-engine DeHavilland Beaver. The plane could only seat five people, including the pilot, a Norwegian named Arnie Timberg.

We flew from Frobisher to Cape Dorset, then to Igloolik, and north to Pond Inlet. From there we flew to Beechey Island and to Resolute. From Resolute we flew to Isaacson and then to Eureka on Ellesmere Island. From there we flew still farther north to Tanquary Fiord and Otto Fiord. Upon returning south, we landed at Grise Fiord, then down the east coast of Baffin Island to Broughton Island. Once there, the plan was to fly across the peninsula and land in Pangnirtung.

The pilot tried to reach Pangnirtung on his radio to check the weather, but got no response. However, the weather looked fine at Broughton Island, so we took off around 2 a.m. Crossing the ice cap on the peninsula was straightforward. It was a clear cloudless night. Since we were north of the Arctic Circle, there were twenty-four hours of daylight in July.

We flew steadily and finally reached the fiord at the end of which (on the east side) was the little community of Pangnirtung. So far so good. We could even see the lights of the houses in the distance and the runway just beyond, nestled up against a mountain ridge. Below us were the dark Arctic waters of the fiord. We were flying at 3,000 feet directly over the fiord. All we needed to do was to fly farther down the fiord a few miles, then execute a broad U-turn to the left and come in to land on the runway.

Suddenly our plane hit a sickening gust of wind and dropped 300 feet. We found ourselves buffeted by a strong wind coming from the east. What had happened was that as we flew out over the fiord, our little plane had come out from the lee of a mountain range, which had sheltered us from the wind. But the last few miles were unprotected and a sweeping wind from the east was now hitting the plane. Had we been able to reach the Pangnirtung airport by radio, they would have told us to delay our trip until the winds died down.

But now it was too late. The plane suddenly dropped another 300 feet. Arnie gunned the engine and tried to climb back up. But every time he seemed to gain a few feet the plane would lurch again and drop. The four of us who were passengers looked at each other wild-eyed. We were all thinking the same thing. Would our plane be dropped into the icy water of the fiord? Another lurch and a sickening drop. No one spoke.

I looked at my heavy outdoor boots. If we hit the water, should I remove them so I could swim? But I knew that this would be pointless. In Arctic water at freezing temperatures, none of us would survive more than five minutes.

As the wind continued to buffet us, Arnie finally reached the end of the fiord and began the slow U-turn to come around to land. We all crouched in our seats, willing him to keep the plane from dropping into the sea, but not saying a word. The plane continued to be buffeted. However, it managed to finish the U-turn and we approached the Pang-nirtung runway. We were now over land, but not out of harm's way. The wind was still treacherous, since it was a direct cross-wind to the runway. Arnie finally brought the plane down, fighting the cross-wind all the way. We landed on the runway and the plane gradually came to a stop. As it did so, the wind pushed the plane towards its side and the left wing touched the ground. We hurriedly climbed out. All we could think about was that we were still alive! Arnie then tethered the plane with ropes to keep it from flipping over.

To this day, I have never had a closer call.

Years later, I was sitting at a football game in the Ottawa stadium and turned around to find Arnie Timberg sitting just behind me. He immediately recognized me. I clasped his hand and we reminded ourselves of our close call in Pangnirtung. He was an experienced bush pilot, but it had been as traumatic for him as it had been for his four passengers.

In the summer of 1976, I was a tour guide for three trips to the Eastern Arctic. This time the mode of transportation was a two-engine Twin Otter, which could carry sixteen people plus a pilot and a co-pilot.

The Twin Otter turned out to be great transport vehicle for trips of this kind. The passenger windows on each side were under the wing so all the passengers had an unimpeded view of the terrain below. The pilots were used to no-nonsense trips for oil or mining personnel, typically ferrying people or supplies from point A to point B. Now they were asked to take the 'scenic route'. Up in the Arctic this often involved following the 'floe edge', where the edge of the ice met the open water, and where you might see polar bears, narwhal whales, walrus and seals. Instead of flying at 3,000 feet or above, we would sometimes ask the pilots to descend to as low as 300 feet so we could see the wildlife.

Most food was flown in from the south and could be pretty basic. For instance, every morning we had Tang instead of orange juice. In Iqaluit, we would have a caribou-steak dinner at the only hotel in town, but this was comparative luxury. In the smaller communities we visited, the group would stay in the 'transient centre', which was essentially a shack. At Eureka, we didn't even have that comfort; we stayed in tents erected at the end of the runway.

We used Iqaluit as a base for day trips to Cape Dorset and Pangnirtung, both of which had active Inuit craft centres. Cape Dorset was the site where James Houston taught the Inuit the art of printmaking. Pangnirtung also had a well-established arts centre and the group would tour it and buy some prints or sculptures.

On one of my day trips to Pangnirtung, we arrived just as a film crew from Eon Productions had finished filming the famous stunt that appears before the opening credits of the James Bond film *The Spy Who Loved Me*. They had used a nearby mountain, Asgard Peak, in Auyuittuq National Park just north of Pangnirtung. The mountain had a long ledge ending in a sharp cliff and a sheer drop of over a mile. Stuntman Rick Sylvester skis off the mountain into mid-air. His skis come off and there are fully twenty seconds of free fall. Suddenly he sprouts a parachute covered with a colourful Union Jack. In the film this is followed by a close-up of James Bond (played by Roger Moore) gently descending, a weary but bemused

With an Inuit child in Cape Dorset, Baffin Island, in 1976.
In consecutive summers in the 1970s, I travelled all over the far north.

smile on his face. The opening credits begin to roll over Carly Simon's rendition of 'Nobody Does It Better', one of the best-known of the Bond themes.

When I arrived in Pangnirtung, the crew had just finished shooting this scene and had shipped the film south for processing. They were waiting with bated breath to see if the shoot had been successful, or if they would have to go back and shoot it again. In the end they learned that one of the cameras had managed to film the whole plunge.

Sylvester received $30,000 for this stunt. But I also got something out of it. Twenty-five years later, I used the story of the plunge, coupled with a story of my visit to the local Inuit printmaking centre, to introduce a chapter of my 2004 book, *Blockbusters and Trade Wars*, dealing with the phenomenon of creative clusters.

On all the Horizon trips, after flying up the interior of Baffin Island, where we saw herds of caribou, we would reach the northern end and stay overnight in Pond Inlet, across from Bylot Island, the famous bird sanctuary. Then on to Beechey Island, with its gravesites from the ill-fated Franklin Expedition.

Ellesmere Island was undoubtedly the highlight of my Arctic trips. This is the northernmost island in the Arctic archipelago, with an area of about 200,000 square kilometres, almost twice the size of Newfoundland. It has only three settlements: Grise Fiord, a tiny Inuit community inserted on the southern coast in the 1950s; Eureka, a weather station halfway up the island; and Alert, the air force base on the northeastern tip. The total population of the whole island was less than 200. Ellesmere gets little precipitation and so most of it consists of brown mountain ridges—in effect a polar desert. Flying over the treeless terrain, we would spot herds of muskox, who would immediately assume their defensive posture (forming a circle with their heads and horns facing outward) whenever the plane came near. We also saw herds of Arctic hare, white against the brown background. These were large animals, the size of jackrabbits, and they all seemed to be hopping in unison.

After landing in Eureka, we would visit the weather station. The fifteen or so employees worked out of a cluster of interconnected buildings at one end of the runway, all presumably waiting to be transferred out. For whatever reason, the staff did not appreciate visitors and preferred to be left alone.

Flying north along the Nanson Sound, we would reach Tanquary

Fiord, a long narrow fiord that led to a grassy area where a short runway had been built in 1963. Flying the length of the fiord was an experience in itself as we skimmed over the water and the mountain ridges closed in from both sides. Then we would land on the runway. The group would get out and walk over to the only sign of life, an unoccupied quonset hut. Inside the hut was a table and an open journal, where they could enter their names and any remarks. We were the very first 'tourists' to sign in. Preceding us were mostly government workers and scientists. In the latter category were a few expeditions to Lake Hazen, a number of miles to the east.

To make the subsequent visits more fun, I buried some mementoes near the hut, with a small cairn above to mark the spot. Then on my next visit, I would direct the group to the cairn and have them unearth the mementoes (usually, spoons or cups with the Canadian flag on them).

After the visit to Tanquary Fiord, we would fly farther north to Otto Fiord, which was at that time entirely covered with floating icebergs, calved from the glacier. Flying just above the icebergs (each the size of a house) was unforgettable. Although we never went all the way to the North Pole, we did fly out over the Arctic ocean, north of Ellesmere Island, where the vista was little more than jumbled ice floes.

Some of the scenes I saw on those trips have undoubtedly changed. With global warming, the Nanson Sound is now typically ice-free for much of the year. But the scenery is just as spectacular. The price of jet fuel makes it much more expensive to take trips of this kind. But even so, it is worth doing. Those memorable trips I took led me to the conclusion that all Canadians should travel to the far north sometime in their lives.

As for Horizon Holidays, it still exists as a boutique travel firm with the name Horizon & Co., although neither Gordon nor Bernie is involved with the company anymore.

3. Becoming a Communications Lawyer

HOW IT ALL STARTED

Not many lawyers can trace their entire career to a paper they wrote in law school. But that in fact happened to me. It is a story that resonates with law students every time I tell it.

At the beginning of the fall semester in second-year law, I had to choose from some elective courses. For some reason, I was attracted to a new course called Legal History, which was being taught by Dick Risk. Only about fifteen students took the course, and Risk himself had no clear idea what the course would involve. There would be no exam. Rather, each student was to write an essay on some arcane topic of legal history, for example, the history of a statute or regulation. Why was it enacted? What impact did it have? He gave us a short list of possible topics (I recall one was Early Canal Law in Upper Canada) but said we could focus on any statute we wanted.

By a stroke of luck, the Report of the Committee on Broadcasting was published on September 1, 1965, just a few weeks before I had to choose a topic. This was a report chaired by Robert Fowler, who had previously headed up a Royal Commission on Broadcasting in 1958.[1] In the 1965 report, the Fowler committee excoriated the newly licensed private TV broadcasters for their inadequate Canadian content performance. He recommended replacing the Board of Broadcast Governors (BBG) with a stronger body with the power to annex and enforce licence conditions on private broadcasters.

The choice for my topic was obvious, at least in hindsight. Why not examine the history of the Canadian content regulations on television? The regulations had only been introduced four years earlier, so this didn't sound too difficult a topic.

Professor Risk was a bit dubious but gave his approval. So I embarked on my research. The *Canada Gazette* provided the text of the regulations. It turned out that the regulations had been amended a surprising number of times since they had been first introduced in 1961. I then visited the CBC library in Toronto and discovered that it maintained a comprehensive clippings file on the BBG. This turned out to be a treasure trove. Every amendment had been discussed at a BBG public hearing and this had been covered exhaustively in the press. The Toronto newspapers were generally no friend of broadcasters, other than the *Toronto Telegram*, which was controlled by John Bassett, who also controlled CFTO-TV. So the *Globe and Mail* and the *Toronto Star* gave the BBG hearings wide coverage.

Armed with these sources and the Fowler committee report, I began writing my paper. But at the same time, I decided to give the paper a wider focus. This would not be just a study of how some particular regulations were adopted and amended. It would be a study of how administrative agencies go about addressing a problem. So I developed a flow chart showing various decision points that regulatory agencies had to go through in enacting a regulation. Gradually my paper took on a more ambitious mandate.

I handed the completed ninety-two-page paper in to Professor Risk in April 1966. He gave me an A. This, coupled with other good marks, put me in the top ten of my class that year and I won the Bernard Newman Award for the best law student combining academic excellence with extracurricular activities (presumably a reference to my musical life and my editorship of the *Advocate*). Dick Risk also passed on my paper to two other professors at the Faculty of Law, both of whom taught administrative law: Albert Abel and John Willis. They loved the paper.

John Willis was a spry and delightful codger of sixty-two who had never progressed past a BA degree but was revered among administrative-law academics. He had written a brilliant survey piece on judicial review of administrative action in the mid-1930s. His fascination was always in the practical realities of administrative agencies: How do they do what they do? He was an early supporter of curial deference. So my paper hit a real chord with him.

As for Albert Abel, he turned out to be the editor of a little-known academic journal published by the University of Toronto Press called *Canadian Public Administration*. And in my third year (1966–67), he approached me to see if my paper might be published in that journal. I agreed, but noted that the paper would need to be updated. By this point, the government had introduced legislation to replace the BBG with a new agency to be called the Canadian Radio-Television Commission (CRTC), implementing many of the Fowler Committee recommendations.

Accordingly, I decided to rewrite the paper to include a speculative section at the end, dealing with the powers of the new CRTC and how it might proceed. (In fact, the new Broadcasting Act came into force on April 1, 1968).

I finished the rewrite while I was articling at the Toronto law firm of McCarthy & McCarthy and handed it in to Professor Abel by the end of 1967. The paper was titled 'The Regulation of Program Content in Canadian Television: An Introduction.' It eventually appeared as a major seventy-five-page piece in the October 1968 issue of *Canadian Public Administration*.[2]

By the fall of 1968, when the paper was published, I was in the bar admission course. But I had been asked back to join McCarthy & McCarthy as a fully fledged associate after my call to the bar in March 1969. But there I was, back in October 1968, having just received twenty-five complimentary reprints of my article from U of T Press. I wondered, What do I do now?

I decided to take the bull by the horns. On McCarthy & McCarthy letterhead, I wrote a letter to the new chairman of the CRTC, Pierre Juneau, a man I had never met. I said that I was interested in broadcasting law and had done a recent study of the Canadian content regulations (see enclosed reprint). But I was interested, I said, in further study of this area, possibly with a view to developing materials for a course in this subject. Could I discuss this with him?

Most of this was pure chutzpah. But to my amazement, I received a phone call from his secretary only a few days later. Mr Juneau would be at the Royal York Hotel next Monday, accompanied by his research director, Rodrigue Chiasson. Could I meet them for breakfast?

I panicked. This was all happening too soon. I was still only in the bar admission course!

I hurried to the Faculty of Law, where I spotted Professor Willis. I told him what had happened. 'What should I do now?' I asked.

Willis laughed. 'That's easy,' he said. 'Ask for money!'

'How much should I ask for?'

'Well, how much would it cost to hire two law students and send yourself and the students to Ottawa for the summer? Then you could spend your time at the CRTC and find out how they operate. Interview them. Make photocopies of everything that looks interesting.' Willis had a gleam in his eye.

I quickly made some calculations. I figured $5,000 would be enough to cover it.

The following Monday, I showed up at the Royal York Hotel. Juneau and Chiasson met me for breakfast. I talked up the importance of broadcasting law as a new discipline. I presented my plan. And to my astonishment, I emerged with their commitment to give me $5,000. And that started my career as a communications lawyer.

As an aside, I should say that in the spring of 1969, after I was called to the bar, I gave one of the reprints of my article to Patrick Vernon, a senior partner of McCarthy & McCarthy. Pat was a Conservative Party fundraiser and he passed the copy on to a young Conservative supporter he knew who was in the radio business—Ted Rogers. A week or so later, Pat passed a letter he had received from Ted to me. It read, in part:

Dear Patrick: I was astounded to receive the reprint from the *Canadian Public Administration* of an article by Peter Stewart Grant. It is a fabulous article and it could almost be called a treatise ...

At the time, of course, Ted Rogers operated an AM and FM station in Toronto, and was also a fledgling cable operator there. His future was still ahead of him, as was mine.

ARTICLING AT MCCARTHY & MCCARTHY

I articled at McCarthy & McCarthy in 1967–68, did the bar admission course at Osgoode Hall in 1968–69 and was asked back to join the firm as an associate in the commercial law group after I was called to the bar in March 1969.

Why did I choose McCarthy & McCarthy?

In the fall of my third year at law school, in 1966, I had dutifully sought interviews at various law firms. But I was in a quandary. I was equally interested in litigation and commercial law. Which firm should I article with?

As I was from a town in Northern Ontario and neither of my parents were lawyers, I didn't know any lawyers in Toronto. Nor did I know anything about the downtown law firms. However, Horace Krever, who had taught me in his civil procedure class in my second year at law school, had also been in private practice—one of the few instructors who had. I felt he might be able to offer me advice, so I wandered into his office and asked him what he thought. He immediately recommended McCarthys. It was the only firm, he said, that combined a strong litigation group, headed by J.J. Robinette, Q.C., acknowledged to be Canada's greatest living litigation counsel, with a commercial law group. In those days, the big commercial firms (Blakes, Oslers, Torys, Davies) had few if any litigators and referred their trial work to the litigation firms like Weir Foulds or Faskens. (Since then, life has changed and all the big commercial firms have litigation groups as well as commercial law groups.) McCarthys was an exception, so I focused my attention there.

Luckily my second-year marks were excellent (I stood in the top ten) so they offered me one of the six articling positions. I would make the grand sum of $75 a week, a big increase from the $60 that was paid to the law students the previous year.

When I started articling at McCarthys in the fall of 1967, the firm occupied the seventh floor of the Canada Life building, on the northwest corner of Queen Street West and University Avenue, and had about sixty-five lawyers. The offices were old and dumpy and the corridors had green linoleum tile. All the articling students worked around a large wooden table in a single interior office. This was typical of law firms at the time. The one bright element was the ritual of high tea. A sweet silver-haired lady would arrive at 4 p.m. with a tea trolley and cookies and biscuits. Of course the students would descend on this poor lady's wares like a swarm of locusts.

In January 1968, however, partway through my articling year, the firm moved into the new Toronto-Dominion Bank Tower, at 66 Wellington Street West, occupying the forty-seventh and forty-eighth floors. Now we had decorator broadloom and a spiral staircase joining the two floors. But where was the tea lady? She had to be let go because the lease reserved all 'catering' to the landlord. This was somewhat ironic, because McCarthys had in fact acted for the landlord and had drafted the form of lease that it then had to sign as a tenant of the building!

During my articles, I was rotated around various sections of the firm: litigation, commercial and real estate. One day the managing partner of the firm, Beverley Matthews, came into the articling student room and asked any one of us who was free to join him in his office in ten minutes for an interesting assignment. After he left the room, the six of us drew straws. Who would have the privilege of taking this on? I won the draw.

A few minutes later, I was in Mr Matthews's office. Our client was Gulf Canada, which was acquiring British American Oil Co. through a merger. All the BA signs on the hundreds of BA gas stations would need to be changed to GULF. But there was a tiny legal question: Did Gulf have to obtain consent from each of the hundreds of independent lessees of these stations? Mr Matthews asked me to do a legal memo for him.

I immediately dove into the law library. The issue was whether the merged entity of Gulf and BA was a 'new' company, in which case consent was necessary for a change in the leases, or was it a continuation of the old company, in which case the existing leases were still operative. I quickly discovered only two cases on point: a lower-court decision in BC and a relatively recent case in the Ontario Court of Appeal, the Denison Mines case. The latter case had held that a merged company was simply a continuation of the old companies. I checked the Supreme Court of Canada reports to see if the case had been appealed and discovered that it had been. However, the decision in the highest court had turned on an entirely different point and there was no mention of the continuation issue. So my memo relied on the Court of Appeal decision and suggested that consent would not be required from the lessees.

A day or so passed. I wandered by Mr Matthews's office. Had he seen my memo? Yes, said his secretary. However, he had shown it to Mr Robinette and he had disagreed with my conclusion.

I was crushed. Where had I gone wrong?

Later I found out what had happened. While the Supreme Court of Canada had not commented on the continuation issue in its written judgment rendered in the Denison Mines case, the matter had been extensively argued. The justices had made it clear during the course of oral argument that they were not sympathetic to the position of the Ontario Court of Appeal on this issue. So Mr Robinette had concluded that if the matter was tested at the highest level, you could not count on the appeal judgment to be the law.

Incredible. But how did Mr Robinette know this? Simple. He had argued the Denison Mines case in front of the Supreme Court of Canada himself.

I was chagrined. But somehow I also felt curiously reassured. I told myself that any other lawyer researching this point in Canada would have agreed with my memo, as far as it went. The fact that Robinette knew better simply proved how unique and special he was, and how lucky I was to be in the same firm. (As a matter of interest, the corporation law was changed some years later to specify that mergers had the effect of a continuation. As for Gulf Canada, all its retail gas stations were later acquired by Petro-Canada in 1985.)

The rest of my articles passed without incident, and the firm invited me back to be a commercial associate once I had passed the bar admission course. This happened in March 1969.

RESEARCHING AND TEACHING COMMUNICATIONS LAW

I had not forgotten about the field of communications law. After all, the CRTC had given me $5,000 to do some research into broadcasting law. So in the summer of 1969, I travelled to Ottawa. Now (finally!) a fully fledged lawyer, I hired two students to work in Ottawa. The students were Dennis Wood, later to become a municipal/environmental lawyer at McCarthys, and my cousin John Gregory, who later became a lawyer at the Ontario attorney general's office. They rented a small set of rooms in a house in Gatineau, and travelled to the CRTC offices every morning by bus. Every few weeks, I came up from Toronto to supervise their work.

We spent the summer doing research. I assembled a complete set of BBG and CRTC decisions (something the BBG and CRTC had never done), and indexed them. Then I interviewed all the senior people at the CRTC. By the end of the summer, I had a comprehensive sense of what the CRTC was doing.

By this time, Dean Ronald St. John Macdonald (probably through John Willis) had gotten wind of my CRTC project. He invited me to start a one-semester course in communications law at the Faculty of Law in the fall of 1969. This would be an elective essay course for third-year students. As a part-time lecturer, I would be paid $4,000. I enthusiastically accepted his offer, and organized materials for the first course in communications law ever offered in Canada. That first year, I had twenty-five students.

Teaching broadcasting law at the Faculty of Law,
University of Toronto, 1970.

For nearly five years, from the fall of 1969 to the spring of 1974, I taught communications law at the Faculty of Law, U of T. At that time the CRTC only regulated broadcasting but I also became interested in how the telephone companies were regulated. So while I started with a single-semester course in broadcasting law, within two years I had added a second course—in telecommunications law. Both courses were 'essay' courses, with no final exam, but I diligently prepared 'cases and materials' for each.

In 1970, the federal government had created the Department of Communications (DOC). The government had also commissioned a number of studies into the communications industry (referred to as the Telecommission studies), focusing on the promise of the 'wired city'. Similar studies had been published in the United States and the whole field suddenly became very hot.

That year, the law school decided to devote the annual Conference on Law and Contemporary Affairs to the topic 'Communications and the Public Interest'. I became the faculty adviser to the conference, held in February 1970, and helped pick the subjects and get the speakers. It was the first conference on this topic in Canada and was a huge success, attracting over three hundred registrants from across the country. The speakers included the chair and vice-chair of the CRTC and over two dozen key people from the broadcast and cable industries. I also asked David Johnston, then an associate professor at the Faculty of Law, to moderate a panel on cable television and the wired nation. David later became the dean of the law school at the University of Western Ontario, the principal of McGill University, the president of the University of Waterloo, and, most recently, the Governor General of Canada. Another panellist was Marshall McLuhan, who later dropped in as a guest for one of my lectures.

I decided to broaden my horizons beyond broadcasting regulation and learn all I could about telephone regulation. The major telecommunications carriers (Bell Canada, B.C. Tel and CNCP Telecommunications) were regulated by the Telecommunications Committee of the Canadian Transport Commission, but there were numerous small telephone companies regulated by provincial regulatory agencies. I was always fascinated with companies like Bell Canada and was imbued with the notion that the regulators may have been 'captured' by the industry.

The first step in my education was to acquaint myself with all the decisions of the federal regulators over the years on telephone rates. There was only one text in the area, H. E. B. Coyne's *The Railway Law of Canada*, which had been published back in 1947.

Why, you may ask, would you look in a railway law text for references to telephone rate cases? For a simple reason. Telephone (and telegraph) rate regulation had been handed to the Board of Railway Commissioners for Canada in 1908 and the applicable statutory provisions were all found in the Railway Act. So Coyne was the logical (and the only) source. (The Board of Railway Commissioners was replaced by the Board of Transport Commissioners in 1938 and this was replaced with the Canadian Transport Commission in 1967.)

The Coyne text did include references to a number of telephone decisions. However, as the former general counsel of the board, Coyne had really only been interested in railways and so he had made only a limited selection of telephone cases. The full text of all the decisions could be found in two reporting services, *Canadian Railway Cases* (C.R.C., published from 1902 to 1939) and a series called *Judgments Orders Rules and Regulations* of the Board of Railway Commissioners (J.O.R.R., published from 1911 to 1938). I went to the Faculty of Law library at U of T and discovered that they had a complete set of C.R.C. but only the Great Library at Osgoode Hall downtown had a complete set of the J.O.R.R.s.

Over the next two years, I reviewed, summarized and indexed all the telecom decisions reported in these services. I rapidly discovered that Coyne had been very selective. There were dozens of telephone decisions, some of them quite interesting, that were not mentioned in his book. There were also a number of decisions after 1947 that weren't referred to because his book had never been updated. I obtained directly from the Canadian Transport Commission xeroxed copies of all its telephone decisions that had been rendered since J.O.R.R. had stopped publishing in 1938.

I became something of a pack rat, collecting everything I could on telephone regulation. During this period, I also applied for more research funding from the CRTC, the Department of Communications and some of the provincial regulatory agencies. This made it possible for me to hire more law students for the next few summers.

In the process, I began to be a bit of an expert on the history of telecom legislation—threading my way through all the arcane amendments and legislative rewrites that had occurred in the period since 1906. These became essential to understanding the judicial decisions that affected telecommunications.[3]

Later on, I discovered that my research gave me a real advantage. Bell Canada's regulatory department had been run for many years by its vice-president and general counsel, a man named Norman Munnoch. Munnoch undoubtedly knew every decision affecting the telephone companies back to the earliest times. But Munnoch retired in 1963. And from 1958 to 1969, Bell had no need to go before the regulator for general rate increases, because of the cost savings of introducing direct distance dialling in that period. So when Munnoch left, he took much of the institutional regulatory memory of Bell Canada with him. By the time I became involved in Bell rate cases for the CRTC in the mid-1970s, I knew as much as Bell Canada did about the history of telephone rate regulation. At that point, Bell regulation was run by a younger team, many of them hired in the 1970s.

In the course of my research into the early history of telephone regulation, I ran across the name Francis Dagger. Dagger had been the first Ralph Nader of the telephone industry. He had written the *Dagger Report*, which led to the creation of Saskatchewan Telecommunications in 1908. He had also been an expert consultant to the Mulock Committee hearings into the telephone industry in 1905, which led to the rate regulation of Bell and B.C. Tel in 1908. In his later years he had worked for the regulator of the provincially regulated telephone systems in Ontario, until he was let go as part of the Mitch Hepburn cutbacks in the 1930s.

I looked up his obituary at the university library. Francis Dagger had died in 1945 at the age of eighty-one, leaving a sole surviving daughter named Mildred Dagger in Unionville. I decided to contact her to see if his papers or memorabilia had survived. There was no one named Mildred Dagger in the Unionville telephone directory so I called the Unionville paper. Had they ever heard of a Mildred Dagger? Why, yes, the editor answered. Mildred Dagger had married Dr Temple and was now Mildred Temple. Dr Temple had passed away but Mildred still lived in Unionville.

Within minutes, I had Mildred Temple's address and phone number. I called her out of the blue. A lady with a quavery but friendly voice answered the phone. Was she Mildred Dagger, the daughter of Francis Dagger? Indeed she was. After I explained my mission, I asked to visit her. She said she would be delighted to welcome me to her home, a little bungalow on a side street in Unionville.

I spent an hour with her the following week, and this led to a number of occasions when she came down to my class at the Faculty of Law to tell them about her father. She was in her seventies but remembered her father like it was yesterday. As a girl of seven, she had accompanied him as he travelled across the prairies, proselytizing against the Bell Telephone Company. She remembered his strong speaking voice and his ability to chair meetings and resolve disputes. She knew very little about telephone regulation, but she did have vivid memories of living in the Parkdale area of Toronto at a time when less than 10 percent of homes in Toronto had telephones.

My class was mesmerized by her stories. She had lived with her father until he had passed away, making her living teaching piano at the Toronto (later the Royal) Conservatory of Music. In the last ten years of her father's life he had become a breeder of cocker spaniels, with a number of Best in Breed to his credit. Unfortunately all his papers had been stored in a barn that burned down in 1956.

Most Sundays, I visited my mother for lunch in her apartment. After Mildred Dagger had appeared at my class at the law school, I mentioned the story to my mother, proud of my detective work in tracking her down. 'Mildred Dagger!' said my mother. 'I just had tea with her last Thursday. She's one of my closest friends. We see each other every month!'

It turned out that they had met when my mother was studying at the Toronto Conservatory of Music in the 1920s. Had I wanted to track Mildred down, I could have simply asked my mother!

I only taught the communications courses for five years. During this period, I also started a new law review, the *Canadian Communications Law Review*, although it only published five issues from 1969 to 1973. By 1975, the Faculty of Law had hired Hudson Janisch, a keen young professor from Dalhousie Law School. Hudson had become interested in communications law when he attended the national conference I had organized in 1970. He subsequently started a course in communications law at Dalhousie Law School, so he was a perfect choice to take over my courses at U of T, which he did to great effect for many years (he retired in 2005).

However, a surprising number of the students who took one of my courses, or who worked for me in the summer, went on to greater fame. They include Larry Grossman, Patrick Boyer, John Gregory, Dennis Wood, Paul Morrison, Elizabeth Stewart, Robert Hage, John Honderich, Murray Rankin, John Hunter and Brian Gray.

Patrick Boyer became a commercial lawyer at Oslers and then a Conservative MP for the Lakeshore constituency. When he was taking my communications law course, I assigned him an interesting topic for an essay: the treatment of directory advertising revenue in telephone rate cases. He did an excellent paper that summarized the complex history of board decisions on this matter. The paper turned out to have a fascinating afterlife! (See p. 96.)

GLORIA

I had married Gloria George in June 1966, and we found a third-floor flat in the annex area of Toronto. For the next six years, we lived there. We acquired a little beagle, and Gloria enrolled in the Arts program at U of T, eventually obtaining her BA. While doing so, she started a dance company called Looking Glass Dance Theatre, which toured public and private elementary schools across Ontario with a short ballet for children, *Clown of Hearts*. It was financed by an outreach program called Prologue to the Performing Arts. The company became popular in schools but Gloria had higher ambitions. She set up a new dance company with the unlikely name Ballet Ys. (The last name was pronounced 'eece' to rhyme with 'peace'.) Armed with some start-up funding from donors, the company employed six dancers and performed in Toronto and on tour. Its best-known work was its premiere of Ann Ditchburn's ballet *Nelligan*, starring Robert Desrosiers and Claudia Moore.

By 1972, however, our marriage came apart. Our agreement to separate was without rancour and we remained friends. Later when Ballet Ys encountered rough weather, as all small dance companies do, I helped hire Celia Franca, the founder of the National Ballet of Canada, to advise the company on what to do. The solution was to merge Ballet Ys (which had an excellent administration) with a dance company in Montreal called EntreSix (which had an excellent artistic director but troubled administration), and move the merged company to Ottawa. This happened in 1981. The new company was called Theatre Ballet of Canada and was under the artistic direction of Lawrence Gradus, the founder of EntreSix. Gloria was billed as co-founder of the new company but was no longer the artistic director. So ended her life in the dance profession.

Armed with her BA, she found employment with the City of Toronto. She remarried in 1980, although she retained the name Gloria Grant, and had a son named Michael. Her marriage did not last and she later bought a small duplex in the Beach, where she currently lives.

Theatre Ballet of Canada eventually folded. Lawrence Gradus left in 1989 and his successor as artistic director, Frank Augustyn, changed the company name to Ottawa Ballet; he worked hard to put its finances in order and to give the troupe more solid roots in the Ottawa area. The company continued to tour under Augustyn, who also broadened its repertoire. However, he resigned in September 1994 and the company suspended operations soon after.

ME AND URI GELLER

As part of the performance of *Clown of Hearts*, the ballet Gloria choreographed while we were still together in the early 1970s, the lead dancer needed to perform some simple magic tricks surrounded by an audience of primary school children seated on the floor. But where do you obtain suitable magic tricks?

I volunteered to acquire the necessary equipment on my next trip to New York. So in due course I showed up at the counter at Lou Tannen's, a famous emporium that sold magic tricks to the trade. There you could buy large or small effects, ranging from small card tricks to large illusions, such as how to 'saw a woman in half.' For $100, I emerged with a number of small illusions (the appearing cane, the disappearing cane, the Zombie Ball effect, appearing flowers, etc.) that were suitable for *Clown of Hearts* and an audience of young children.

I got on the Lou Tannen mailing list and every few months, I received their new magic catalogue. I became quite interested in magic and bought a few how-to books. One day in 1975, the new catalogue arrived. 'Bend Spoons and Keys Like Uri Geller' trumpeted the headline on the front page. For $5, Lou Tannen would send you the Uri Geller secret. For $10, they would send it to you by airmail. I sent $10 and a few days later a small package arrived from New York. I opened it eagerly and within minutes had learned the 'secret'. Now I was able to bend keys and spoons as if by the use of psychic powers.

Coincidentally, around that time, the real Uri Geller, the Israeli mystic, had just appeared on a CITY-TV show called 'The World of the Unexplained'. In the show, he had worked his magic powers and bent various spoons and keys provided by guests. There was no suggestion that this was just a magic trick. Geller presented himself as a true psychic. I knew Joan Schafer, the producer of the show, and I called her up to complain. She protested that her cameras had followed his every move and could not detect any sleight of hand. So he had to be a psychic. I told her that I could duplicate his trick. Joan immediately came over to the McCarthy offices along with her crew and I went to meet her. There we sat in the reception area and I proceeded to bend her keys without detection. She was genuinely mystified until I disclosed how it was done.

You, gentle reader, may also be interested to know the Uri Geller secret. And since I am not a card-carrying magician, I feel free to tell it to you.[4]

What Lou Tannen had sent me was a short piece of metal cut from a curtain rod—a 5-centimetre-long piece of brass with an open slot running through it. This can easily be concealed in the palm of a hand. To bend a key, all you need to do is slip the end of the key into the slot (with your fingers wrapped around the piece to conceal it) and then press the head of the key with your thumb. The leverage thus obtained easily bends most keys. The metal piece with which this is accomplished can then be slipped into a pocket or (if tied to an elastic cord) pulled up a sleeve.

Once bent, only the head of the key is shown to the audience at first. Then you slowly withdraw the key from your hand, all the time rubbing it mystically and calling on it to bend. As the body of the key comes out of your hand, it appears to bend.

Over the years, I continued to be interested in magic and I enjoyed taping TV shows like *Siegfried & Roy* or *David Copperfield*, then figuring out how the illusions were performed. But I was never interested in performing magic tricks. In this regard, it was similar to my interest in music—I was fascinated by how musical effects could be created and how to orchestrate, but I had little interest in actually performing in public.

BOB RICHMOND AND MUSICFEST CANADA

When I recruited the pit orchestra for each of the college musicals, I was intrigued to find that a surprising number of the student musicians had come from North Toronto Collegiate Institute. North Toronto Collegiate had a superb music program, headed up by a renowned music educator named Jack Dow. (Much later, I was delighted when two of my sons, Rory and Robbie, went to North Toronto Collegiate and Rory became involved in the music program as an excellent tuba player.)

One of the trumpet players in the stage band I assembled for *Skule Night* was Robert R. Richmond, a North Toronto graduate. Bob later became a music teacher in the Scarborough school system. I struck up a friendship with Bob and his wife, Shelley. On November 26, 1966, on my birthday, Shelley gave birth to a daughter, Randi, and I was named godfather. Bob was an avid boater, and I still remember a wonderful trip with Bob, Shelley, Randi and my first wife, Gloria, in their power boat, going the length of the Trent-Severn canal system, from Georgian Bay to Lake Ontario. Bob's boat was called *Trumpet One* and at several of the locks, Bob would bring out a long herald trumpet and play a fanfare for the amusement of the gallery of spectators.

Bob was a real entrepreneur and in 1969 he created the Cummer Valley Concert Band. This was a community band based in North York. In 1970, he organized a trip to bring the band to the world's fair in Osaka, Japan, where it played at the Canadian Pavilion.

Then, in 1972, Bob had an even more ambitious idea. He asked me to incorporate a new organization to be called the Canadian Stage Band Festival. I was pleased to do so, and for the next few years, he acted as president of the festival. Later additions were the Canadian Choral Festival in 1981 and the Canadian Concert Band Festival in 1988. To reflect these additions, the organization changed its name to MusicFest Canada in 1987. I was invited to join its board of directors in 2011.

MusicFest Canada is now an annual national event that brings together more than eight thousand of Canada's young musicians who perform for recognition in the country's foremost musical ensembles. Participants range in age from twelve to twenty-five years and are drawn from the elementary, high school, college and university levels. The festival is held each year in May, usually near the holiday weekend. The participants in MusicFest Canada are chosen from the winners in over fifty affiliated festivals across Canada where as many as four hundred thousand young musicians perform and seek an opportunity to come to the national festival.

Unfortunately, Bob's ambitions always exceeded his ability to finance them, and in 1984, he had to step down when the festival ran into financial difficulties. His marriage fell apart and he had some major health issues. He moved to Vancouver and I lost touch with him. Years later, in 2007, I got a tragic call from his daughter, Randi Richmond, who, by this time, was a production manager in Hollywood. Bob had fallen into a depression and taken his own life. I was asked to preside over a sad memorial reunion of his Toronto friends where we reminisced about his life. It is a great tribute to his enthusiasm and dedication that his legacy, MusicFest Canada, lives on.

HOW MY COMMUNICATIONS LAW CAREER BEGAN

In 1971, the government decided to set up a task force to look at communications policy in regard to data communications. The task force was headed by Dr Hans J. von Baeyer, a communications engineer who had designed the Mid-Canada line of radar stations in the late 1950s. I was hired to help the task force with legal issues. In that capacity, I used my recently won knowledge about telecom regulation to write a detailed fifty-page study summarizing the state of play across Canada in regard to telecom policy, including the hot topics of terminal attachment and system interconnection. My study, 'Jurisdictional and Legal Aspects of Computer/Communications in Canada,' was included as part A in volume II of *Branching Out*, the two-volume report of the Canadian Computer/Communications Task Force, which was published in 1972.

In 1973, I organized and chaired the first continuing-education legal program given by the Law Society of Upper Canada on broadcasting law. It was held in Toronto and, as part of the program, the Law Society Department of Continuing Education published a two-volume handbook that I authored: *Broadcasting and Cable Television Regulatory Handbook*. (A French-language edition was later published as well.) These two volumes, coupled with my earlier work for the von Baeyer task force, cemented my emergence as a communications lawyer.

The 1973 continuing legal education program also led to a long-time relationship with the Law Society of Upper Canada, the governing body of the profession in Ontario. Over the ensuing years, I was involved in dozens of conferences on communications law and policy (see p. 186).

By this point, I was committed to being a communications lawyer although I didn't have any broadcast or telecom clients. At that time, McCarthy & McCarthy did no work for any broadcasters or telecom carriers. The only link we had to the field was through John Robinette, who acted on libel matters for Canadian Press and its subsidiary Broadcast News.

I wanted to follow my teaching and research with a full-length textbook. However, I was still generating very little money for the firm. So I approached John Clarry, the managing partner of the firm, and asked for an unpaid one-year sabbatical to continue my research without having to bill any hours. Mr Clarry was sympathetic but wondered how I would make ends meet. No problem, I said, I'll survive on my law school honorarium of $4,000. And so I did. I kept my office at McCarthys but continued to work on a textbook.

However, I did get regular phone calls from the CRTC. It became known that I had studied and indexed the decisions of the Commission and its predecessor, the Board of Broadcast Governors. So occasionally a staff member would call me and ask me a question. For example, I might be asked for any precedents on whether religious stations were permitted. And I would check my notes and say that the BBG ruled back in 1965 in a case in Richmond Hill that it was not prepared to license a religious radio station. And the staff member would go away happy.

During this period, I had lunch with Pierre Juneau, the CRTC chairman, in a week when the CRTC was having a public hearing in Toronto. Mr Juneau asked me, well, how are we doing? I told him that I thought the Commission was off to a good start, but I was curious about one' case. What was that, he asked. I told him that at this very hearing, the CRTC was dealing with the renewal of a Quebec FM radio station on a non-appearing basis (meaning that the applicant did not have to appear and answer any questions, so it was considered routine). This struck me as odd, I said, since this station was controlled by a group that also controlled another FM station in the same market in the same language.

Yet I noted that the BBG had clearly established a policy in the mid-1960s that precluded anyone from owning two FM stations in the same market in the same language, although owning a joint AM-FM station was permitted.

Juneau listened to my comment with interest. It was clear that no one had ever pointed this out to him. A few weeks later, the Commission issued its licence decisions arising from the Toronto hearing. And in the renewal decision for the Quebec radio station, the CRTC added a condition that the owner divest one of the two stations before the next licence renewal. (Later, in 1998, the CRTC changed the policy and allowed persons to own up to two FM stations in the same language in the same market, as well as up to two AM stations in certain cases.)

Gradually I did more and more work for the Commission, rendering opinions on various matters. Normally, a government agency like the CRTC would have to use the federal Department of Justice if it needed additional counsel. However, because the CBC already used the Department of Justice and the CRTC regulated the CBC, the CRTC was not subject to this rule and could use outside counsel from the private sector.

Looking over my early opinions for the CRTC, I must say that they covered a broad range of topics. Among other things, I looked at the US rules on diversification of program control (the FCC 'fin-syn'[5] and prime-time access rules), the legal implications of stripping commercials from US border stations carried by cable systems in Canada, the extent of possible liability of CRTC members in actions for damages (mercifully quite limited) and the constitutional jurisdiction of the federal government over cable television. I also did a report on the jurisdiction of the Commission over master antenna systems (cable-like systems serving individual apartment buildings) and drafted an order exempting such systems from the need to have a CRTC licence. (That order, as amended and updated many times over the years, still exists.)

UNESCO

In 1974, UNESCO, the Paris-based international organization, decided to have a committee of experts draft a new declaration on the role of the mass media in combatting racism and apartheid. Canada was invited to appoint a 'media law expert' to this committee at the last minute, after China had declined to do so.

The Canadian foreign service was hard pressed to find anyone to fill this role and called the CRTC. Could they suggest someone? John Lawrence, the general counsel of the CRTC, was approached. But the meeting was to take place in Paris the following week and he was tied up drafting the CBC licence renewal decision. So he couldn't go. John called me. Would I like to go to Paris, France, the following week to be the Canadian nominee on the committee of experts? UNESCO would pay all my travel and accommodation expenses.

Why not? I was thrilled. This was my first taste of international cultural policy and I had never been to Europe in my life.

I lacked a passport. However, the foreign affairs department issued me a diplomatic passport overnight. So off I flew to Paris, knowing very little about UNESCO. When I arrived in Paris, I checked into a small Left Bank hotel on the Quai des Grands Augustins. The following morning, I showed up at the UNESCO headquarters and was ushered into a conference room where eleven other 'experts' were gathered. There was four-way simultaneous translation.

Within minutes, I was approached by a UNESCO official. Would I consent to being the rapporteur for the week-long session? I agreed and within minutes of the opening of the meeting I found myself elevated to this status. For the next five days, March 11–15, 1974, I participated in the review of a draft declaration.

The story of what happened at the meeting of experts is told in a detailed confidential report I provided to the government in August 1974. The 'experts' were from a cross-section of countries: Argentina, Canada, France, India, Kenya, Lebanon, Mexico, Poland, Senegal, the USSR, the United Kingdom and the USA. At thirty-two, I was the youngest delegate by at least five years. Most of the delegates were between forty-five and fifty.

I had been chosen to be the rapporteur by the UNESCO Secretariat sight unseen. Why? Because, as one of the staff told me, 'Canadians make good rapporteurs: they're intelligent, bilingual, independent, and—most important—*not* the United States.'

Over the next few days, we worked our way through a draft declaration. The Kenyan delegate acted as chairman of the meeting. To my amusement, whenever matters bogged down in real conflict (which

Manning the desk for the Canadian delegation at UNESCO, in Paris, 1974.
With me is A. A. (Frank) Keyes (at left), a career bureaucrat who in 1977 co-wrote
the Keyes-Brunet report on copyright reform.

happened fairly frequently) he would typically resolve it by suggesting
that the rapporteur attempt to come up with a draft of the disputed
clause for consideration at the next day's meeting that would 'take all
these views into account.' For some reason this usually proved acceptable
to everyone.

At the outset of the meeting, the UNESCO Secretariat expressed the
view privately to me that they thought it was most unlikely that the
meeting would produce a text that would be acceptable to all the experts.
But this in fact occurred. I played a large part in achieving this by suggesting wording at various junctures that would be acceptable to each side.

Later, in October 1974, I went back to Paris for a week as part of the
Canadian delegation to the UNESCO General Conference. The main
topic of discussion was to be the Mass Media Declaration. However, at the
outset of the conference, the Arab bloc, supported by many of the
developing countries around the world, presented an amendment to
define *racism* as including Zionism. When this was approved in a
controversial vote, the entire Western bloc walked out (including
Canada) and boycotted the deliberations for the rest of the week. That

stopped dead our participation in any discussions at UNESCO. In lieu of attending the UNESCO sessions, I ended up going out for dinner each evening with the Canadian delegation, a number of whom were in the foreign service and who unerringly chose the best little-known restaurants in Paris. So it was a wonderful week!

Four years passed and on November 28, 1978, after much pushing and shoving, UNESCO approved an amended version of the declaration with the unanimous consent of all 146 states. It no longer had the offending definition of racism. The full name of it is The Declaration on Fundamental Principles Concerning the Contribution of the Mass Media to Strengthening Peace and International Understanding, to the Promotion of Human Rights and to Countering Racialism, Apartheid and Incitement to War.

Some time later, I had a much more significant encounter with UNESCO (see p. 204).

THE BORDER BROADCASTING WAR

I was back in Canada when, on May 1, 1974, the CRTC attached a condition to the licence of Rogers Cable and other cable companies in Toronto authorizing them to delete the commercials on the signals of the three Buffalo commercial TV stations and to replace them with public service announcements. Thus started the 'border broadcasting war' between Canada and the United States. The three TV stations in Buffalo, New York, retained Gordon Henderson, Q.C., of Gowling & Henderson to sue the Commission and the cable companies, and he did. The CRTC suddenly found itself in court.

For years, the Buffalo stations had sold advertising time to Canadian advertisers seeking to reach the Toronto market. By this means they could take advantage of their 'overflow' audience in Canada. But they were not licensed to serve Canada and had no obligation to broadcast Canadian programming. The border broadcasting war arose out of the efforts by the CRTC and the Canadian government to 'repatriate' the Canadian ad revenue of the Buffalo stations for the benefit of Canadian TV stations, and the attempt by the Buffalo stations to hold on to that revenue.

The Commission orders took advantage of the fact that more and more Canadian viewers were receiving the Buffalo TV signals through cable. To begin with, the Commission ordered the cable companies to substitute the signal of a local Canadian station (including its commercials) for that of the Buffalo station whenever the same program was being carried at the same time by both stations. Since the Canadian station had bought the exclusive Canadian broadcast rights to the program, this only seemed fair. And as a matter of interest, the Federal Communications Commission applied a similar policy in the United States, so the Buffalo stations could hardly complain when Canada did the same.

However, the commercial deletion order went further. Even when the Canadian rights to the program were not bought by a Canadian station, the order authorized the cable company to flip a toggle switch and replace the commercial on the US signal with a Canadian public service announcement. By doing this on a random basis, the cable company could completely undermine the ad revenue of the border stations.

Three years earlier, I had provided an opinion supporting the Commission's jurisdiction to make such an order. Now the Commission called me to retain John Robinette, Q.C., our premier litigator, to defend the Commission in court. Tom Heintzman, then an associate with the firm, and I acted as his juniors. Although the action also targeted Rogers Cable, the counsel acting for Rogers deferred to Mr Robinette and we ended up carrying the weight of the case.

On behalf of the Buffalo TV stations, Gordon Henderson pulled out all the stops, arguing among other things that the CRTC had no jurisdiction over cable television in the first place. The case went all the way to the Supreme Court of Canada, which eventually ruled in the Commission's favour in 1977.[6] The decision was important and precedent-setting since it established clear federal jurisdiction over cable television under the constitution.

Another part of the Canadian strategy to repatriate the ad revenue going to the US border stations was contained in Bill C-58, an amendment to the Income Tax Act enacted in 1976, which declared that the advertising expenses of advertisers placed on US border stations to reach Canadian audiences could not be deducted from their income as a business expense. This had the effect of increasing the effective cost of any ads placed by Canadian advertisers on the Buffalo stations. (Bill C-58 also disallowed expenses for ads intended for Canada placed in foreign newspapers and periodicals, a provision that continues to this day.)

To fight Bill C-58, the Buffalo stations enlisted the US Congress to help them. Retaliatory 'mirror' legislation was introduced and eventually passed which disallowed expenses by US advertisers for ads placed on Canadian border stations. But this only affected two radio stations in Windsor which sold time to Detroit advertisers, so it was a price worth paying.

I was involved in all of these moves and counter-moves, as a back-room observer if nothing else. At one point, the Buffalo TV stations made an overture to the Commission. Couldn't they sit down and negotiate a deal? Perhaps they could agree to contribute to a Canadian programming fund as a condition of being able to sell ads in Canada? To US business-men, this seemed eminently reasonable. But Pierre Juneau, the CRTC chair, declined to bite.

Looking back on this period, it is clear that Canada won the border broadcasting war, although the 'war' was not without cost. Eventually, the CRTC dropped its commercial-deletion policy in most markets and this concession was included in the 1988 Canada-US Free Trade Agreement. However, the simultaneous-substitution rules continue in force as does Bill C-58, now enshrined in section 19.1 of the Income Tax Act.

Today, the Canadian audience of the US border TV stations has declined precipitously, as other viewing options have been introduced and as the Canadian stations make more aggressive use of the simultane-ous substitution policy, aided by the fact that over 90 percent of Canadian households now receive the US signals through Canadian cable or satellite distributors.

4. Working for the CRTC

BEING SECONDED TO THE CRTC

In late 1974, another call came from the CRTC. Could they 'borrow' me from McCarthys for two years under what was called the Executive Interchange Program? The CRTC undertook to pay my travel and accommodation expenses as well as whatever my salary and fringe benefits would have been at the law firm. I would be called Special Counsel and would help them with a variety of matters. I would report to John Lawrence, the general counsel of the CRTC.

This was particularly exciting because in 1975 the CRTC was to be handed jurisdiction over the federally regulated telecommunications carriers: Bell Canada, B.C. Tel, CNCP Telecommunications, and Terra Nova Tel and NorthwesTel, the last being two small telcos serving parts of Newfoundland and the NWT. Effective on April 1, 1975, the name of the agency changed from the Canadian Radio-Television Commission to the Canadian Radio-television and Telecommunications Commission, allowing the acronym CRTC to stay in place. In my new role, I would be in a position to act as Commission counsel for its first telephone rate cases. This sounded like a wonderful opportunity even though it would postpone any possible textbook.

The firm still had no broadcast clients (other than the CRTC itself) and some in the firm were probably dubious about whether there was any future in communications law. But John Clarry, the managing partner, agreed with this plan and for the next two years (extended to three) I maintained an apartment in Ottawa on Somerset Street West, about four blocks from the CRTC offices at 100 Metcalfe Street. (I kept my third-floor flat on Sussex Street in Toronto.) I was still employed by McCarthys but the firm was paid my salary and fringe benefits by the CRTC.

The deal with the CRTC included the rental cost of a furnished apartment in Ottawa. But instead, I rented an unfurnished apartment and applied the difference in cost to acquire some furniture. I put in some attractive pre-Confederation-style pine furniture along with Art Deco tub chairs. I also bought a Yamaha C-3 grand piano. So my second-floor apartment in Ottawa was quite enjoyable to live in.

The 1970s was an exciting decade for broadcast regulation in Canada. In early 1970, the CRTC had thrown the gauntlet down and called for much tougher Canadian content rules for television and (for the first time) Canadian content rules for music on radio stations. Over the 1970s, the Commission also issued new policies for FM radio, and awarded cable licences for major cities across Canada.

I have already mentioned the Capital Cities case, in which the Buffalo TV stations sued the CRTC and Rogers Cable, and I was involved in the successful defence. And, as I have noted earlier, the government enacted Bill C-58 in 1976, which amended the Income Tax Act to preclude those Canadian advertisers who used foreign periodicals or US border TV stations to reach Canadian viewers from deducting the cost of those ads on their tax returns. This too was highly controversial.

As special counsel to the CRTC in the 1975–78 period, I did a variety of tasks. Most of them were concerned with the regulation of the telecom carriers (see p. 94–105). However, I dipped my toes into broadcast regulation, too. In particular, I drafted much of the FM radio policy and the accompanying regulations, issued by the CRTC in 1975.

I actually managed to have some fun with the regulations. For instance, in describing the different types of radio interview, I needed to have a definition of the term *celebrity*, so I used the well-known zinger based on a 1962 quip by Daniel J. Boorstin: 'A celebrity is a person who is famous for being famous.' This actually passed muster at the Department of Justice and became part of the regulations, although it was removed in a later amendment.

I also remember attending a hearing where Northrop Frye, the president of Victoria College and Canada's greatest literary critic, sat on the CRTC panel in his role as a part-time commissioner. For a number of CRTC hearings, Dr Frye had dutifully sat on the panel but had never asked a single question. Some of us wondered how the great man could stand listening to the mindless presentations by applicants and interveners, but that is another story. At this particular hearing, however, there was an intervention by Israel (Sruki) Switzer, a consulting engineer who was also a well-known gadfly. Switzer concluded his passionate objection to the application by quoting the masthead motto of the *Globe and Mail*: 'The subject who is truly loyal to the Chief Magistrate will neither advise nor submit to arbitrary measures—Junius.' (Switzer also had that motto emblazoned on his own letterhead.) After quoting the motto, Switzer added for dramatic effect, 'And I only wish I could have delivered it in the original Latin!'

The CRTC panel was chaired by Pierre Juneau and he looked around to see if any of his fellow commissioners wanted to ask questions. Suddenly he noticed Dr Frye's hand raised. 'Oh, Dr Frye, do you have a question?' he asked.

'Just a matter to correct the record, Mr Chairman,' Frye replied. 'Junius was the pen name of a British writer in the late eighteenth century who only wrote in English.'

There was a pregnant pause as this information sunk in. Pierre Juneau later told me laughingly that he felt suddenly very proud of his commission—there can't be any subject that at least someone on the panel doesn't know something about!

Another memorable occasion was a hearing in 1972 when the Commission heard an application for renewal of a cable licence in the Eastern Townships. The owner was a US citizen from Texas who had apparently won the cable television system in a poker game, but had ignored the CRTC notices indicating that he had to sell the system to Canadians in order to maintain the licence in good standing. To the astonishment of the audience, the Texan, who had arrived wearing a ten-gallon hat and cowboy boots, engaged in direct conversation with the CRTC chair, at one point saying in a long drawl, 'Weeell, Pierre ...'

After that item was finished, the CRTC called the next application. It was for the original Global television licence, presented by Al Bruner. After setting up an easel with a map of southern Ontario, Bruner asked the chairman if he could go over to the easel and make his oral presentation using a travelling microphone. The chairman said, 'Well, okay, but *you can't call me Pierre.*' The audience broke into laughter and applause.

A few years later, Floyd Chalmers, the chairman of Maclean-Hunter Cable TV (later acquired by Rogers), called up the CRTC chairman. Chalmers was the chancellor of York University and he told Juneau that York had decided to confer an honorary doctorate on him. Juneau was of course delighted and travelled down to Toronto to accept the honour. In the anteroom just before the ceremony, Chalmers explained that Juneau would have to kneel before him, whereupon he would throw an ermine sash over Juneau's head and shoulders and say, '*Admitto te ad gradum.*'

Juneau dutifully went through the ceremony although he felt a bit silly kneeling before Chalmers, who was after all an executive of a broadcast licensee. But later, when he was back in Ottawa, Juneau brightened as he regaled us with the story. 'A thought suddenly came to me!' he said. 'This would be a hell of a way to grant broadcast licences!'

During my stay in Ottawa in 1975–78, while I focused on my work, I also enjoyed playing my new grand piano. One evening I took a date to dinner in the restaurant at the National Arts Centre. The NAC had hired a well-known local jazz pianist, Aurele Lecompte, to play piano. After 8 p.m. the restaurant emptied as patrons left to attend the concert in the NAC theatre. I noticed that the piano in the restaurant was a Yamaha C-3 Conservatory Grand, the same model I had back in my apartment. I approached the pianist and commented on this. One thing led to another and soon Lecompte and I were playing jazz standards with four hands at the piano. This went on for a half hour and we thoroughly enjoyed ourselves. At the conclusion, as I got up to rejoin my date, Lecompte asked me if I was available on Mondays to replace him at the NAC! Of course, I had to beg off.

Later, I thought about it again. What if I failed as a communications lawyer? In my mind, I could imagine Pierre Juneau coming to dine at the NAC restaurant. Suddenly he would look over at the grand piano. 'Isn't that Peter Grant?' he would say. 'I always wondered what happened to him!'

REGULATING THE TELEPHONE COMPANIES

On the telecom side, as I have noted, the CRTC was handed the jurisdiction to regulate Bell Canada and B.C. Tel on April 1, 1975, inheriting this from the Telecommunications Committee of the Canadian Transport Commission (CTC). A few staff people came over from the CTC, but none of the former CTC commissioners were appointed to the CRTC. Many people thought that the CTC had been subject to regulatory capture so this was seen as a good thing. In fact, this resulted in a CRTC that was keen to reinvent telecom regulation and to make it more accessible to the public.

Almost the first task I had at the CRTC was drafting a public notice calling for a review of 'practices and procedures' in the telecom field. In it, we proposed that:

- notices of impending rate hearings be stuffed in the monthly bill;
- informal hearings be held in smaller communities, where people could intervene without the need for lawyers;
- the regulated companies pay for the cost of consumer interveners.

All these changes were duly implemented.

The general rate of inflation in Canada in the 1970s was over 8 percent a year. This meant that the telephone companies had to come in for rate increases every few years to 'catch up'. (Inflation continued at 7 percent a year in the first half of the 1980s, but dropped to only 4 percent in the latter half of the 1980s. In the following twenty years, from 1990 to 2010, inflation averaged less than 2 percent a year.)

The year after the Commission acquired jurisdiction over the federally regulated telephone companies, Bell Canada applied for a major rate increase. It was seeking a 9.5 percent increase in residential telephone rates and a 12.5 percent increase in business rates. I was asked to act as Commission counsel in the case. The panel consisted of Charles Dalfen, the newly appointed vice-chair of the Commission, and two commissioners, Roy Faibish and Jean-Louis Gagnon. Bell Canada was represented by formidable counsel: Ernie Saunders of O'Brien, Hall & Saunders, and his young associate, Bernard Courtois.

This was my first rate case and it was not a small one. The main hearing lasted six weeks. There were some eight hundred written interrogatories, and more than five thousand pages of hearing transcript. In addition, the Commission held twelve regional hearings in various communities throughout the Bell service area.

This was an important case for me, providing my first experience in cross-examining witnesses. As is no doubt true for many tribunals, the counsel appearing in front of the Commission varied greatly in terms of competence. And even experienced litigators did not always do well when faced with technical material. My chief failing was being too eager. Consequently I was frequently called out by Bell Canada's counsel, who would interrupt my questioning to ask that their witness be given a chance to answer the question. Over time, however, I improved my style of questioning. I also discovered the benefit of using creative exhibits to move the questions along and keep the panel of commissioners interested.

In terms of the content of the case, the most interesting feature related to the treatment of the revenue from telephone directory advertising. In 1971, Bell had moved all its directory advertising to a company named Tele-Direct Ltd., itself a subsidiary of a tiny Ontario telephone company named the Capital Telephone Company Limited, a subsidiary of Bell Canada. (At the time, under its federal charter, Bell was only allowed to directly own companies that owned and operated telephone lines. So it used its tiny telephone subsidiary to own the directory company.) The benefit of Bell's manoeuvre was to shelter the revenue from directory advertising so that the only revenue that could be applied against Bell Canada's revenue requirement would be the licence fee paid by Tele-Direct to Bell for exclusive access to its telephone number database.

All of this had been exposed in the paper on directory advertising written in 1973 by one of my law students, Patrick Boyer, which exhaustively canvassed the lengthy jurisprudence on this issue. After graduating from law school, Boyer had joined the Toronto law firm of Osler, Hoskin & Harcourt. Then, to my great surprise (and secret delight), Boyer sent in a written intervention to the Bell rate case, attaching a copy of his paper from my course. He was allowed to speak briefly about it at a regional hearing.

When it came time for Bell Canada's president to appear at the main hearing, I was well prepared. In a carefully worded question, I asked Bell's president, James Thackeray, whether he agreed that telephone directories were an integral part of the operation of a telephone company. He acknowledged that they were.

That was all we needed. In its decision, the Commission ruled that Tele-Direct was, in its view, 'engaged in an enterprise which is an integral part of the operation of its corporate parent.' The Commission then ruled that for regulatory purposes the total net income of Tele-Direct would be included in 'other income' for Bell Canada, effectively reducing Bell's revenue requirement for 1977 by $5 million. Bell was awarded most of the increases it sought. However, because of the Tele-Direct adjustment, the Commission was able to order pay telephone local calling rates to be reduced from 20 cents to 10 cents a call. The decision also included commentary on quality of service and non-urban service that broke new ground. It clearly showed that a very different Commission was in town.[1]

Bell was upset with the Tele-Direct adjustment. Its carefully laid plan to shelter the directory revenue had come to nothing. But even more problematic was the Commission's later decision to take the same approach with Bell's consulting subsidiary, Bell Canada International Management Research and Consulting Ltd. (BCI). Through this subsidiary, Bell loaned out its employees to install and troubleshoot a new telephone system in Saudi Arabia. This was a highly lucrative contract for Bell, and Bell had planned to shelter the revenue under BCI. But the Commission declined to allow this, effectively ruling that any profits from BCI should be applied against Bell Canada's regulated revenue requirement. BCI, it ruled, was subject to the same integrality principle that lay behind the Tele-Direct decision.

To say that Bell was enraged by this decision would be an understatement. In fact, it led directly to the decision by Bell Canada to reorganize the company in 1983, creating a new parent, Bell Canada Enterprises, Inc. (BCE). When this corporate shuffle was announced, there was a firestorm of protest and the government referred the matter to the CRTC for a hearing and recommendations. The reorganization was ultimately approved but the government later amended the Bell Canada Act to implement the recommendations of the Commission. One of the sections of that Act specified that if an activity of an affiliate of the carrier was, in the opinion of the Commission, 'integral to the provision of the service by the carrier' the Commission could treat some or all of the earnings of the affiliate as if they were earnings of the carrier. (This provision later became section 33 of the 1993 Telecommunications Act.)

And all of this derived from a paper by one of my students! (Later Patrick Boyer left Oslers and became a Conservative MP for the Lakeshore constituency.)

SUPPORT STRUCTURES

My first practical exposure to the exercise of rate setting for a particular service (as opposed to an application for a general increase in rates across the board) came in 1977 with the Support Structures case. There were two issues of interest: first, potential competition between cable and telephone companies, and second, the determination of the appropriate rate to be charged by Bell Canada to cable companies for access to its poles and underground conduits for their strands of coaxial cable going into residential homes. Bell would also provide the coaxial cable itself for an extra charge.

On the competition side, Bell had included the following clause in its contract with cable companies:

The Customer (cable system) covenants to use the Bell facilities (the poles, ducts and coaxial cable) only for distribution of signals conveying television and/or radio programs.

This meant that Bell was using its effective monopoly on poles to keep the cable companies from competing directly with the telephone company. At the time, section 5 of the Cable Television Regulations (later section 3 of the Broadcasting Distribution Regulations) precluded cable companies from using their facilities to distribute programming services 'except as required or authorized' pursuant to their licence or the regulations. But the Commission saw little point in allowing Bell to dictate what cable companies could or could not do with the cable facilities.

Accordingly, I drafted the following wording in the decision, which turned out to be remarkably prescient:

Although the two transmission technologies—coaxial cable and copper pair—provide distinct services into the home at present, new services may develop which could be provided by either technology. In such cases, neither technology should be burdened with artificial barriers preventing their development in a fair and reasonable manner …

There are to be no restrictions imposed by the Company [Bell] on the services to be provided via the coaxial cable. In the Commission's view section 5 of the *Cable Television Regulations* should provide a sufficient regulatory basis for examining any questions raised as to the possibility of unfair competition.

The rates issue was more difficult to resolve. At the CRTC hearing, Bell presented an expert witness who used an incremental costing approach to arrive at a rate of $5 per main pole, plus 50 cents per drop pole. The cable industry countered with an expert witness who used a fully costed approach, which resulted in a rate of $3.72 per pole if only telephone and cable lines were attached to the pole, and $1.49 if hydro lines were also attached. Both witnesses were aggressively cross-examined by the other side and there turned out to be major flaws in both reports. The contradiction of having an incremental rate higher than a fully loaded rate also did not escape notice. So the CRTC was left with a challenging problem: If neither expert report was acceptable, what should the rate be? And how would the Commission justify that rate?

I was asked to draft the decision. Lacking any acceptable basis upon which to anchor the decision, I decided to follow two principles: first, pick a rate somewhere between the rates proposed by the two sides; second, have a phased increase over a five-year period to reflect inflation. With this in mind, I plunged in and created a rate structure largely out of whole cloth. The rate was $4.50 per pole for two years, with no fee for drop poles, rising to $5.50 per pole for two years and then $6.50 per pole in the final year.

I then attended a meeting of the commissioners to acquaint them with my proposal. 'Sounds good to me,' said one commissioner. The others agreed. But how to justify it? I came up with the following wording:

In the long term, the Commission believes that rates for support structures can only be established with complete confidence after fuller study based on access to appropriate data, collected in light of the factors set out above. In the absence of such data, however, and in the face of immediate requirements, the Commission has decided to exercise its best judgment on appropriate rate levels to cover a period of time sufficient to permit some degree of stability in the rate structure and to permit the development of data which could be used to provide a more refined calculation in subsequent years.

With these considerations in mind, the Commission has reached the following conclusion: [and then the rates and other terms were laid out].

Of course, there was nothing in the record of the case pointing to the particular rates chosen. But using my wording, the CRTC issued its decision.[2]

The reaction of the industry was intriguing. The cable industry declared victory, since the initial rates were somewhat lower than those proposed by Bell. A few weeks later, I ran into Ed Skelton, the rates supervisor for Bell Canada. He also commended the CRTC for its decision. I said, 'But Ed, you must have noticed that there was precious little backup for the rates.' 'Oh, that doesn't matter,' he said. 'The thing is, you made a *decision*. We now have a rate that is certified to be just and reasonable.' So both sides were happy.

Since that case, I have had occasion to cross-examine over a dozen economists or 'experts' on rate cases, whether before the CRTC or the Copyright Board. I have also presented evidence myself to support or oppose various rate levels. However, I have to say that my experience in the Support Structures case gave me a somewhat cynical view of the rate-setting process!

Shortly after the Support Structures and Bell Rate Increase decisions were issued by the Commission, I received a letter from the vice-chair, Charles Dalfen, who had chaired both hearings:

May I express my sincere thanks to you for your efforts in producing the decisions. Without your efforts and talents those decisions would not be of the high quality and calibre that I believe they are. As the token radical in the place (the McCarthy Brothers would roll over in their graves!), you have infused the kind of soul into the decisions that only Pat Pearce could equal. [Mrs Pearce was a commissioner who frequently expressed left-wing views.]

TELESAT CANADA

During my stay at the Commission, I also had a baptism by fire in regard to the relationship between communications regulation and politics. This involved the 1977 Telesat Canada case.

Telesat Canada had applied for approval of an agreement with the nine major telephone companies who were members of the Trans-Canada Telephone System (TCTS). The deal allowed Telesat to gain financing for a new series of satellites. However, it came at a cost: Telesat would not be allowed to compete with the telephone companies. After an extensive hearing, the CRTC decided not to approve the agreement largely because of its detrimental effect on competition.

I had a hand in drafting the lengthy decision and the commissioners were quite proud of its compelling arguments.[3]

However, the carriers lobbied the Federal Cabinet and to the surprise of the CRTC, the decision was reversed by the governor in council. The argument made by the carriers was that unless the government itself was prepared to step up with a guarantee of financing, the new series of satellites would not be built and launched by Telesat unless the TCTS deal was approved. The government blinked, and varied the decision from a no to a yes. While this came as something of a shock to the Commission, it was also a lesson to all of us—don't underestimate the power of politics!

I should add a note here about the relationship of my law firm with Telesat Canada over the years. In 1990, McCarthy & McCarthy merged with the Quebec-based law firm Clarkson Tétrault to become McCarthy Tétrault. The Ottawa office included Tony Keenleyside, a young partner who had been acting for Telesat Canada. As a result, we inherited both Tony and his main telecom client, and so, for a few years, our firm acted for Telesat in rate cases before the CRTC. In the 1992 rate case, in fact, Tony and Hank Intven of our firm were instrumental in rebutting a major intervention from Cancom.[4] When the government sold its shares in Telesat to BCE Inc. in 1993, however, we lost the account. But the account came back in 2007, when BCE sold Telesat Canada to a consortium headed by Loral Space & Communications Inc., for whom we acted.

CHALLENGE COMMUNICATIONS

One day in August 1977, I got a call from a lawyer in Toronto who was well-known as a plaintiff's lawyer in personal injury cases. He had a problem. One of his clients, a company in which he was a significant investor, was about to go bankrupt. He came to my office at McCarthys, accompanied by his client, Sheldon Kideckel, the president of a small mobile phone supplier, Challenge Communications Ltd. He also brought along a lawyer from Philadelphia who specialized in FCC work.

Bell Canada was the problem. In those days, mobile telephone service involved the use of radio apparatus in the customer's car, and Bell permitted this equipment to be owned and maintained by the customer. But there were only a few analog frequencies available and the channels were heavily congested with traffic, all of which interfaced with Bell's telephone network through a Bell operator. In 1977, Bell decided to introduce a new service called Automatic Mobile Telephone Service (AMTS). The units would use UHF frequencies and would interconnect with the Bell system without the interface of an operator. But Bell decided that it alone would own the equipment.

It was clear to Challenge that this would decimate its business. A similar service had been introduced in the United States some years earlier but there the Bell companies allowed competitive companies to supply and maintain customer-owned equipment. In Canada, Bell Canada intended to have a monopoly on the automated side of the service.

But what relief was available to Challenge Communications? The lawyer from Philadelphia noted that the key statute supporting competition in the United States was the Sherman Act. Surely the Canadian equivalent—the Combines Investigation Act—could provide the basis for relief? I quickly disabused him of any such notion. At the time we were talking, in the 1970s, that Act applied only to goods, not services. (Since then it has been replaced by the Competition Act, which does embrace services.) Nor was there much help under the Bell Canada Special Act. True, it had been amended in 1968 to add a provision dealing with the interconnection of equipment not provided by Bell. But the Federal Court of Appeal had effectively gutted this provision in the Ottawa Cablevision case in 1974, ruling that this provision did not empower the Commission to order interconnection.

However, there was another basis for relief. As I had discovered in the course of working on the Telesat Canada case, there was support for competition policy in a little-known section of the Railway Act that was applicable to telephone companies. Subsection 321(2) read:

A company shall not, in respect of tolls *or any services or facilities provided by the company as a telegraph or telephone company,*

(a) make any unjust discrimination against any person or company,

(b) make or give any undue or unreasonable preference or advantage to or in favour of any particular person or company or any particular description of traffic, in any respect whatever, or

(c) subject any particular person or company or any particular description of traffic to any undue or unreasonable prejudice or disadvantage in any respect whatever...

Looking at all the early telephone cases cited by Coyne on Railway Law and my more extensive research, it was clear that historically this provision had only been used to deal with discriminatory *rates* charged to consumers, not with competition policy. However, the italicized words, embracing discrimination in *services and facilities* as well as rates, had been added to the subsection in 1970.

The subsection also referred to an undue preference in favour of 'any person or company.' Bell Canada thought this only referred to *customers* of the telephone company. But the word *company* was defined elsewhere in the Railway Act to include the telephone company itself. Accordingly, the subsection was susceptible to a much broader interpretation. Arguably, by monopolizing the ownership of the equipment, Bell Canada had given an undue preference or advantage *to itself*. And as a potential supplier of customer-owned equipment, surely Challenge had been subjected to an 'unreasonable disadvantage' by Bell's decision to disallow customer-owned equipment in the automated mobile service.

So I told my visitors from Challenge their only hope was to apply to the CRTC for relief under subsection 321(2) of the Railway Act. The Challenge lawyers went away and drafted a pleading on behalf of their client, accompanied with affidavits. It was based entirely on subsection 321(2).

Since I had been involved in the early discussion with Challenge, I decided it would not be appropriate for me to act as counsel to the CRTC in the hearing of the application. Instead this task devolved to David Osborn, the deputy counsel. The CRTC panel then proceeded to hear the case. Bell raised a number of legal points to try to justify its position. But the hearing panel was frankly appalled at Bell's high-handedness. Challenge not only won its case but the Commission awarded costs against Bell, an unprecedented step.[5]

Bell promptly appealed the CRTC decision to the Federal Court of Appeal. McCarthys was retained to defend the CRTC decision, and Tom Heintzman argued the case with my assistance. And in April 1978, the court dismissed the appeal.[6] Bell immediately sought leave to appeal the decision to the Supreme Court of Canada. I attended the hearing along with Tom Heintzman and the Supreme Court dismissed Bell's leave application without even hearing from our side. I remember walking back from the court to the Chateau Laurier with Ernie Saunders, Bell's counsel in the case. He was well aware of the implications of the decision. 'I don't think the Commission will want to have that broad a jurisdiction,' he said, crestfallen. I begged to differ. In fact, the use of subsection 321(2) of the Railway Act turned out to be the key to the introduction of competition in the telecommunications industry in Canada over the next fifteen years. Its current equivalent, subsection 27(2) of the 1993 Telecommunications Act, is one of the most important provisions of that legislation.

The idea of using an 'undue preference' provision to address competition policy later morphed into the broadcasting sector. Starting in the 1990s, the CRTC applied the notion of prohibiting undue preference in its regulations, licence conditions and exemption orders applicable to broadcasters, cable and satellite distributors and even Internet sites. The concept of using undue preference in this way was firmly based on the Challenge case.

DECISION 79-11:
THE FIRST INTERCONNECTION CASE

All of these cases were just a prelude to the granddaddy of telecom cases in the 1970s, namely, the Interconnection case. This was an application by CNCP Telecommunications to interconnect its lines with those of Bell Canada, so as to permit the interconnection of private line networks and public data network services to Bell's facilities. The application did not involve direct competition for Bell's lucrative 'message toll service', i.e., public long distance service, although Bell argued that this represented a 'slippery slope' towards such competition. However, it was clear that CNCP's application would involve a major step towards increased competition, so all the major telephone companies in Canada fought the application tooth and nail.

I acted as Commission counsel in the case. There was a lengthy interrogatory process and then twenty-five days of hearings, involving dozens of witnesses, which took place in Gatineau in March and April 1978. This was followed by final and reply argument in writing.

My real work took place later on, since I was largely responsible for drafting the key parts of the CRTC decision. This took an enormous amount of time. I was back in Toronto for most of this work, and as I finished drafts of major parts of the decision, I would send them by bus to

Ottawa. (This was before e-mail.) A standard refrain from me to anxious CRTC staff members would be, 'It's on the bus!'

A major part of the decision elaborated on the legal principles involved. I particularly enjoyed drafting this part because my early research paid off in an amusing way. Bell had argued for a certain rate-making principle, based on some early railway cases. It helped that I was aware of a 1964 telephone case that had come in front of the Board of Transport Commissioners, involving the Town of Kenora, and where Bell had argued the converse. No one in the CNCP proceeding had known about this case or referred to it but I was happy to add a reference to it in the decision.

Eventually we completed the decision and it went into translation. Finally, the decision was released on May 17, 1979.[7] The English version alone was fully 284 pages long. It granted the CNCP application subject to detailed technical conditions and compensation conditions.

Ten years later, on May 17, 1989, some of the CRTC staff members from that period met in a bar in Ottawa to reminisce about Decision 79-11. We all felt that it had marked an enormous increase in sophistication for the Commission and we were quite proud of our work. Despite its significance, Bell had not appealed the decision to the courts.

Later of course the decision was superseded by CRTC decisions that opened up telecom competition much more widely. I was involved in some of these as well, acting for business users (see p. 111–118). However, Decision 79-11 marked a major milestone in my career. It was also the last decision of the Commission that I had a hand in drafting.

ACTING FOR THE CULTURAL INDUSTRIES

My duties as special counsel to the Commission took up most of my time from 1975 to 1978 and I spent much of this period in Ottawa, although I maintained an office at McCarthy & McCarthy in Toronto.

In 1975, I got a call from Paul Audley, who was the executive director of the Independent Publishers' Association (IPA). This was a breakaway group from the Canadian Book Publishers' Council (later the Canadian Publishers' Council), which had been founded in 1910 but which was dominated by the multinational book publishers active in Canada.

Reflecting the spirit of cultural nationalism that was emerging in this period, the Canadian-owned book publishers wanted their own trade association.

Paul wondered if I could help them incorporate the IPA as a not-for-profit trade association. I was pleased to do so, and the Association of Canadian Publishers (ACP) was born. I also gave them some help on interpreting the Copyright Act in regard to book importation.

A little later, I got a similar call from the owner of a small Canadian record label. He wondered if I could incorporate a trade association for the Canadian-owned sound recording industry. The small Canadian labels wanted to break free from the Canadian Recording Industry Association (CRIA), which was dominated by the multinationals. Again, I was happy to help. And so the Canadian Independent Recording Industry Association (CIRPA) came into being. (It is now called the Canadian Independent Music Association.)

I rapidly learned that there was a big difference between acting in the telecom and broadcast sectors and acting for companies in the book publishing or sound recording industries. The broadcast and telecom clients could generally afford me, even at the rates charged by McCarthy & McCarthy. But this was not true of the small Canadian-owned book publishers or music labels. Accordingly, I frequently worked for the latter sectors on a *pro bono* basis. In effect, I cross-subsidized this work with my more lucrative work in the communications sector.

Then in the early 1980s, I incorporated the Foundation Assisting Canadian Talent on Recordings (FACTOR) and MUSICACTION, its equivalent for the French-language music sector. And I carried out a tele-ordering study for the Canadian book industry that led to the creation of Telebook Canada, a non-profit organization that developed a searchable database of published book titles.

In 1982, I served as chairman (Books) for the large invitation-only National Strategy Conference on Books, Records and Films, hosted by the Banff Centre. There were participants from each cultural sector, for a total of seventy people. The other chairmen were Peter Steinmetz (records), Michael Levine (film) and David Silcox (plenary). My work for the Association of Canadian Publishers had sensitized me to the importance of having vibrant Canadian-owned firms in the cultural industries. Relying on foreign-owned companies to seek out and promote Canadian cultural products was not likely to be an effective policy. However, the conference included a number of executives and lawyers representing the multinational companies active in Canada and they did not appreciate my views.

Insofar as the cultural industries were concerned, I was enthusiastic about assisting the Canadian-owned sector even when it could scarcely afford me. In fact, I went out of my way to distinguish McCarthys as a firm that would side with the Canadian-owned publishers, distributors, record labels and broadcasters in any dispute with their foreign counterparts. This undoubtedly cost us some lucrative work. But other law firms were happy to get work from the multinationals, whether it was Gowlings acting for the Buffalo TV stations, or Oslers acting for Time Warner in the *Sports Illustrated* dispute. By focusing on the Canadian-owned sector, I felt that I could keep relatively free from conflicts. But more important, I felt we were acting for the underdogs and on the right side in terms of cultural policy.

FREEDOM OF INFORMATION

The mid-1970s was an exciting time for advocates of greater government openness. In the United States, the Watergate scandal combined with the rise of Ralph Nader had resulted in meaningful freedom of information legislation by 1976. But in Canada, although many members of the bar supported the notion, the government resisted.

In August 1976, the Canadian Bar Association made freedom of information the central theme of its annual convention in Winnipeg and after extensive debate the delegates voted overwhelmingly for a resolution calling for access-to-information legislation. Having helped to start a Media and Communications Law Section in the Canadian Bar Association, I pushed to have a special committee created to lobby for meaningful freedom-of-information legislation in Canada. I ended up heading the committee. But we were pushing up a steep hill. The Liberal government resisted the notion. They suggested that it would be inconsistent with our parliamentary system. In particular, they argued, 'ministerial responsibility' would be imperilled if a court was able to overrule a minister of the Crown and order disclosure of a government document. No court should be given that power.

In the fall of 1976, I happened to be up at the University of Toronto Faculty of Law and ran into a former student of mine, Murray Rankin. He told me that he was now getting his LLM at Harvard. 'That's great,' I said. 'What's your thesis topic?'

'Well, I haven't picked one,' he replied.

I jumped in. 'Why don't you look at freedom of information in a parliamentary system?' I said. In particular, I suggested that Murray devote his thesis to rebutting the 'ministerial responsibility' defence, using precedents from jurisdictions that had a parliamentary system, like the UK.

Murray's eyes lit up. 'That sounds like a great idea!' he said.

A few months passed. Then, two events happened in quick succession. First, the government published a Green Paper on freedom of information. Reading it gave me a sickening feeling. Reflecting the views of Trade and Commerce minister Mitchell Sharp, himself a former civil servant, the document reiterated the idea that no government documents should be disclosed unless a minister agreed.

Around the same time, in March 1977, I received a thick envelope from Harvard. It was Murray's LLM thesis. I read it through quickly. It was a superb piece of work. Based on English jurisprudence, it effectively demolished the idea that ministerial responsibility trumped access to information.

I called Murray and congratulated him. And I had a brilliant idea. I suggested he come to Ottawa at the expense of the Canadian Bar Association and spend a week rewriting his paper. In particular, I explained, we would need a chapter at the end rebutting the Green Paper. And we would need the entire paper written in a more exciting polemic style. Then we would have the bar association publish it at a press conference. 'We'll call it the Rankin Report,' I said.

Murray arrived in Ottawa and for a week we fed him coffee and sandwiches as he converted his thesis into a hard-hitting report. Meanwhile, I designed a cover with the attention-grabbing title *Freedom of Information in Canada: Will the Doors Stay Shut?*

In May 1977 all was ready. The Canadian Bar Association held a press conference in Ottawa and unveiled the Rankin Report.[8] The president of the association read a speech I had drafted, with some good quotable lines. The press conference was an incredible success. Press coverage over the next few days was dominated by favourable coverage of the bar's initiative. We all basked in the glory. The government was on the defensive. The Conservatives immediately picked up the issue and made freedom of information a campaign promise in the 1979 federal election.

We kept the heat on. At a conference in Victoria in March 1979, the CBA unveiled a model bill on freedom of information prepared by my committee under my direction. The Liberals were caught flat-footed, having introduced nothing in Parliament up to that point. In the election that spring, the Conservatives won the right to lead a minority government under Joe Clark. Following their election promise, the Tories tabled the first draft legislation on freedom of information, Bill C-15, for first reading on October 24, 1979. But the Clark government fell in December of that year. In the ensuing election, the Liberals swept back into power. Finally taking action in the face of political pressure, they tabled Bill C-43, which was given first reading on July 18, 1980.

In order to facilitate an understanding of Bill C-43, and under the auspices of the CBA and the Law Society of Upper Canada, I organized a major international symposium on freedom of information and individual privacy. It took place in Toronto before more than two hundred and fifty delegates on September 26 and 27, 1980. A highlight of the symposium was a mock trial using the language of Bill C-43, with top-ranked counsel arguing each side. Our committee continued to keep up the pressure and we tabled a ninety-two-page submission to the Standing Committee on Justice and Legal Affairs in March 1981, proposing various amendments to the bill.

Eventually, the legislation was enacted by Parliament and it became law in 1983. While the Access to Information Act is by no means perfect (a recent Supreme Court of Canada decision has undermined its applicability to cabinet documents), it does allow the courts to overrule a government's decision to withhold a document in a number of circumstances. I have no doubt but that the pressure brought by the Canadian Bar Association on this issue was instrumental in bringing the legislation to fruition. My role in all of this was relatively minor and behind the scenes, but I like to think it had an impact.

As for Murray Rankin, he moved to British Columbia to teach at the University of Victoria Faculty of Law, where he became a recognized expert on access to information. Later he went into private practice, focusing on environmental and public law. Since 2012, he has been the NDP member of parliament for the riding of Victoria.

5. Return to McCarthys

RETURN TO MCCARTHY & MCCARTHY

By 1979, it was time for me to return to McCarthys, and I did so happily. The CRTC had asked me to stay on an extra year to handle its review of the TransCanada Telephone System agreements, but I declined. I was keen to start working in the private sector. And needless to say, the firm was keen to make some money.

With that in mind, I closed my apartment in Ottawa and moved back to Toronto full-time. I needed a much larger apartment to accommodate my pine furniture and my grand piano, so I rented a co-op apartment in Rosedale.

My first client came almost immediately. I was contacted by a consultant who acted for the Ontario Hospital Association (OHA). Hospitals, like other big businesses, operated a switchboard (a so-called private branch exchange, or PBX) that connected with all the phones on the premises. But Bell Canada insisted on supplying and maintaining ownership of all this equipment. Hospitals enviously looked south of the border, where there was a thriving market for a variety of PBX equipment that could be purchased from different companies at different prices, many of the units coming with features not offered by Bell. Bell's own subsidiary Nortel was a successful supplier to the US market with its digital PBX unit called the SL-1; the SL-1 offered some features in the United States that Bell did not offer to its own customers in Canada.

The OHA wanted to get the CRTC to overturn the rules preventing subscribers from owning their own phones so as to open up the PBX market to competition. The OHA was aware of my involvement in the Challenge case and felt I could help them. In the end, I was retained not only by the OHA but also by a number of other business-user groups, all of which wanted to own their own phones.

On November 13, 1979, Bell filed an application with the CRTC to bring the issue of terminal attachment before the Commission. Bell had recognized the inevitability of subscriber-owned terminal equipment but wanted to control the process. It proposed self-serving 'interim' requirements, but these were shown to be hollow. In reality, Bell proposed a protracted four-stage procedure that each proposed type of connection would have to undergo, as well as a lengthy process to develop and approve a standard that would have required technical certification of subscriber-owned equipment by a Canadian lab. Under this approach, liberalization would have been delayed for years.

On behalf of the OHA and the Telephone Answering Association of Canada I filed an application for interim relief on January 15, 1980. In the application, I proposed that the Commission use the technical standard already promulgated a few years earlier by the Federal Communications Commission in the United States. After all, the telephone system across Canada operated according to a North American standard. A month later, Bell filed its own proposed standard and we responded by filing detailed comments on the unsuitability of that standard.

On August 5, 1980, the CRTC granted my interim application and liberalized terminal attachment for Bell Canada subscribers, allowing the FCC standard to apply for the interim period.[1] I can still remember the feeling when this decision was announced; it was my first telecom victory in front of the CRTC. However, Bell promptly appealed to the Federal Cabinet to reverse the interim decision. I drafted a seventeen-page rebuttal to Bell's petition and, in the end, the cabinet upheld the CRTC interim decision.

In the main hearing that followed, I presented an array of witnesses from the business community to talk about the benefits of competition in subscriber equipment. Probably my most effective witness was the head of the St. Joseph's Hospital in London, Ontario. She was an engaging and intelligent business-minded executive who also happened to be a nun. In all our preparatory meetings, she wore conservative business attire. But thinking of the impact on the Commission, I asked her if she would wear her nun's habit when she appeared at the CRTC hearing.

She did so. Her evidence went in beautifully as she described the hospital-specific features that she wanted for her PBX and that the Bell equipment would not have. Ernie Saunders, Bell Canada's counsel, recognized her effectiveness and could not help but notice that she was dressed in a nun's habit. He decided on the spot not to ask her any questions!

The final decision by the Commission granted our application in its entirety, and approved consequential tariff changes. This was followed by a similar decision relating to B.C. Tel. Suddenly most of the telephone subscribers in Ontario, Quebec and British Columbia could own their own phones.

In preparing and fighting the terminal attachment case, I had the help of Lorne Salzman, an associate in the firm who had been working with the computer law group. Lorne's background was in drafting and negotiating deals for the acquisition of computers and other high tech equipment, including the licensing of intellectual property. Within a few months of our victory in the case, he was asked to deliver a presentation at a conference organized by business users on how to acquire a PBX system. These systems typically cost millions of dollars. For this purpose, Lorne drafted a proposed contract between two made-up companies, Titanic Telephone Inc. (the equipment vendor) and Iceberg Industries Ltd. (the business user). The contract was drafted entirely from the perspective of the business user, with all the warranties and other clauses biased in favour of the user. Lorne presented this contract as an example of what a sophisticated business user might ask for, but cautioned that no equipment vendor would be likely to agree to all of these conditions. In fact, Lorne envisaged a burgeoning career acting for business users in negotiating these contracts.

It was not to be. Very little of this kind of work materialized. A year or so later, Lorne was talking to an executive from a major PBX supplier at a conference when the executive suddenly broke off and told a colleague to send a potential customer 'the Iceberg contract'. Lorne enquired further and learned to his amusement (and chagrin) that his draft contract had evolved to become the standard contract in the industry. What had happened was that the business users had played the PBX vendors off against each other, seeking all the conditions and warranties specified in Lorne's draft. Gradually each vendor caved and agreed to these conditions in order to get the multimillion-dollar deal.

Lorne continued to work with me on telecom matters for a number of years. But he never forgot the Iceberg story.

FIGHTING BELL CANADA FOR FUN AND PROFIT

In 1980, the same year I won the terminal attachment case, I was also made a partner in McCarthy & McCarthy. My entry into partnership had been delayed because of the sojourn at the CRTC but the firm finally recognized that there was a future in this new burgeoning area.

The terminal attachment case also marked the beginning of a relationship in which I acted for a number of business users to fight Bell Canada (and sometimes B.C. Tel) at CRTC rate cases and other regulatory proceedings. The group was led by the Canadian Industrial Communications Assembly (CICA), a not-for-profit association of executives in Canadian companies who were responsible for purchasing telecom services. It later changed its name to the Canadian Business Telecommunications Alliance (CBTA). That relationship lasted for almost a decade.

Presenting telecom cases in front of the CRTC was not inexpensive. Back in 1980, a six-week rate case could easily run up a legal bill of $100,000 or more (which in 2013 dollars would be more than $250,000). CICA alone could not afford to hire me so, based on the approach taken in the terminal attachment case, a number of other trade associations joined the fray in order to share the cost. In a typical case, I would be described as acting for 'CICA et al'. The other clients embraced within this framework included, from time to time, the Ontario Hospital Association, the Canadian Bankers Association, the Canadian Business Equipment Manufacturers Association (CBEMA), the Hotel Association of Canada, the Association of Competitive Telecommunications Suppliers (ACTS), the Canadian Association of Data Processing Service Organizations (CADAPSO), the Canadian Radio Common Carriers Association, the Canadian Manufacturers Association and the Canadian Petroleum Association. This approach turned out to be very cost effective for the business clients, as I would agree to work within a specific budget (say, $125,000) and the associations would agree among themselves at the start of the case how they would apportion the cost, with no single client paying more than $25,000.

There was never much conflict about my instructions. Essentially, the group wanted more competition and lower business rates. But how I managed to achieve this result was largely left to me. None of the clients understood the details of rate regulation or how the CRTC worked, so I was given a relatively free hand to take what I called 'targets of opportunity'. In this, I was aided by access to telecom consultants, but the overall strategy was primarily my concern.

Over the next few years, I appeared at virtually every Bell and B.C. Tel rate case. Because of the latitude given me by my clients, I was able to make a real difference for business users, although fighting the telecom carriers was no picnic. My first rate case acting for business interveners occurred in 1981, and it provided a useful lesson in how to proceed.

In order to justify any rate increase, telephone companies would present what they called their 'construction program,' involving millions of dollars of cost to extend service, rebuild exchanges and so forth. For interveners intent on challenging the proposed rate increase, the construction program was always a tempting target. However, it was next to impossible to attack. One might ask for a list of all projects over $100,000 to be produced, and then pick a few items from the list to attack. But, of course, Bell Canada would be able to justify each project. You have questions about the expenditures to be made in a local exchange serving a suburb of Kitchener? Bell would produce engineering reports showing the buildup of new houses and the complaints about delays in that suburb. Bell would also refer to earlier judgments of the Board of Railway Commissioners, where the predecessor tribunal had ruled that it would not substitute its judgment for that of the company management in such matters.

So as an intervener, what could you do? I wandered into the law school library and started reading the reports of rate decisions south of the border. These were found in a series of law reports called *Public Utility Reports* (PUR). I particularly focused on the decisions of the New York State Public Service Commission and the California Public Utilities Commission, both of which were activist agencies, not afraid of cutting rates.

Browsing through the cases in 1980, I discovered an interesting case in front of the California Public Utilities Commission. Just the year before, it had cut back a Pacific Tel rate-increase application because the company had delayed implementation of teleprocessing in its business offices. A number of gas utilities and a few telephone companies in the United States had computerized their order-taking and customer-billing systems, with the result that they could handle the same customer base with a much smaller workforce.

I called up the California PUC to find out more. I was put in touch with a Commission employee named Harry Strahl, who had developed the evidence and presented it to the PUC. Strahl was delighted to help and soon I flew out to the PUC offices in San Francisco to interview him more closely. I secured the permission of the California PUC to bring him to Ottawa, at the expense of my client, to be a witness before the CRTC. At the same time, I contacted the Consumers Association of Canada, which was pleased to present a Canadian economist as a witness to speak to the applicability of Strahl's evidence to the Canadian situation.

As I suspected, Bell had done nothing to introduce teleprocessing in 1981 and its ratio of customer service representatives to telephone subscribers was therefore far higher than it needed to be. Nor did it have any incentive to change its systems, as long as the Commission approved all its proposed business office expenses as part of the rate case.

So on behalf of business users, I mounted a frontal attack on Bell. The company felt mortally wounded. It cross-examined both witnesses to try to show that this was a foreign development and that the Canadian situation was entirely different. At the same time, Bell indicated that its executives had visited one of the telephone companies that had implemented teleprocessing in its business offices with great success. (It was the Winter Park Telephone Company, which served the area surrounding Disney World in Florida. Doubtless the Bell Canada executives also brought their families along for the ride!)

In the end, the CRTC declined to rule in my favour. It dealt with my arguments in the following passage:

The Commission recognizes the desirability of introducing methods, including teleprocessing, that are intended to improve business office productivity. However, the Commission considers that the desirable rate at which such methods are introduced depends on the circumstances of the particular telephone company ... [T]he Commission accepts Bell's argument that, in a large telephone company serving a large geographical territory, a gradual mechanization of business office operations is prudent ...[2]

As a result the Commission made no adjustment in regard to teleprocessing in its rate decision. My only consolation was that the message did get through to Bell Canada, and in the next few years it reportedly accelerated its program to introduce teleprocessing in the business office.

I have to say that my experience in Bell and B.C. Tel rate cases generally supported Richard Posner's observation that utility-rate regulation was largely ineffective in addressing perceived abuses.[3] As my experience in the 1981 case demonstrated, regulators would always be reluctant to substitute their judgment for that of company management in regard to its capital or operating budget. That said, I did have much more success in addressing comparative rate levels for business services. In many cases, Bell or B.C. Tel would try to use the general rate case to adjust rate levels for particular business services in ways that were problematic. I frequently challenged these adjustments and often won significant victories for business users. But it was clear to me and my clients that the only effective way to lower their rates was to introduce competition. (Later, after amendments to the telecommunications legislation were made in 1993, the Commission moved away from rate-of-return regulation and introduced so-called price-cap regulation over baskets of monopoly services, with deregulation of competitive services. This is a far superior approach.)

DECISION 85-19:
THE SECOND INTERCONNECTION CASE

In 1984, I acted for business users in what became known as the IX-2 case. Having won a limited right of interconnection back in 1979, CNCP Telecommunications applied for full rights of interconnection in 1984. This application was to allow it to compete directly with the telephone companies for public long distance traffic.

Business users fully supported the CNCP application and I participated actively in the case on behalf of CBTA et al, which embraced twelve different clients. A number of user witnesses were presented at the CRTC hearings, all supporting the benefits of increased competition. CNCP focused its attention on winning its application to provide a competing long distance voice service. On behalf of CBTA, I supported this completely. But I also focused on the benefits of resale and sharing of private lines, with evidence from the hotel industry, the book publishing and distribution sector and the university sector.

The Commission's decision was issued on August 19, 1985.[4] CNCP had prepared for a favourable decision by booking a reception room where champagne was waiting to be poured. But to its great surprise and chagrin, the Commission denied its application. The decision was a curious one, since it summarized the benefits of long distance competition at great length, but then pulled its punches at the end. I am told that the

CRTC staff supported full competition, but the commissioners were concerned about the impact of rate rebalancing. The only consolation for business users in the decision was that the Commission did approve resale and sharing to provide interexchange service other than public long distance traffic, something CBTA had strongly supported.

The decision delayed the introduction of full competition in long distance calling in Canada for seven years. Eventually, Unitel Communications Inc.—the successor to CNCP—applied in 1990 and in 1992 won the right to compete directly with the telephone companies.[5] In the interim period, enhanced resale and sharing increased, and Call-Net, a small would-be competitor to the telcos, tried to offer lower long distance rates through 'enhanced' services that flirted with the rules. (The CRTC at Bell's behest tried to stop Call-Net but the Federal Cabinet staved off the regulator for a time.)

The result was that real reductions in long distance rates did not occur until after Unitel won its interconnection application in 1992. But it was tough sledding for Unitel and the other competitors to the telcos, and they lost millions of dollars in the ensuing battles for market share. Technology also played a factor as the cellular market exploded and the cable companies entered the telephone market through Voice Over Internet Protocol (VOIP) services. The Commission's hesitance to upset the status quo in 1985 was a major disappointment for those seeking a more competitive framework at that time. But eventually competition arrived.

ACTING FOR PEOPLE WITH DISABILITIES

In 1986, I became involved in addressing the problems people with hearing impairment had in dealing with the telephone network. My client was the Canadian Hearing Society, then headed by Judy Rebick.

They called me because of the introduction of teletypewriters that could be attached to the telephone system. With one of these devices (called a TTY) at each end of the line, people with hearing or speech disabilities could communicate over the phone system by typing their messages where they could be read on a small LCD screen. But how could they communicate if the person on the other end of the line did not have a teletypewriter unit? The solution would be to have a live person receive the call (armed with a TTY unit) and then relay the message orally to the desired recipient.

The previous year, the Commission had ordered B.C. Tel to provide a call relay service for people who were hard of hearing in British Columbia, to be paid for by adding the expense to its general revenue requirement, which would be recovered through its general rates.[6] The Canadian Hearing Society asked me to persuade the Commission to order Bell Canada to do the same in Ontario and Quebec. This required me to present evidence at the next Bell rate case, where I was already acting for business users. However, the business users did not oppose me doing so, so I did not have a conflict in taking on the Hearing Society application.

At the CRTC hearing in Gatineau, Quebec, I arranged to have TTY devices installed both at the witness table and in front of each commissioner. The evidence went in quite well, as I had the witnesses show the panel how the system worked in practice. But my most effective witness was a beautiful teenage deaf girl who spoke directly to the Commission in a voice that showed the telltale signs of her disability. Her message was quite simple. If she wanted to call a boy to have a date, *she had to ask her mother to call the boy for her.* But with a call relay service, she could do it herself. Her story immediately resonated with everyone in the room. We could all imagine how embarrassing it would be to have to 'go through your mother.' It was incredibly moving to hear her describe the problem.

Bell argued that a service of this kind should be done with government funding, not by recovering it from subscribers. But the Commission disagreed. It approved my application in its entirety, and the call relay service has operated across Ontario and Quebec ever since.[7] The Commission also ordered Bell Canada to pay my legal fees. Many years later, in 2009, the Commission required the telecom carriers to add an Internet version of the service.[8]

This was not my only exposure to the challenges facing people with disabilities. In 1989, I was approached by the National Broadcast Reading Service, Inc. to help it get a CRTC licence for a satellite-delivered audio service for people who were blind or visually impaired. The service was to be called VoicePrint. Volunteers would read current articles in newspapers and magazines and this would be transmitted as part of basic cable service, with the cable operator paying a penny per subscriber per month to cover the cost. An earlier application for the service had been turned down by the Commission because of organizational and governance problems, so I was approached to rescue the situation.

I was pleased to help. I helped them redesign the application to address the Commission's concerns and then presented the application at a hearing in Hamilton, Ontario. The Commission approved it in 1990.[9] (Later, in 2012, VoicePrint changed its name to AMI-audio.)

CROSS-OWNERSHIP
BETWEEN BROADCASTERS AND CABLE OPERATORS

By 1978, I was free to act for private broadcast clients. But I had none.

This changed in 1979. I got a call from John C. Clark, the chairman of Connor, Clark, a broker-dealer concerned over a Vancouver application. Western International Communications (WIC), the owner of the CTV station in Vancouver, had applied to the Commission for approval to acquire Premier Cablevision, which operated the largest cable television system in BC. Clark was secretly acting for the Belzbergs, who had a minority stake in Premier Cablevision and were concerned with the low price being paid for their shares.

Of course, the Commission couldn't care less about the interests of minority shareholders or what price applied for their shares. To stop the acquisition, I had to come up with arguments based on public policy. Bearing this in mind, I drafted a hard-hitting intervention and an oral presentation for Clark to present to the CRTC at its hearing in June 1979. Among other matters, the intervention laid out all the potential conflicts of interest that could occur between a cable television company and a local TV broadcaster. In the end, the Commission denied the application. That allowed Rogers Cable (then only operating in Ontario) to enter the bidding war and purchase Premier Cablevision instead. Phil Lind, a senior executive for Rogers, called me and asked if Rogers could retain me to do a minor memo in regard to the CRTC process. I declined, knowing they were simply trying to conflict me out of acting against them. But, of course, Clark was not interested in opposing them anyway, since he was happy with the increased price obtained for his shares. So Rogers was successful in acquiring Premier Cablevision. (It sold the system to Shaw Cable in 1994.)

The issue of cross-ownership between cable television systems and television programming services did not go away. As I recount later (see p. 151–152), I was involved in a number of later cases where the issue was hotly debated.

REQUIRING PRIVATE BROADCASTERS
TO AIR CANADIAN DRAMA

During this period, I was also kept busy with the CTV case. This case arose from the Commission's decision in 1979 to renew the licence of the CTV Network for three years. As part of the renewal, it also imposed a licence condition requiring CTV to present twenty-six hours of original new Canadian drama during the 1980–81 broadcast year and thirty-nine hours during the 1981–82 season.

The CTV stations had been licensed in the early 1960s but since then had commissioned little or no Canadian drama (the term *drama* as used by the CRTC includes comedy). Instead they filled the Canadian part of their schedule with news, sports and inexpensive game shows. There was an obvious reason. Drama or comedy was expensive and they could acquire the Canadian broadcast rights to popular Hollywood shows for a fraction of the cost of acquiring a Canadian drama series. But the Commission was unhappy. After years of calling on CTV to broadcast some Canadian drama without significant result, the CRTC finally decided to make it a licence condition.

Eddie Goodman, the senior counsel at Goodman & Goodman, who had helped John Bassett win the original licence for CFTO-TV in 1961, acted for the CTV Network, assisted by his junior, Kathy Robinson. He rolled out a long list of arguments. The licence condition was discriminatory, it offended freedom of expression, control of program content could only be by regulation, the hearing was unfair, proper notice of the proposed condition was never given to CTV, and so on. In the Federal Court of Appeal, most of these arguments failed. But he won on two points: first, that the CRTC should have given the precise wording of the licence condition to CTV in advance; and second, that the hearing was flawed because one of the commissioners who participated in the decision did not attend the last few hours of the hearing. So the court ordered the CRTC to rehear the matter. Instead the CRTC decided to appeal the decision to the Supreme Court of Canada. So did CTV, since it was not happy with the limited nature of its initial victory.

Tom Heintzman acted for the Commission, assisted by me. And when the matter came before Canada's highest court, the CRTC won on all counts.[10] We successfully argued that the CRTC was a unique regulatory body where the normal rules of 'he who hears, decides' simply did not apply. Under the 1968 Broadcasting Act, we argued, it was the entire executive committee of the CRTC that made licensing decisions, not just the hearing panel. Moreover, the CRTC did not have to give prior notice of the precise wording of a proposed licence condition as long as the subject matter of the condition was clearly dealt with at the hearing. The court also ruled against Goodman's argument that a condition requiring so many hours of original Canadian drama was an unacceptable limit on freedom of expression.

To say that this was an important decision for the Commission is an understatement. Following the decision, the Commission has imposed specific programming obligations by way of licence condition on most of its broadcast licensees, typically tailored to address perceived shortfalls in under-represented Canadian program genres, like drama, long-form documentary, or local news in smaller markets. The legal underpinning for all of these conditions is the 1982 CTV case.

In one respect, however, the case has been overruled. In 1991, a new Broadcasting Act was enacted. In it, the decision-making power for licensing decisions was handed to the CRTC hearing panel, not to the full Commission.

THE GENESIS OF 'TRANSFER BENEFITS'

A second court case in which I was involved during this period also had significant implications for future CRTC policy. The Courtenay-Comox case arose from a 1978 decision of the Commission to approve the transfer of assets in a cable television system. A public-interest intervener argued that before the Commission could approve such a transfer, it should have a competitive hearing at which other parties could compete for the licence. We were retained by CableNet, the purchaser, to defend the

Commission's decision not to do so. I assisted Tom Heintzman to make the necessary arguments to the court and we won the case in 1980.[11] Leave to appeal the decision to the Supreme Court of Canada was later refused.

The Courtenay-Comox case endorsed the CRTC practice not to have a competitive hearing at the time of the transfer of control of a broadcasting undertaking. But this led to another major CRTC policy. In lieu of such a competitive hearing, how could the Commission ensure that a proposed transfer was in the public interest? The answer was to impose so-called transfer benefits on the would-be purchaser. These would be financial or other commitments made by the purchaser on behalf of the broadcast licensee to enhance the broadcasting system during the term of the licence.

Over the next thirty years, the benefits policy of the Commission emerged as one of the key elements in its panoply of broadcast policies. Over time, in a series of proceedings, the Commission elaborated on how the policy should be applied in particular circumstances. In the end, hundreds of millions of dollars were required to be expended by virtue of this CRTC policy on hard-to-finance Canadian programming, infrastructure expenditures and other measures to support the Canadian broadcasting system. Of course, would-be purchasers often tried mightily to avoid or minimize the application of such benefits to their deals. With the consolidation in the industry, there were many such cases, and over the years I was involved in some of the largest transactions, advising either the applicant (seeking to minimize benefits) or the interveners (seeking to maximize the benefits).

FIRST CHOICE

In the spring of 1981, I received a call from Peter Legault, a man who ran a small investment company and who was raising money for a group that wanted to get a national pay television licence. Would I meet with him? Certainly. That led to my being retained to prepare the application by First Choice for a pay TV licence, the first in Canada.

First Choice Canadian Communications Corporation was a company created out of whole cloth. The organizers (Peter Legault, Gordon Sharwood and David Roffey, all of whom were investment brokers) had secured commitments for up to $19 million from over a dozen well-heeled investors across Canada. They included Donald Sobey, J.R. McCaig, Norman Keevil, Royfund Equity Ltd., AGF Management Ltd. and Manulife. Legault told me that they had initially approached Jerry Grafstein to act for them. (Jerry was a Liberal lawyer who had been one of the founding shareholders of CITY-TV, Toronto; he later was appointed to the Canadian Senate.) Jerry had apparently told them that he was critical to winning the pay TV licence but Legault and his group did not find this credible. Other law firms were conflicted so they ended up coming to me.

Our first task was to put together an executive team. David Roffey had studied the US pay TV situation and he nominated himself to be the financial analyst. Don MacPherson, an affable fellow who was head of CBC Sports, was brought aboard to be the proposed president. Joan Schafer, a young producer from CITY-TV, was enlisted to be vice-president of programming. With this team in place, we put together the application.

The deadline for submitting applications to the CRTC was midnight on July 10, 1981. While I was heavily involved in drafting the application, the actual job of printing it had been delegated to a computer processing firm. The group finally signed off on the content of the application in the late afternoon. Don MacPherson had booked a flight to Ottawa at 7 p.m. and so we felt comfortable that he could deliver the application to the CRTC offices in Gatineau, Quebec, in time.

However, the application was still stuck at the computer firm by 7 p.m. Don booked a flight at 8:30 p.m., the last Air Canada flight to Ottawa that evening. But the snafus in production continued. We did not get a complete copy of the application until 8:45 p.m. What to do? Luckily, Don was an expert in getting something from point A to point B in record time. (As head of sports at CBC, he had frequently been involved in emergency efforts to get a time-sensitive videotape delivered on time.) He chartered a jet plane, which took off from Pearson Airport at 10 p.m. and arrived in Ottawa an hour later. From there he took a taxi to the CRTC offices across the river in Gatineau, arriving at 11:30 p.m., just half an hour before the midnight deadline. A security guard at the door accepted the application, but to be sure, Don had him write a 'receipt' on the back of his business card. Then Don returned to Toronto on the same jet that had brought him to Ottawa. In recounting the story later, Don noted with amusement that as he was leaving the CRTC building, another applicant came into the building to deliver an application.

Later, Don had his business card with the receipt written on the back mounted inside an acrylic cube. Years later, Don died of cancer and I attended at the funeral parlour to meet his children. When I told them of my connection to First Choice, one of them showed me the acrylic cube. What was this, they wanted to know, since their father had told them that it was a very important memento, and had always kept it on his desk. I was pleased to explain its significance.

In the end, the CRTC was presented with six applications for a national 'general interest' pay television licence, three applications for regional pay TV licences, and two applications for a national arts channel. So it was a hot competition. Apart from First Choice, the national competitors included well-financed applications backed by the cable industry (fronted by Moses Znaimer, a founding investor in CITY-TV), by Astral and Telemedia (fronted by André Bureau, later to be chair of the CRTC from 1983 to 1989), by CTV and TVA who had combined forces and by Standard Broadcasting.

At the CRTC hearing, I focused on the key attributes that would distinguish First Choice from the rest. A critical point was that First Choice was owned by a group of entirely independent investors who had committed $19 million to fund the start-up. So it was not subject to the conflicts of interest that might apply if it was controlled by the cable industry, by film producers, or by conventional broadcasters (factors which I argued tainted some of the other applications). Second, the First Choice application proposed national services for both English and French viewers, something only one other applicant had proposed. Third, its Canadian content commitments were higher than the others', driven by optimistic penetration estimates. And finally, unlike the other national applicants, First Choice was prepared to accept regional competition although it was pointed out that this would come at a cost to its Canadian content commitments.

As part of the application process, each applicant could present a short videotape showing what their service would look like 'on the air'. Joan Schafer put together a four-minute videotape with clips of a number of Canadian films. A highlight was a clip from the film *Atlantic City*, in which Moses Znaimer had played a hoodlum dressed in a white suit who threatened the protagonist with a knife, sneering, 'All I want is the money …' Joan put this line through an echo chamber so that the word *money* reverberated.

At the hearing, Moses Znaimer fronted the application funded by the cable industry. When it came time for the First Choice application to be presented, he sat in the front row of the audience at the CRTC hearing. When the First Choice audiovisual presentation was played, including the clip showing Znaimer as the hoodlum seeking the money, the hearing room rocked with laughter. Znaimer was not amused. He was fit to be tied.

On March 18, 1982, the Commission announced its decision. First Choice was awarded a national pay TV licence in English and in French, beating out all the other national applicants.[12] Three regional pay TV services were also approved that would compete directly with First Choice. And C-Channel, a national arts channel, was given a licence.

This was my first major broadcast victory in front of the CRTC and I was exhilarated. But it also meant that I was plunged into tons of legal work. I had to draft and negotiate affiliation agreements with every cable company in Canada. These were the first such agreements ever put together. I had to help negotiate long-term supply agreements with the Hollywood studios, as well as agreements with Canadian distributors and producers. And I drafted an endless series of interventions to the CRTC, to try to delay the entry of regional pay licensees in provinces not yet approved.

All the pay TV services launched on the major cable systems on February 1, 1983. This was preceded by a barrage of TV commercials and billboard ads, so public interest was intense. To subscribe, you had to rent a set-top decoder, often combined with a converter, and the price was $14.95 per service.

The regional pay services in Ontario and Alberta, both of which were controlled by Dr Charles Allard of Edmonton, adopted the same name, Superchannel, so the competition in those provinces was between First Choice and Superchannel. (A third regional service called Star Channel launched against First Choice in the Maritimes.) The Commission had precluded the services from acquiring exclusive rights to the Hollywood movies so the same movies appeared on both services. In one of its most controversial steps, however, First Choice had negotiated an output deal with Playboy, entitling it to show a two-hour block from the Playboy channel on Friday evenings. In addition, the deal called for the production of a series of programs for Playboy that would be made in Canada and would qualify as Canadian content.

The Playboy deal made headlines across Canada and led to protests from women's groups outside the First Choice offices in the Eaton Centre in Toronto. The protests were remarkable in that they combined right-wing evangelical women (who criticized the portrayal of explicit sex) and left-wing feminists (who had no problem with explicit sex but criticized the involvement of bubble-headed playmates). It is interesting in retrospect to compare this with the complaints years later that led to the cancellation of the Miss Canada pageant that had run for many years on the CTV Network. In that scenario, right-wing evangelical women had no problem with the Miss Canada pageant, but feminists decried it.

In the result, the Playboy segment on Friday evenings turned out to be quite tame. In a magazine show anchored by an articulate playmate, a typical sequence would take the viewer into a condom factory in New Jersey. Purportedly erotic sequences would show topless women but not much else. However, the publicity did wonders for First Choice subscriptions, which soared past those of Superchannel.

By the fall of 1983, however, the overall penetration of pay television had barely reached 10 percent, and C Channel, the arts channel, had gone bankrupt. Star Channel also went under. First Choice had run out of money and needed to be rescued. This came in the form of an infusion of funds from Astral (controlled by Harold Greenberg and his family), backed by the Bronfman family in Montreal. Superchannel opposed the rescue and tried to stop the CRTC hearing to approve it with an eleventh-hour action seeking a prohibition order in the Federal Court of Canada. However, acting for First Choice, I assisted Tom Heintzman to appear in court and we defeated Superchannel's attempt.

At the CRTC hearing, I persuaded the Commission to approve the change of control. When the chairman asked me how urgent the application was, I famously replied, 'If you look up the word *urgent* in the dictionary, you'll find the First Choice logo.'[13] Ironically, two years earlier, I had argued to the Commission that it would not be appropriate to give the pay TV licence to Astral, due to its direct involvement in film production. However, Harold Greenberg, the president of Astral, was now happy to get the company out of film production as the price of its entry into broadcasting, so there was no longer a conflict of interest. As a result, the Commission approved the deal and I acquired a new client, Astral.[14]

By 1984, pay television penetration had not significantly improved, and it became clear that something had to be done. Ian Greenberg, Harold's youngest brother, flew out to Edmonton to commence discussions with Dr Allard. I flew out to Edmonton to join them in a subsequent meeting and eventually they decided to solve the problem by splitting the country between them. I drafted a term sheet under which Superchannel would have Western Canada, and First Choice would have all the pay subscribers east of the Manitoba border. This gave First Choice about 60 percent of the total English-language pay subscribers in the country, which was about the same as its then ratio of subscribers. First Choice would continue to have the obligation to offer its French-language pay service on a national basis. The key benefit of the deal from both sides was that it allowed each company to control its destiny in a separate region of the country without any competition.

The reorganization of the pay television industry was approved by the Commission in 1984, but not without a hearing in which Lawson Hunter, the director of investigation and research under the Combines Investigation Act, opposed it.[15] Hunter's position was simple. You can still have competing pay TV companies, he said. All you have to do to make them viable is lower the Canadian content rules. I had great fun attacking his position at the hearing. Years later, Lawson Hunter came back into my life in a more positive way, which I describe later.

In 1986, responding to the application of the pay television licensees, the CRTC amended their licence conditions to reflect the real economics of pay TV.[16] The application involved lowering the unrealistic Canadian content conditions that had applied since 1982. It was not an easy task to convince the Commission to do so. In many ways, I considered this application far more challenging than the bid to win the original licence. The problem was to balance the need for financial viability with the need to make a significant contribution to Canadian content. One aspect of the application was to create the Foundation to Underwrite New Drama (FUND) with an injection of $1 million each year from First Choice. To run the FUND, I suggested the company hire Phyllis Yaffe, the former head of the Association of Canadian Publishers, whom I knew well. Phyllis ended up doing a superb job. And from this point forward, the pay industry prospered.

Before I move on to other events, I should pause briefly to talk about Harold Greenberg. The Greenberg family were Montreal Jews who had started in business with a modest photo concession in a department store in the early 1960s. That would have been the end of the story except for the fact that they won the concession to set up photo outlets at the site of Expo '67. The revenue from this allowed them to expand and they eventually got into the film business through the acquisition of Bellevue Pathé, a film lab. This benefited from the growth of the Canadian film sector in the late 1970s, and by the 1980s Astral Bellevue Pathé, as it was then known, was a well-recognized Canadian film production company, with over twenty feature films to its credit. Its first major film was *The Apprenticeship of Duddy Kravitz*, released in 1974 with co-financing from what is now Telefilm Canada. In 1982, it released its most lucrative film, *Porky's*. Observers joked that this was something of a consolation prize for Astral, it having lost its bid for a pay television licence earlier that year. However, as I have noted, once Astral became the owner of First Choice in 1983, it agreed to get out of the film production business.

Born in 1930, Harold was the oldest of the four brothers and they took direction from him. He was a delightful, sweet man and a smart businessman, never succumbing to the temptation to 'go Hollywood.' He loved to quote the old Jewish adage: 'Act British, think Yiddish.'

Harold passed away in 1996 and was succeeded by Ian. After his death, the FUND was renamed the Harold Greenberg Fund. First Choice changed its name to The Movie Network (TMN) in 1993. And in 2013, Astral sold TMN, along with other broadcast assets, to Bell Canada.

THE LEADERS' DEBATES

In the summer of 1984, I got a call from Chaviva Hosek, the president of the National Action Committee on the Status of Women. A federal election had just been called and the NAC had managed to convince the leaders of the three main political parties (Liberal, Conservative and NDP) to participate in a debate on women's issues. The TV networks were keen to televise the event, and Chaviva asked me to negotiate the arrangement between the networks and NAC.

Over the next few days, I drafted a term sheet between the NAC and the networks. The NAC covered the cost of the event, which was to be held in a large ballroom in the Fairmont Royal York Hotel in Toronto. But the term sheet was intended to ensure that the networks would cover all their own costs and would be responsible if, for example, a camera fell over and hurt someone.

I negotiated the deal over the phone with the head of TV news at the CBC, who was acting for the three networks carrying the debate. At one point, he wondered why I was helping a feminist organization like NAC. My response was, 'Because I'm a feminist,' to which he had no answer. (Years later, when I told this story to my wife, she scoffed, 'If you're such a feminist, why aren't you helping around the house?' Point taken!)

The debate on women's issues held on August 15, 1984, turned out to be a signal event in Canadian political history, with an audience of bright, involved women confronting three rather nervous men—Brian Mulroney, John Turner and Ed Broadbent. But the event remains in my memory for another reason.

In agreeing to help the NAC on a *pro bono* basis, I had requested a front-row seat for my mother. The NAC was happy to oblige, and my mother was thrilled to attend the event. I drove her down to the Royal York Hotel and she joined close to a thousand women in the audience. She was then in her eighties. But like other women in the room, she felt a palpable sense of excitement and entitlement in being able to confront our political leaders with questions of particular concern to women. She told me later that it was one of the highlights of her life.

But there was never to be another leaders' debate on women's issues. The federal government cut back the funding to NAC and the organization lost ground. However, in 1992, I got another call from Chaviva Hosek. By this time she was in the inner circles of the Liberal party, and she wondered if I would like to be the broadcasting arbitrator in federal elections. More on this later.

6. Family Matters

From the time my first marriage ended in 1972 until 1984, I was an eligible bachelor. Not surprisingly, I had relationships with a number of women during this period. These included the executive secretary to a provincial deputy minister of communications, a law student at the University of Ottawa, a documentary filmmaker from San Francisco, a librarian from Cornell University in Ithaca, New York, and a British woman who was a simultaneous translator at UNESCO in Paris.

All of these women were attractive, intelligent and interesting, and some them lived with me in Toronto for a few months. But none of these relationships matured into an engagement. Instead, I would typically move on to someone else after a period of time. In fairness, I was probably a frustrating date, since I was a total workaholic. But I learned a lot about myself and about the kind of girl I was attracted to. All of which undoubtedly primed me for the thunderbolt that hit me in 1984.

On August 8, 1984, my life changed when I met my future wife at a job interview.

By this point, my communications law practice was finally taking off. Lorne Salzman was helping on the telecom side, but with my big victory on pay TV in 1982, I badly needed a new associate. I had enlisted a bright young commercial lawyer, Cheryl Belkin, to help. However, she eventually came into my office and said, 'I've fallen in love with an Israeli and I'm moving to Tel Aviv.' So she left.

My next associate was Heather Howe. She was bright and intelligent, and had a good feel for the area, having acted as the executive assistant to Bernard Ostry, the deputy minister of communications, in Ottawa. She helped me for a year or so, but then she walked into my office and said, 'I've fallen in love with a management consultant from McKinsey, and I'm moving to New York.'

Now what to do? Hiring someone from within the ranks of the junior associates at McCarthys no longer seemed the right option. We needed to make a lateral hire. So Lorne Salzman and I put an ad in the *Ontario*

Reports, the weekly law journal that goes to the entire legal profession in Ontario. Our half-page ad described the new field of communications and entertainment law in upbeat terms and invited applicants from lawyers one to three years out with good marks. While we suggested that applicants should have 'sensitivity to the interests of Canadian cultural industries', we did not insist that they have any direct experience in the field. We realized this would be highly unlikely. Instead, we focused on trying to attract someone with a good general background who could respond to the challenge presented by the new areas of law and learn on the job.

This ad appeared in the *Ontario Reports* on July 20, 1984.
One of the applications was from my future wife, Grace A. Westcott.

We had no idea how many applications we would receive. So we were pleasantly surprised to receive 120 letters responding to the ad. Working through the raft of letters, and sorting the wheat from the chaff, we winnowed this down to twenty applicants. Each of them was invited to attend an interview with Lorne and me. Based on the twenty interviews and the resumés, Lorne and I agreed that the top three candidates were Grace

Westcott, then a research lawyer with Osler, Hoskin & Harcourt; Randy Pepper, also a junior at Oslers; and Chris Pibus, a junior associate at Lang Michener. All three met the qualifications and were excellent possibilities. We called their references and they were all positive.

But who to choose? Lorne and I agreed that Grace was the best candidate. She was attractive, personable and articulate. She had stood in the Dean's List at the Faculty of Law, University of Toronto, and had an LLM at Columbia. But Lorne expressed a concern: 'Should we hire a woman lawyer? You know what happened with our last two associates. They both fell in love, got married and left.'

'Don't be sexist, Lorne,' I responded. 'That isn't going to happen three times in a row.' So we hired Grace.

A few weeks later, I took Grace to a classy midtown restaurant, Scaramouche, to celebrate her hiring. I remember spending most of the time educating Grace on the intricacies of the IX-2 case, the application by CNCP Telecommunications to the CRTC for interconnection with Bell Canada's local exchanges so as to offer a competing long distance telephone service. She bravely tried to express interest but must have been bleary eyed by the end.

A month later, in September 1984, having given her notice at Oslers, Grace Westcott started work at McCarthys. I immediately got her involved in some telecom matters. In the middle of her first week at work, we were all working late and I suggested that Lorne, Grace and I go for dinner. This was agreed. However, at the last minute Lorne got tied up and begged off. So Grace and I went for dinner at an upstairs restaurant on Yonge Street north of Eglinton.

This time we started talking about personal matters. What schools had she gone to? What were her extracurricular activities? Why did she go to New York for an LLM?

Grace's background was intriguing. She had been to Victoria College, as I had, and had won the Moses Henry Aikins scholarship, as I had (but in her case, she had maintained good enough marks to renew it, which I hadn't!). She had gone to the Faculty of Law at U of T, as I had. But, most fascinating, she had spent a year at the Eastman School of Music in Rochester, studying performance flute. I told her that I too had been at Eastman, for two summer courses in arranging. I gave her a summary of my own musical career. It didn't take me long to invite her to come over to my apartment sometime so that we could play flute and piano.

The next morning, Grace arrived at work and dropped into my office. She dumped a pile of music on my desk. 'What's this?' I asked. 'Flute and piano music,' she said. I quickly looked through it. There was a wide range of pieces: Bach sonatas, Debussy pieces, the Mozart Flute Concerto arranged for flute and piano, and many other pieces. I'd never seen this music before, but it all looked like fun. So we agreed to meet in my apartment on Sunday afternoon to work through the repertoire.

Grace arrived on Sunday and got out her silver flute. I sat at my Yamaha grand piano. We began playing the pieces. Soon I became aware of three things: (1) she was a great flute player, (2) this was really fun, and (3) I was enormously attracted to her.

By the end of the afternoon, I was smitten. This was too wonderful to be true. She seemed to like me. But how could this work out? I was her boss.

We sat at my pine dining table to relax. I took my heart in my hands. I reached over and took her hand. I told her that I was really attracted to her. But I didn't want to hurt her. So if she didn't want to go further, that would be okay. And if we did want to go further, we would need to keep it completely private until we had decided whether it was the 'relationship of the century' (I remember using that term). If not, we would simply go on as before, and not let it affect our professional life. What did she think?

Grace did not take her hand away. Instead she held it affectionately. And with that, we began our relationship.

We were careful to keep it all hidden from the firm. Luckily our offices at the firm, while on the same floor, were on opposite sides of a major conference room, so we could work quite independently. Nor did we share a secretary. During this period, I maintained a charade that I was dating a female stockbroker. No one caught on. (Grace tells me that a contributing factor to the deception was the fact that once I was in the office, my workaholic disposition took over and I was entirely focused on work.) At one point, we decided to have dinner again at Scaramouche. But as we approached the concierge, I spotted a client seated at a table in the restaurant. So we hurriedly left to avoid detection.

Within a few months, I got to know Grace's parents, who suspected something was up when I gave Grace a diamond necklace for her birthday on October 10, 1984. On Sundays, when I often had lunch with my mother at her apartment on Alexander Street, I invited Grace to join me. My mother immediately liked Grace. Her only concern about our relationship was whether Grace would be too career-oriented to want children. I reassured her.

By January 1985, on one of the Sunday lunches I had with my mother, we were joined by my brother's two boys, Adam and Hamish. They were seventeen and fourteen at the time. After lunch, Grace departed on her own, and I drove Adam and Hamish home. I couldn't resist asking them what they thought of Grace. There was a brief huddled discussion between the two of them in the back seat of my car. Then Adam spoke up. 'We think you should go for it,' he said.

INTRIGUE

By May 1985, I was ready to go for it. I invited Grace to go with me on a two-week vacation in Italy. Secretly, my plan was to propose in Venice. Grace agreed to go on the trip. But we had to camouflage this so that the firm would not catch on. Luckily, Grace's brother was getting married in Vancouver the week of our return. So she said she would be going hiking in BC, after which she would attend that wedding. My cover story was that I was going to Italy with my stockbroker friend.

As it happened, we left for our respective vacations not only on the same day, but at the same hour in the afternoon. So if anyone had been alert, they would have caught on. Our careful plans for secrecy almost came undone in the taxi ride to the airport. The taxi driver suddenly announced that he was running out of gas and would have to transfer us to a different cab. Of course, he stopped on King Street West, right across from the TD Bank Tower. With our hearts in our mouths, we nervously boarded a different cab. But luckily no one saw us. We barely made it to the airport on time.

The trip to Italy was wonderful. I had never been in Italy before. But I pulled out all the stops. We began in Rome, then rented a car to drive to Siena, Florence, Ravenna, Venice, Como and Milan. I had not organized hotels in advance except for Rome and at each stop I asked the concierge to call ahead and get us first-class accommodation at the next city. We ended up staying at the Villa San Michele in Fiesole, just outside Florence, a small hotel reputedly designed by Michelangelo as a convent. It had only a dozen rooms but a restaurant to die for. Booking ahead, we were unable to get into any of the top hotels in Venice itself but we were able to get into the Excelsior Hotel on the Lido, the island just off Venice, which also featured the only casino in Italy. The hotel was on the beach.

I decided to propose to Grace after dinner at the Excelsior. However before I could get any words out, she waved me off and we walked out to the beach instead. It was a moonlit evening and very romantic, but I was terribly nervous. In a few words (which I recall were largely incoherent) I proposed marriage. She immediately said yes.

Of course, unknown to me, Grace had long before fully expected me to propose in Venice. But she was damned if she was going to accept marriage in the pink walls of the Excelsior Hotel's restaurant. So she had propelled me to the beach.

We celebrated by collecting some sand from where we had been standing when I proposed. It was put into a glass decanter, which sat on our dresser for a number of years before one of our children found it and, not knowing what it was, dumped all the sand out somewhere in the garden. So much for mementoes of the past!

Later that evening we dropped in on the casino and I put my money on the number 10 on the roulette wheel, since it was May 10, 1985. Incredibly, the number won. We celebrated by splurging—spending the money on a dessert.

From Venice we drove to Bellagio on Lake Como. We had lunch in a beautiful outdoor lakeside café across from the Hotel du Lac. At the next table were three elderly British tourists, two women and a man. They seemed very friendly and we began talking. One thing led to another and we divulged the fact that we had just become engaged. They were the first people we told. They were delighted and exuberantly showed us their wedding rings. One of the women had just been widowed and so she was very moved by the occasion.

Later that day, we drove around the south end of Lake Como to check in at the famous Villa d'Este, one of the great hotels of the world (and also one of the most expensive). For a night we joined the company of the rich and famous. Just behind the hotel was a high-end fashion boutique and I bought Grace a lovely Italian-designed pantsuit in taupe.

After we arrived back in Toronto Grace promptly flew to Vancouver to attend her brother's wedding. A few days later she arrived back in the office. So far no one had caught on. However, Grace was now wearing the new pantsuit. It looked very Italian. Could Grace have gone to Italy? Her secretary sneaked into her office when she was out to check the label on the jacket. Yes, it said *Milan*. But it also said *London* and *New York*. So the result was inconclusive.

Meantime, Grace and I attended on European Jewellers on Bloor Street West to pick out a diamond engagement ring. A diamond was selected and her ring size was taken. The cost was about the same as the cost of our trip to Italy!

A week later, I got a call from European Jewellers. The ring was ready, a day early. I picked it up and had Grace come over to my apartment for dinner. With due ceremony, I presented the ring to her. We decided on the spot that this was the moment to inform our parents. So we travelled over to my mother's apartment to announce the news, and then to Grace's parents' home to do the same. It was an exhilarating evening.

Now it was time to tell the firm, but when and how? We decided to tell Lorne first at a Sunday dinner at my apartment, and then to let the firm know on Monday morning.

I invited Lorne and his wife to Sunday dinner, telling them I had a surprise to announce. When they arrived, Grace was already there and we told them the news. Lorne laughed and presented me with a greeting card that said, *Congratulations, Peter and Grace*. He had never caught on, but his wife, Nancy, had guessed that this might be the news

As an aside, I should note that I was the matchmaker who brought Lorne and Nancy together. Nancy Vitriol had been my publishing editor at the Law Society of Upper Canada and I had taken her out once or twice. She was also a canvasser for John Roberts, a Toronto-area Liberal member of parliament. She invited me to an election rally for Pierre Trudeau to be held in Maple Leaf Gardens on May 9, 1979. I accepted the ticket and told her that either I would come or I would make sure someone would be there. I then gave the ticket to Lorne, telling him that there would be an attractive girl in the next seat. The rest is history. Lorne met Nancy in Maple Leaf Gardens, they hit it off and they were married on January 10, 1980.

But back to my story. Following my Sunday dinner with Lorne and Nancy, I went in on Monday morning to see the managing partner of the firm, Harry Macdonell. I told him Grace and I were going to be married and that we had decided that she would move to a different firm. Harry smiled and congratulated me. He hadn't had the least idea that we were seeing each other. In fact, when I had called to set up a meeting to discuss

A photo taken in 1988,
three years after Grace Westcott and I were married.

a personal matter, he had feared that I might announce I was leaving the firm myself to go to a competitor. So if anything he was relieved.

A note was immediately circulated to every lawyer in the firm announcing our engagement. To say the firm was stunned would be an understatement. No one had caught on. I remember Dale Robinette telling me how disappointed she was that they were deprived of the gossip that would have accompanied a more public affair.

(As it turned out, one person *had* caught on: Susan Peacock, then a lawyer with First Choice pay TV. Susan had attended a luncheon at the Sutton Place Hotel some months before and had sat at the same table as Grace and I. Out of the corner of her eye, she noticed Grace putting butter on my bread plate. *Ah-ha!* she guessed to herself. *Peter and Grace must be an item!* But luckily, she shared this guess with no one else.)

In the summer of 1985, we attended some engagement parties. One was held in the backyard of Chris Johnston in Ottawa. Six years older than I, Chris was the founding partner of the law firm of Johnston & Buchan but he had worked for the Commission in the 1970s, where we had first met. Despite being in a competing law firm, Chris was a respected and admired friend, as was his law partner Bob Buchan. Chris invited the entire Ottawa communications Bar to the engagement party. Even the counsel from Bell Canada attended and wished us well!

Grace and I were married on October 12, 1985, at Bloor Street United Church in Toronto. The reception was held on the top floor of the Four Seasons Hotel.

MIXING FAMILY WITH CAREER

After my marriage to Grace, she moved to Blake Cassels & Graydon, where she worked on major real estate transactions. Then she was approached by Cassels, Brock & Blackwell. She accepted their offer, and in her work with that firm she focused on general commercial law with a specialization in copyright. She became a partner there in 1992.

I frequently joked to friends that Grace was the only lawyer I knew who had worked at all four corners of Bay and King Streets in downtown Toronto: Oslers was on the northwest corner, in the First Canadian Place; McCarthys was on the southwest corner, in the TD Bank Tower; Blakes

Then the children arrived!
Christmas 1998, with Rory, Kristin, Robbie and Tom.

was on the southeast corner, in the CIBC Tower; and Cassels Brock was on the northeast corner, in the Scotia Plaza.

In 1986, we bought a house on Highbourne Road in the Chaplin Estates area near Yonge and Eglinton. The house had formerly been owned by David Galloway, who later became the CEO of Torstar. The purchase turned out to be a wonderful choice: the street was tree-lined and relatively traffic-free. It was a friendly area, with lots of kids around. And we had a two-car garage.

Soon Grace and I added some kids of our own. Kristin was the first to arrive, on October 15, 1989. Then Tom arrived on June 12, 1992.

Grace and I were keen to have a third and we kept trying. Soon enough she became pregnant again and we trooped down to Mount Sinai Hospital to have an ultrasound. The technician passed the wand over Grace's tummy and the image of the baby's head came up on the screen. Then a second head appeared. The technician turned the screen towards himself and checked out the image more closely. There was a pause. Then he smiled at us. 'Congratulations!' he said. 'You're expecting twins!'

In fact, it turned out to be identical twin boys: Rory and Robbie were born 15 minutes apart on December 18, 1993.

This necessitated two big decisions on our part. First, Grace decided to quit the partnership at Cassels Brock. Second, we bought a minivan!

Grace later opened a legal practice of her own, specializing in publishing contracts and copyright law. She acted as the vice-chair of the Canadian Copyright Institute and she is a recognized Canadian expert on copyright reform. She also became the chair of the City of Toronto Legacy Project, which has organized the naming of parks and the mounting of plaques honouring Toronto's creative artists and scientists. And as if this were not enough, she also served for over six years on the board of directors of the Canadian Centre for Diversity (formerly the Canadian Council of Christians and Jews).

THE GARAGE

In 1992, we bought a cottage in Cedar Springs, a little seasonal community north of Burlington on the Niagara Escarpment. Once the twins arrived, we continued to use the cottage on summer weekends and occasionally in the winter. But soon this became incredibly difficult. The work of maintaining two households with four children under the age of five was particularly demanding on Grace. So we sold the cottage and decided to stay in the city.

This turned out to be a smart decision. Within a few years, the twins discovered the wonders of our unused two-car garage, and this became their home away from home, and a kind of clubhouse for their neighbourhood friends. In 2007, Grace wrote the following piece about the Garage Band, which she has given me permission to include in this memoir.

THE GARAGE BAND
by Grace Westcott

It was the raccoon that finally did it.

That was what prompted me, one Saturday in June, to clean out our two-car garage. This garage had not seen a car since 1986 when I steeled myself to drive ours down the narrow driveway, just to see if it could be done. After the nerve-shattering experience of then backing it out, we never ventured to park the car in the garage again.

So the raccoon and the junk took over.

This particular Saturday, I approached the junior members of the family, our twelve-year-old twins, Robbie and Rory, and their thirteen-year-old brother, Tom. They were sprawled in the basement watching television with R, the boy from next door and a buddy from down the street. I cleared my throat and offered to buy each of them a giant slushy from the corner Petro-Canada station if they would clean out the garage. No need to worry, I assured them: I personally would deal with the raccoon poop, and would bleach the floor afterwards, too.

No reaction. Nothing.

I gave up and went away.

Later I looked out and saw that they had actually set to work, hauling stuff out onto the driveway, sweeping up last year's dead leaves, and tossing old junk down from the loft, a small storage platform built on the rafters. By the time they had finished and I had cleaned up after the raccoon, the boys surveyed the empty garage and saw…potential.

By late afternoon, a sorry-looking purple couch appeared in the garage, a cast-off carried in from the curb. Two excited twelve-year-olds urged me to try out this most fabulous, most comfortable couch ever built.

'Can we keep it?' they asked.

I could see where this was going.

'Check for bugs,' I said.

Over the next few days, the boys kept their eyes open for anything useful left at the curb. They came home with two discarded garden chairs, a blue La-Z-Boy, a non-functioning stereo system and a shelving unit. This was the beginning of a summer-long scavenger hunt, which ultimately netted them four couches, three rugs, two coffee tables, two speakers, a perfectly functioning solid wood colour television console, a ratty armchair, two beanbag chairs, a mirror, several road signs, a straw Piglet and sundry other things I might charitably call 'objets d'art.' Blithely immune to the yuck factor, they even hauled home a cast-off futon for the garage loft.

'Cover it with a sheet,' I said.

The twins brought out the PlayStation and hooked it up to the garage television, the better to luxuriate in modern boyhood with their pals. They arranged their games neatly on a shelf. A buddy contributed two more speakers and a music system that actually worked. After begging some spare speaker wire, they triumphantly produced surround sound rap. They took our extra television set, heaved it into the loft, and, with pooled technical know-how, connected the two televisions with a splitter. They collected their savings and bought wireless controllers for the system. Now they could play four-man games on two screens on two levels at once.

They installed a doorbell.

And they hung up the obligatory NO GIRLS sign.

Having built their personal domain, they set rules for themselves. These rules looked a lot like the rules they habitually ignore in the house. Everyone was to take his shoes off in the garage. Anyone putting his shoes on the couch was to sweep the garage as a penalty. They made a place for everything and occasionally put everything in its place. They recycled. They tidied up. And believe it or not, they begged to be allowed to use the 'good' vacuum cleaner. Really.

Then the word got around.

Yep, the garage became *the* summer project and *the* place for the neighbourhood boys to hang out. R, next door, brought his three best buddies to join up, and his fearless little brother came along. J from down the street moved in the moment he discovered it. Far-flung school friends had themselves delivered for play dates. They arrived on bikes and skateboards. They took the subway. As for me, I got used to finding eight or nine boys lounging in the garage at a time. And the sleepovers started, with up to twelve of them spending nights of questionable comfort and perfect happiness in the garage.

Consumed with ideas for garage improvements, they pooled their allowances in what came to be known as the Garage Fund. A bulletin board disappeared from Robbie's bedroom and reappeared on the wall of the garage, along with the garage to-do list, the Garage Fund account and—get this—the collected receipts for garage purchases, neatly tacked in place.

Their proudest purchase was a mini-fridge, costing a colossal $149.99. A buddy's windfall birthday money brought the Garage Fund to a sufficient amount, so six boys piled into the van for the trip to Future Shop for the Big Acquisition.

At this point, they thought to worry about the electrical load on the single garage outlet, which by now carried the overhead light, the PlayStation, two televisions, two fans, a sound system and an electric clock. So they ran an outdoor extension cord to the neighbour's house, to draw down power next door, and ran another to our outdoor plug. Then they suspended a couple of power bars on the wall. They haven't blown a fuse yet. At least, not at our house.

A garage literature sprang up. They created a quote board to immortalize their *bon mots*. When school started they wrote up the garage in their obligatory 'What I did on my summer vacation' school assignments.

There were witticisms too.

They found an old toilet seat in somebody's trash. I regret to say they brought it home. ('Wash your hands,' I said.) Soon it was up on the garage wall, framing a colour print of the *Mona Lisa*. It was only later that I saw the connection between this and the NO DUMPING sign they hung up next to it.

They decapitated the plastic snowman, and nailed his cheery head to the wall.

They hoisted all but one of the garden tools into the rafters to make more space. Then they got hammer and nails and suspended the garden hoe on the wall. When next I looked they had written above it, in bold chalk lettering, the words *dirty hoe.*

(Okay, so maybe the innocence was slipping here, but it *was* amusing.)

And they didn't lack for sports. They wheeled the basketball hoop in off the street and placed it in the driveway in front of the garage. Between that, the broomball and the football, soon every blade of grass in the backyard had been beaten into dust.

All they lacked was a fishin' hole.

We learned how to make mac and cheese by the bucketful. Better still, *they* learned how to make it by the bucketful. We sent out plates piled high with hot dogs, burgers and peanut-butter sandwiches, corn on the cob, bagels and cut-up fruit. They made cookie batter, and ate the whole batch raw.

Pizzas started to arrive unbidden around dinnertime, the thoughtful contribution of various of the garage gang's parents. The pizza-delivery man soon knew to deliver direct to the garage. Offerings of muffins and drinks and fruit and snacks materialized. The boys put this unlooked-for good fortune down to 'garage guilt' on the part of the parents of our regular visitors.

And the boys? They simply couldn't believe their luck. Lest the charm be broken, they thought it prudent to listen to me, the Mom of the garage-host boys and wielder of ultimate power of life and death over the garage. I experienced the unaccustomed and dizzying sensation of *respect for my authority.*

And when school started, the kids of the grade-eight class and their parents and teachers soon heard all about the now-famous garage, as the entire grade took to dropping in Fridays after school for a party. Yep, the girls too.

Okay, okay, I confess, not everything they did was exactly adorable. They did get slap-happy with a can of spray paint, and left the garage door looking like a storefront in Harlem. In their zeal to rid the garage of unwanted clutter, they took an outgrown bicycle—one I was saving for younger cousins—hauled it up a tree and flung it to the pavement below, before sawing it in half with the hacksaw. They broke a window with a misplaced soccer ball, (though they paid for most of it with the Garage Fund). I could have done without the derelict shopping cart hauled in from somewhere and left in our driveway. Then there was the sortie to the Petro-Canada station at 3:00 a.m., to take advantage of the awesome special on monster-size hot chocolates. And it was unfortunate that my son Rory decided that the best way to unstick the top drawer of the chest of drawers—an heirloom stored temporarily in the garage—was to saw the front of the drawer completely off.

And while I'm confessing, it's true they may have startled some passers-by when seven of them ran, glorious and half naked, out onto the sidewalk, late on a dark night in a torrential downpour, whooping for the sheer joy of getting drenched in the rain. But is there not something deeply elemental in that? Is that not a splendid natural birthright? Can you fault me for letting them whoop awhile before dutifully calling them in?

Does boyhood get better than this? Does parenthood?

Not if you ask me.

Shortly after Grace wrote this piece, we decided to rebuild the backyard deck. As part of the project, we ran a heavy-duty power line out to the garage to support six outlets. We also ran a coaxial cord to connect our satellite television service to a television set in the garage. So on a typical Friday evening, we would find up to nine boys sleeping over in the garage.

Once the deck was completed, I decided that it might be fun to invite the parents of the kids who came to the garage (by now over forty in number) to attend a backyard BBQ and a 'tour' of the garage. This became an annual event in late June, and the parents were finally able to see where their kids hung out. The Garage Band continued until the boys went off to university in the fall of 2011.

7. Communications Law in Action

PURSUING A NEW FM STATION IN TORONTO

My first exposure to presenting radio cases to the CRTC occurred in 1984, when I was retained by a radio executive named J. Robert Wood to help him apply for a new FM station in Toronto. Bob Wood worked for the CHUM radio organization but he had always nourished a dream of owning his own FM radio station in Toronto, Canada's largest market.

In 1984, there appeared to be only one FM frequency available for the Toronto market, so we put together an application for that frequency. Bob's investors included Anne Murray, the owners of the Trivial Pursuit game, Pat Keenan and David Campbell. To win the application against potential competitors, Bob also had to propose a music format that would be distinctive. He decided to have the station focus on urban dance music, a variant of rhythm and blues that was popular in many US markets but not found in Canada. The format was associated with black musicians but had broad cross-over appeal. In the end, however, the CRTC granted the licence to an applicant who had proposed an easy-listening station.

But Bob Wood was not ready to give up. The problem was that there were no more FM frequencies assigned to Toronto. To find one took a considerable amount of engineering ingenuity. Bob started searching for a drop-in frequency that could be used for Toronto and he retained Mark Tilson, a gifted broadcast engineering consultant who eventually found a full-coverage frequency that would work. I helped Bob file an application for the frequency in 1986 and his was the only application. However, the major broadcasters were shocked to learn that a viable frequency was available and lobbied the Commission to turn down the application, arguing that it was a public frequency and everyone should have a shot at it. So Bob was denied a second time.

Bob reapplied in 1990. This time he had strengthened his application by finding some minority investors from the black community. But he had formidable opposition.

The application was heard in Toronto by three CRTC commissioners.

The hearing went very well for Bob's application. In the end, two of the commissioners voted for Bob's application and the third voted for a country music applicant. Unfortunately, the CRTC decision was not taken by the hearing panel, where he would have won the nod. Instead, the decision was made by the full executive committee of the Commission, and it decided to overrule the hearing panel and support the country music applicant. The two commissioners who wanted Bob's application to win filed a strongly worded dissent. But there was nothing Bob could do.

Ironically, the Broadcasting Act was changed the following year so that the licensing decisions are now taken by the commissioners who actually sit on the hearing panel. Had Bob's application been heard a year later, in other words, he would have won the Toronto FM licence.

The urban dance format that Bob had proposed did not go away, but morphed into R&B/hip-hop. In 2000, a company called Milestone Radio Inc., involving some of his black investors, obtained an FM licence for Toronto for a station to be called the Flow, on 93.5 MHz. In 2010, that station was bought by CTV and the format changed. But in 2011, with the help of my law firm, a station was licensed targeting the local Caribbean and African communities with a music format that embraced R&B/hip-hop as well as calypso and world music.[1] But Bob Wood had no involvement in the application.

THE ARMSTRONG CASE

In early 1986, at Bob Wood's suggestion, I was retained to assist with the filing of an application to the CRTC for permission to transfer control over the licences for two radio stations in Victoria. A man named David Armstrong had been the founder and owner of CKDA-AM and CFMS-FM, Victoria, BC. They had been highly profitable stations.

Armstrong himself was by all accounts an honest and generous man. But he was also an inveterate womanizer, an alcoholic and in his later years became badly addicted to pills. On April 22, 1985, at the age of sixty-six, he was found dead in a room at the Laurel Point Inn in Victoria, accompanied by a twenty-six-year-old mistress. He was dead apparently of a drug overdose. He left his third wife, Sherry Armstrong, and their four children.

Some years earlier, Armstrong had agreed to give an option to buy the stations to a broadcaster named Wayne Stafford, who had rescued the stations from financial distress. But Armstrong had second thoughts when his wife, Sherry Armstrong, objected, and when Stafford would not give up the option, he was fired.

The will required the executor to sell the stations and give the proceeds to the widow. However, Sherry Armstrong had other plans. Despite having no broadcast experience, Sherry wanted to take over the stations. After a brief period during which she managed the station but the revenue declined precipitously, the co-executor brought in Bob Wood to run the stations while he found a buyer. Wayne Stafford stepped forward and made an offer. This was accepted by the co-executor conditional on CRTC approval, and I was hired to file the application to the Commission. Sherry hired a number of lawyers, including my old friend Chris Johnston, to oppose the application.

This is the background to what I recall as the single most bizarre CRTC hearing that I have ever attended. Years later, I obtained a copy of the transcript of the two-day hearing and it reads like a soap opera script. With David Armstrong's checkered history as a backdrop, the hearing explored the financial ups and downs of the stations, the emotional conflicts between all the parties, the lawsuits flying left and right, and the decidedly mixed opinions on the suitability of the widow for business management. Employees at the station split down the middle, with those opposing Sherry Armstrong filing an intervention with their names held in confidence to avert what they feared would be retaliation.

In the result, the CRTC decided to give Sherry Armstrong a chance and it turned down the application by Stafford.[2] In due course, the stations were transferred by the executors to a company 75 percent owned by Sherry and 25 percent owned by Charles Camroux, with CRTC approval.[3] Unfortunately for those who believed in the advancement of women in the broadcast industry, Sherry did not prove to be as effective a manager as they might have hoped. A bitter lawsuit between her and Camroux ensued. Eventually, in 1995, the OK Radio Group Ltd. purchased CKDA-AM, flipped it to the FM band, and relaunched it with new call letters. After a number of format changes, the station was sold to the Jim Pattison Group in 2006. As for CFMS-FM, it was sold to the CHUM Group.

The Armstrong case had a small influence on two other cases in which I was involved: the application for the Family Channel pay television licence, which I prepared for Astral and Allarcom in 1987, and the Showcase specialty licence, which I prepared for Alliance Communications in 1993. Although Sherry Armstrong had not had a great success in managing the Victoria radio stations, the case demonstrated the Commission's strong support for the involvement of women in senior management in the broadcasting sector. So I went out of my way to find a highly qualified woman candidate to be the president of Family Channel in 1987 (see p. 151). Later, in 1993, I found another well-qualified woman to be the president of Showcase (see p. 165).

FAMILY CHANNEL

During the discussions between Harold Greenberg and Dr Allard about the reorganization of pay television in 1984, the idea of bringing Walt Disney to Canada came up. Disney had launched the Disney Channel in the United States as a pay channel with some success. Allarcom had tried to licence a block of Disney programming for inclusion in its Superchannel service, but Disney had declined. It wanted to bring its channel directly into Canada.

Astral and Allarcom came up with a better idea. Why not approach Disney on a combined basis to create a Canadianized Disney channel for Canada? Like the Disney Channel in the United States, the service would have no commercials and it would be limited to family-friendly entertainment. But in addition to programming from the Disney library, it would carry Canadian family programming and it would be scheduled and controlled by Canadians.

The only problem was to convince Disney that it had no chance of coming into Canada directly. At our suggestion, the Disney executives called the head of the CRTC. André Bureau, then chairman of the CRTC, made it clear that the CRTC would not allow Disney to come in directly. So Disney agreed to negotiate a deal with Allarcom and Astral.

Accordingly, I flew down to Los Angeles along with Ian Greenberg from Astral and Doug Holtby from Allarcom. Sitting in a boardroom in the Disney offices, we negotiated for three days with the Disney executives, ending up with a term sheet that I drafted. Apart from the economics, a key issue was control. Disney understandably wanted to ensure that its brand was not diminished by being associated with offensive programming. So I needed to draft elaborate references to Standards and Practices that would be acceptable to everyone.

Eventually, everyone shook hands and we proceeded to draft the CRTC application for what became the Family Channel. I was assisted by Yves Mayrand, then an in-house counsel at Allarcom. But we also needed someone to be the president of the new service. I suggested approaching Susan Rubes, the founder of Young People's Theatre in Toronto. Neither Harold Greenberg nor Dr Allard had ever met her but in the end they agreed with my recommendation.

Susan was an excellent choice to lead the application but she knew nothing about broadcasting. To make her appearance more compelling, I took her to the offices of Annick Press in North York to introduce her to the publishers of the Robert Munsch books for children. (I had run into Rick Wilks and Anne Millyard, the publishers of Annick Press, through my earlier involvement with the Association of Canadian Publishers.) Then, armed with copies of *The Paper Bag Princess*, I wrote a speech for Susan to deliver to the Commission describing the book and indicating that this would be a wonderful title to make into a short video for the Family Channel. At the CRTC hearing, Susan brought down the house when she told the commissioners that after rescuing the prince from the dragon, the princess told him he was a bum and she wouldn't marry him after all.

At the same CRTC hearing, an application was brought for a basic cable children's service called YTV. It was fronted by Kevin Shea, and 50 percent funded by Rogers Cable and CUC Cable. The CRTC rules allowed us to reserve our intervention on the YTV application to the final day of the hearing. On the eve of that day, I met with the Family Channel application team in Dr Allard's hotel suite in Gatineau. What position should we take with regard to the YTV application? Both Dr Allard and Harold Greenberg were firm. Surely cable companies should not be permitted to own specialty services, they said. So I was delegated to draft a hard-hitting negative intervention against YTV. I did so, and read it out to the team; the owners approved every word. But Susan Rubes shrank from delivering it at the hearing. After all, she had spent the week being friends with everyone in sight, including Kevin Shea, the head of YTV. Accordingly, I was given the task of delivering the intervention at the hearing, with Susan by my side. In it, I described the conflicts of interest that would occur if cable companies were permitted to own programming services.

Needless to say, YTV was upset. It retaliated with a hastily drafted blast at the Family Channel application, arguing that it was really controlled by Disney.

In the end, the Commission granted both applications.[4] Since then, both services have prospered. Family Channel became entirely owned by Astral and YTV is entirely owned by Corus, a Shaw company.

However, Ted Rogers and his second-in-command, Phil Lind, never forgave me for attacking cable ownership of programming services. This was not the first or the last time that my opponents could not understand that my positions at a hearing were dictated by my clients, not necessarily by me. One day, Harold Greenberg called me in high spirits. He had just got off the phone with Ted Rogers. Ted had told him that if he only dropped Peter Grant as his counsel, life would be a lot better for Astral. I was the first person that Harold called to report this conversation. Luckily, Harold considered that Ted's attack on me constituted high praise for my work!

As for the issue of cable ownership of programming services, the Commission applied a policy against such ownership for a number of years. However, in 2000, it permitted Bell Canada—which owned Bell ExpressVu, the satellite distribution company—to acquire control of CTV. This prompted the cable industry to seek a change in the cable ownership policy and the CRTC did so in 2001. Since then, of course, the floodgates opened and most television programming services in Canada are now owned by companies that also operate broadcasting distribution undertakings.

In 2013, this consolidation culminated with most of the Astral broadcast assets being purchased by Bell. Family Channel, however, ended up being purchased by Rogers, subject to CRTC approval. The irony of having Family Channel wholly owned by a company which—as a shareholder in YTV some twenty-five years earlier—had opposed it being licensed did not escape me!

My work for Family Channel was not the only time that I acted for both Astral and Allarcom on matters of mutual interest. On June 23, 1988, Flora MacDonald, the minister of communications in the Mulroney government, tabled Bill C-136, which would have enacted a new Broadcasting Act. A quick perusal of the proposed legislation turned up a major problem. The draft statute would have exempted any programs 'transmitted on demand' from the definition of 'broadcasting.' Given the imminence of pay-per-view and video-on-demand services and their likely importance to the broadcasting system, Astral and Allarcom retained me to lobby the government to remove this exemption. I did so and when the legislation was reintroduced as Bill C-40 on October 12, 1989, the problematic exemption no longer appeared in the legislation. Bill C-40 eventually became law in 1991. Since then the Commission has licensed numerous video-on-demand services, requiring them to contribute to Canadian content. However, the CRTC has also exempted Internet broadcasting services from licensing, which raises other difficult questions (see p. 231).

EXPANDING INTO ENTERTAINMENT LAW

In 1985, I persuaded the firm to make an offer to Stephen Stohn to join the firm. Stephen had been called to the bar in 1979 and was a rising star in the entertainment law field. I had long felt that the area of content was just as important as carriage, and that having a foot in the door of entertainment law would be a useful adjunct to our communications law practice.

Stephen turned out to be a wonderful addition to the firm, bringing with him a roster of music and TV industry clients. He also had a disciplined approach to his practice, developing excellent contract precedents that were tailored to the Canadian situation. Soon Stephen was joined by one of our junior associates, Graham Henderson, who also decided to focus on entertainment law.

I was a strong supporter of both lawyers and through my efforts both of them were made partners of McCarthy Tétrault. However, it was not to last. Stephen married one of his clients, Linda Schuyler, the producer of the Degrassi series, and left to set up his own law firm and to join her company as a senior executive in 1995. Graham also left—to join Stephen's boutique firm. He married Margo Timmins, the lead singer of one of his clients, the Cowboy Junkies. Still later he became president of Universal Records Canada and then president of the Canadian Recording Industry Association (renamed Music Canada in 2011). Both lawyers continued to be close friends of the firm.

It is clear in hindsight that an entertainment law practice is difficult if not impossible to maintain in a mega-firm like McCarthys. The reason is twofold. First, in the Canadian market, the clients are small and generally cannot afford the rates charged by a large firm. Instead they can turn to a number of sole practitioners with low overheads who can provide a package service on an efficient basis. While some larger firms may be able to maintain an entertainment practice by relying on earnings from bank financing or tax shelter work, the great bulk of entertainment law work is best handled by small boutiques or, if the entertainment company itself reaches any significant size, done in-house.

It was also difficult to meld the nature of this kind of practice with that of a big firm. In an environment dominated by billable hours, entertainment lawyers are hard pressed to clock the kind of hours typical of commercial or litigation lawyers involved in big cases. So in the yearly 'allocation' debate as to how the partners focusing on entertainment law will be compensated they inevitably suffer.

That being said, my interest in and exposure to entertainment law turned out to be extremely useful. While I avoided the prosaic day-to-day work of entertainment lawyers (e.g., drafting recording and publishing contracts, film deals and the like), I did gain a working knowledge of the field. That materially helped me in what turned into a significant area of my practice, that is, focusing on the larger industry-wide issues of interest to the production sector, like copyright reform, and appearances on behalf of the industry trade associations before the CRTC or the Copyright Board of Canada.

On these kinds of matters I was in a unique position to provide a useful service. The best example is the work I did in setting up the Canadian Retransmission Collective (see p. 160).

THE BELL DISPUTE

In 1986, I managed to lure Hank Intven to join the firm. He had been the general counsel of the Consumers' Association of Canada (CAC), and then joined the CRTC, eventually becoming executive director of Telecommunications. He was bright, personable and a superb regulatory lawyer. After a six-month interlude during which Hank and his wife, Lyndsay Green, sailed in the Caribbean with their baby daughter, he joined the firm.

I was delighted to have him join our communications practice. However, within months, we were hit with an internal crisis. BCE, the parent company of Bell Canada, acquired control of TransCanada Pipelines (TCPL). This was part of an ill-conceived move by Jean de Grandpré, BCE's CEO, to diversify BCE and transform it into a conglomerate. (BCE's ventures in this regard all ended unhappily for the company and later BCE sold them off at a loss and retrenched. But that is another story.)

The crisis arose because TCPL was one of McCarthy's largest commercial clients. The firm had acted for TCPL since it was created in the 1950s. One of our commercial lawyers, Gary Girvan, had moved to Calgary to look after its needs. But now that BCE was in control, a phone call came from Jean de Grandpré. Why was TCPL giving its legal work to McCarthys, where Peter Grant was busy 'Bell-bashing' in front of the CRTC? An ultimatum was issued. Unless the firm stopped Bell-bashing, it would lose the TCPL account.

There was a lot of support for me in the firm. But it was also clear that the loss of TCPL would be problematic for our commercial group. At that time, McCarthys acted for relatively few public companies. The loss of TCPL was thought to be devastating.

The firm had a number of partner meetings to agonize over what to do. We came up with strategies to spin Hank, Lorne, Stephen Stohn and myself into a friendly boutique firm. (We even experimented with letterhead to see what the new firm would look like on paper.) I also entered into confidential talks with senior management at the Tory law firm, who indicated they would welcome me as a partner with open arms.

As all of this was happening, our principal telecom client, CBTA, approached me with a question: Given all their CRTC work, wouldn't it make sense to have it handled by an in-house counsel? And would I help by interviewing and selecting an appropriate candidate?

At the same time, it was becoming clear to us that our domestic telecom work would inevitably decline. Reason: once the CRTC opened the door to more competition, Bell's rates would become more competitive and there would be fewer reasons to appear at the CRTC on behalf of business users. While full interconnection had not yet been ordered, it was only a matter of time before that too would occur. So what were we arguing about?

Responding to CBTA's request, Hank and I interviewed a number of candidates to act as its in-house counsel. We chose Ken Engelhart, a young litigation lawyer who was tired of insurance cases and who relished the opportunity to fight Bell. Ken had previously worked as a student lawyer for Hank at CAC and Hank thought highly of him. CAC had given Ken his first taste of regulatory work. So Ken was hired to handle CBTA's work as in-house counsel. Within a few years, however, as the CRTC ruled in favour of more competition, CBTA's main reason for existence disappeared. And by the mid-1990s, the organization actually declared bankruptcy and went out of business. (In 1990, Ken went on to become vice-president regulatory for Rogers Communications Inc., and today is a key player in Canadian communications regulation and policy.)

Back at McCarthys, we took a number of steps that addressed the decline in domestic telecom work. I concentrated almost entirely on broadcast matters, which increased in scale significantly over the next decade. As for Hank, he handled a few energy rate cases initially but then developed a stunning international telecom practice, travelling around the world to advise governments and others on telecom policy. The team he led ultimately worked on projects and deals in over forty-five countries. Hank also became involved in advising the Canadian government on a new Telecommunications Act, which came into force in 1993, and he acted for Telesat Canada in its 1992 rate case and for the CCTA in the 1994 regulatory framework proceeding, and later for Telus, Teleglobe and a number of other major Canadian telecom companies. Hank and I also collaborated on one of my most enjoyable cases—the creation and development of the Canadian Retransmission Collective (see p. 160).

It is intriguing to speculate on what would have happened if the TCPL dispute had not occurred. In 1988, I was approached by the president of CNCP Telecommunications, by then called Unitel Communications, to act as its counsel in their next interconnect application. But I had to turn them down, given the Bell ownership of TCPL. After Rogers became an investor in Unitel, the legal work for Unitel was directed to Bob Buchan at Johnston & Buchan, who had long acted as outside counsel for Rogers. Over the next few years, J&B acted not only for Unitel but also for Cantel, the wireless company controlled by Rogers, which morphed into Rogers Mobility. (Unitel won its interconnect application in 1992. It later became AT&T Canada, and Rogers sold off its interest in the company at a loss. Still later, AT&T Canada became Allstream and was acquired by the Manitoba Telephone System after MTS had been privatized by the Manitoba government. And in 2013, Allstream was sold to Wind Mobile.)

However, given my involvement in so many broadcast matters on the other side of Ted Rogers, I doubt that we could have ended up with either the Unitel or Cantel accounts. In retrospect it is clear to me that we made exactly the right decision in redirecting our telecom practice the way we did.

As for McCarthys, it retained the TCPL account. It also completed a long-standing quest to become Canada's first national law firm. Its efforts to start a firm in Calgary with Toronto partners in the 1980s had been opposed by members of the Alberta bar, and the Law Society of Alberta enacted rules to prohibit its entry. But McCarthys appealed this all the way to the Supreme Court of Canada and on April 20, 1989, the court ruled in our favour, striking down the Alberta Law Society rules on Charter grounds.[5] That allowed a full merger of the Toronto firm with firms in Vancouver, Calgary and Montreal, and the firm became McCarthy Tétrault LLP in 1990. For a number of years McCarthys was the largest law firm in Canada, until a number of other law firms also 'went national.' The firm's profile increased dramatically, and its commercial group ended up acting for a stellar client base that dwarfed its earlier practice. Gary Girvan became one of Canada's best-known mergers and acquisitions lawyers.

Even more ironically, the management of Bell Canada changed dramatically and in 2003 I got a call from its vice-president asking if I could do some work for them (see p. 228).

STANDARD RADIO

In the spring of 1988, I got an urgent call from Allan Slaight, a radio station owner. He had started as a disc jockey in Edmonton, invested briefly in Global Television when it was in trouble, then invested in some successful radio station start-ups. In 1985, he 'traded up' by acquiring the radio stations owned by Standard Radio in Toronto, Montreal, Ottawa and St. Catharines. (These stations were then owned by Argus Corporation, which Conrad Black had taken over some years before.)

The two Toronto stations—CFRB-AM and CKFM-FM—were very

popular and profitable. Allan had installed his oldest son, Gary Slaight, to run the Toronto FM station.

At that time, the CRTC required FM radio stations to observe a fairly strict regime, to distinguish themselves from AM radio stations. In addition to running 35 percent Canadian content in music, FM stations were limited to no more than 49 percent 'hits', i.e., songs listed on one of the top-100 charts. The Commission did not want FM stations to follow the lead of the commercial AM radio stations, which typically devoted virtually their entire playlist to hit records.

The FM stations in Toronto were highly competitive, led by CHUM-FM (owned by Allan Waters), CHFI-FM (owned by Ted Rogers) and CKFM-FM (owned by Allan Slaight). Over the years, the stations had progressively ignored the CRTC rule and the number of 'hits' climbed past 50 percent to 60 percent and then as high as 70 percent. The Commission did nothing. CHUM-AM, which played nothing but hits, was being badly hurt. So CHUM decided to blow the whistle and complain to the CRTC.

The Commission dutifully did an investigation and audited all the commercial FM stations in Toronto for a sample week. CKFM-FM was the worst offender and was called to a public hearing on April 12, 1988. Gary Slaight appeared for CKFM, accompanied by his lawyer. He acknowledged that he was guilty, but said he could not correct the situation overnight; it would take time to adjust the station's computer program. Gary Slaight had not been properly prepared by his lawyer for the hearing and the panel was unhappy with his responses. The Commission decided to make an example of him and on April 28, 1988, it issued a notice calling CKFM-FM to a hearing to show cause why its FM licence should not be suspended or revoked for a breach of its condition of licence. That same day, Allan Slaight fired his lawyer and called me in panic. Could I act for CKFM-FM on the hearing and save the station from possibly losing its licence?

So began a twenty-year relationship with Standard Radio. But the immediate problem was how to rescue CKFM-FM and Gary Slaight from this crisis.

I was very familiar with the FM conditions of licence in question. In fact I had drafted them back in the mid-1970s, when I was working for the Commission. So I carefully reviewed how the conditions applied in the context of the damning evidence of the sample week monitored by the Commission. There was no question but that CKFM had exceeded the 49 percent level—it was well north of 65 percent.

My strategy was threefold:

First, have Gary Slaight express contrition, explain that everything was now in full compliance and state how he had learned an important lesson and would never stray again. Accompanying this would be statements from the music industry attesting to Gary's commitment to Canadian music. This presented no problem, for Gary had a wonderful track record of supporting Canadian musical talent.[6]

Second, I would develop a strong legal case maintaining that although Gary had admitted he was 'guilty,' in fact he was not—that properly interpreted, the station had not breached its condition of licence. In making this case, I was laying the groundwork for an appeal to the courts if the Commission suspended or revoked the licence.

Third, I would show that the station had already been hurt in the market simply because of the threat of suspension. What advertiser would place an ad on the station for a time-sensitive campaign if the station might not be on the air?

To build the legal case I needed some admissions from the CRTC. So I threatened to subpoena their staff unless I got them. This tactic succeeded and the CRTC admitted that in a previous case a different station, with the call letters CKO-FM, had not been held to be in breach of a licence condition when it broadcast sports 10 percent of the time, despite being licensed as an all-news station. I then developed my arguments.

My argument was based on a close reading of the licence condition in question. The condition actually did not require CKFM-FM to meet the hit ratio. Instead, it required FM stations to substantially meet, *on an overall basis*, four different requirements, of which the hit ratio was only one. As shown in the CKO-FM case, the word *substantial* could allow at least a 10 percent variance. And since CKFM-FM entirely met the other three requirements, I argued that its failure to meet the 49 percent rule on the hit ratio did not mean that it was not in substantial compliance if you looked at the overall licence condition.

On August 25, 1988, the Commission released its decision.[7] Most of the text of the decision was devoted to trying to prove that CKFM was guilty and to trying to rebut my legal case.[8] In that regard, the Commission ruled against me, but they announced a curious penalty. CKFM's licence would be suspended for three days but the suspension would not affect its ability to broadcast; only its ability to run commercials on those days would be suspended. And CKFM could pick the three days when the suspension would be effective!

I looked through the decision and felt confident of my chances on a legal appeal. But there was no point in appealing. The penalty was a slap on the wrist. In fact, CKFM chose three days in the week that ratings were being measured in Toronto and announced in advance that it would broadcast commercial-free for three days. Needless to say, its ratings went up during the crucial ratings period!

Shortly after the CKFM decision, Allan Slaight appointed Gary to run his entire radio operation. This turned out to be an inspired move as Gary was a brilliant radio operator. In recognition of his abilities, he was named Broadcast Executive of the Year in 1992, 1993, 1996 and 1998.

Over the next few years, I helped Gary to win new FM radio licences in competitive hearings for Calgary and Ottawa and to acquire AM and FM radio stations in Vancouver, Edmonton and Winnipeg. In 2002, I helped him get CRTC approval for the acquisition of all of Telemedia's radio stations in English Canada, except for a few that were divested to Rogers and Newcap. This deal, worth $385 million, made Standard Radio the second largest private radio operator in Canada. In 2007, Allan Slaight decided it was time to sell, and all of his radio stations were bought by Astral Media. The price was $1.2 billion, the largest radio deal in Canada. Gary continues to be active in the music scene and he also runs the Slaight Family Foundation, a major contributor to philanthropic causes.

In 2013, most of the Astral radio stations, including the ones acquired from Standard Radio, were sold to Bell Canada. As for CKFM-FM, Toronto, it now operates under the name Virgin Radio.

THE CANADIAN RETRANSMISSION COLLECTIVE

In 1988, the Copyright Act was amended to create a new 'retransmission right' for the owners of TV shows. This was the right to obtain equitable remuneration from cable companies when they carried the programs on so-called distant signals. (Distant signals were signals received more than 32 kilometres beyond the Grade-B contour of a television station.)

For many years, cable companies had paid nothing for the carriage of distant signals, relying on a 1954 decision of the Exchequer Court of Canada to escape liability. In the United States, cable companies had similarly been excused from paying any royalties for retransmitting TV signals, but this had changed in 1976 when Congress amended the US Copyright Act. In the free trade negotiations between Canada and the United States in the late 1980s, the Hollywood studios had sought a similar amendment from Canada and this was included as part of the Canada-US Free Trade Agreement (see p. 198). But the actual rates and who would be paid were left to be determined by the newly created Copyright Board of Canada.

Needless to say, the Hollywood studios were quick to set up a 'collective society' in Canada to receive such royalties, and they offered to handle collections and payments for any copyright owners who chose to affiliate with them. They called their collective the Copyright Collective of Canada.

As all this was developing, I happened to be speaking to Stephen Ellis, who was a client of the firm. His company, Ellis Enterprises, was an independent television producer specializing in wild life and nature films as well as distributing British and Australian content in Canada. Stephen was also on the board of the Canadian Film and Television Association (the CFTA), which represented producers of TV shows. There was also a rival association of Canadian film producers called the Association of Canadian Film and Television Producers (ACFTP). The two associations had tried to merge the previous year but the attempt had failed and there was much mutual recrimination between them.

I told Stephen about the recent amendments to the Copyright Act and asked him why Canadian producers didn't create their own collective to get their money from distant signal retransmission, instead of going through the Hollywood collective. Stephen was immediately intrigued. He approached the CFTA and got a green light to proceed.

On further analysis, I could see three big problems:

First, how could Canadian producers present a unified front—and a single collective—to the Copyright Board if there were two rival trade associations representing them (not to mention the Quebec producers, who had their own association)?

Second, even if all the Canadian producers worked together, their total claim would probably be quite small, since most of the distant signals were US TV stations where there was little or no Canadian content. If the claim was small, the overhead expenses might dwarf any royalties that could be claimed.

Third, how would Canadian producers finance an application to the board, given the significant likely expense of such an application and their limited resources?

So there were three problems. In the end I figured out a way to address each of them.

In regard to the first problem, I proposed incorporating a not-for-profit collective whose board membership would be controlled equally by the two associations. This took a lot of persuading and cajoling but eventually succeeded. We called the new collective the Canadian Retransmission Collective (CRC). (Later, the two producer associations did merge, becoming the Canadian Film and Television Production Association [CFTPA], and some of the credit is due to the success of CRC. The CFTPA changed its name to the Canadian Media Production Association in 2010.)

The second problem was more fundamental. Could we lure other program rights holders to join our collective and not the Hollywood collective? I did some research into the US retransmission royalty scheme and found that the PBS stations had not joined with Hollywood but had formed a separate collective. So I called their general counsel, alerted her to the Canadian situation and asked if the PBS stations along the US border with Canada could affiliate with CRC in Canada. PBS confirmed that it did not see eye to eye with Hollywood, and after some negotiation, they agreed to join forces with CRC, in exchange for two board seats and a veto on decisions affecting their interests. Then I contacted TVOntario and the National Film Board and both of them came aboard. However, the CBC stood apart. In the end, the CBC formed a separate collective together with the three US commercial networks, ABC, CBS and NBC.

By this time, the deadline for filing claims with the Copyright Board was coming up the following week. I suddenly had a brainwave. What about European producers? No one was coming forward to represent them. And if they missed the deadline, no doubt the Hollywood collective would purport to represent them by drafting its claim as widely as possible. I did some research and discovered that retransmission royalties to producers in Europe were handled by a Swiss-based organization named AGICOA. The largest single member of AGICOA by far was the trade association for the Hollywood studios but they did not control the organization. I contacted the AGICOA general counsel by phone. He was stupefied to learn that the Canadian legislation had come into force and that claims had to be filed within a week. The Hollywood studios had carefully kept this information to themselves, so they could assert a claim for all European productions by default. I described CRC and its mandate. Within a day I had a fax from AGICOA confirming that it would affiliate with CRC!

Armed with this, CRC duly filed its claim with the Copyright Board.

But we still had a third problem. Who would pay for bringing the case before the Board? (In the end the legal expense of bringing the CRC case to the Board was over $850,000.) The associations could only come up with $50,000. I approached McCarthy Tétrault senior management and proposed a contingent arrangement. Any amount owing over $50,000 would only come out of royalties if any.

On this basis, I proceeded with the case. With help from Hank Intven, I drafted the application and developed the evidence for CRC. At the hearing, I appeared as the principal witness for CRC, and Hank acted as their counsel. My second day of testimony before the Copyright Board was on October 15, 1989, the day my daughter, Kristin, was born! This did not go unnoticed by other counsel, who amusingly referred to it at the hearing.

The case took over a year and a half to resolve. However, the upshot was remarkable. The Board ordered the cable companies to pay royalties of more than $50 million a year, an amount that was entirely based on my evidence. Of that amount, CRC was awarded 13 percent. So CRC immediately garnered revenue of over $6 million a year. Needless to say, the McCarthy bills were promptly paid with interest. But more important, I had created a long-time client of the firm.

In 2010, CRC celebrated its twentieth anniversary. By that point, it had paid over $146 million in retransmission royalties to its affiliates.

SHOWCASE

On November 28, 1991, I delivered the keynote address to a conference in Ottawa organized by the Canadian Film and Television Production

Association. My speech was titled 'International Developments and the Canadian Production Industry: New Challenges, New Strategies.' A new Broadcasting Act had just come into force earlier that year. In my address, I proposed that the CRTC should call for more licences for Canadian specialty services that could be included in basic or extended basic cable service. Why couldn't Canada have its own equivalent of US services like A&E, I asked. Within a year, the CRTC decided to call for applications for such licences.

In the fall of 1992, I got a call from the office of Robert Lantos, the chairman and CEO of Alliance Communications Corporation. Would I have breakfast with Mr Lantos at the Park Plaza Hotel the next morning? I was delighted to do so. Lantos was Canada's best-known independent film producer, with a string of successful Canadian films, including *Black Robe*, and a number of TV dramas to his credit, including *Due South*, the CTV drama series. Together with others, Lantos had founded Alliance in 1985 and by the time of his call to me was in the process of taking the company public. (A number of other producers followed suit during this period, so that there was a growing number of production companies with public financing, including Atlantis Films, Nelvana, Cinar and Salter Street. But Alliance was the biggest. It also had a growing business distributing independent productions [including Miramax and New Line films] in Canada, and Canadian shows abroad.)

Robert now wanted to get into the broadcasting business. And he had a new idea for a channel. He was tired of the scheduling practices of the private broadcasters, which relegated Canadian drama to less-watched periods and focused their prime-time schedule on US shows simulcast with the American TV networks.

Robert's idea was revolutionary. Why not create a Canadian specialty channel devoted to drama, with the prime-time block of 7 p.m. to 10 p.m. entirely devoted to *Canadian* drama? I looked at him with widened eyes. The policy attractiveness of the idea was obvious. But was there enough Canadian drama production to fill three prime-time hours seven days a week? And there were few precedents for such a channel—the only one I could think of was UK Gold, a rerun channel that had recently launched in Britain and that carried old UK programs. There was certainly no US precedent at the time.

Being in the distribution business, Robert had a good sense of the inventory available for such a channel. Many of the older Canadian drama programs came from the CBC, so it made sense to bring the CBC in as a partner. But the CBC had no money to invest in a new channel. No problem. Why don't we have the CBC pay for its investment with program rights? Robert also offered a small investment position to other independent producers (many of whom had no money to invest, but Robert put up the money for them).

I accepted Robert's retainer and proceeded to draft the CRTC application. It came together quite quickly as I developed the economic scenario. Clearly it would be predominantly a rerun channel, but it would also have some original Canadian drama productions. The key promise would be the all-Canadian prime-time block from 7 to 10 p.m. But after 10 p.m. there would be room for an independent film festival block of programming, with independent films and series from around the world. After much discussion, it was decided to call the service Showcase.

As I developed the application, it became clear that we would need a proposed president and CEO. But who to choose? Robert thought of Peter O'Brian, a well-known Canadian film producer. But he turned us down, focused as he was on producing a film to be shot in BC for Twentieth Century Fox (it was released in 1995 under the title *Far from Home: The Adventures of Yellow Dog*).

I then came up with what turned out to be a brilliant suggestion— Phyllis Yaffe. Phyllis, a former librarian from Winnipeg, had been the executive director of the Association of Canadian Publishers, and I knew she was bright, personable and organized. In 1986, I had tapped her to be the first chair of the First Choice $1 million Fund to Underwrite New Drama Production (later the Harold Greenberg Fund) and she had done a wonderful job. So I introduced her to Robert and she became the proposed president of Showcase.

In 1993, we reached the CRTC hearings to present our application. I had put a lot of work into it and to this day, I think it is one of my best efforts. No one else had thought of the concept and the private broadcasters frankly scoffed at the application. How could any channel succeed with a condition of licence requiring all-Canadian drama from 7 to 10 p.m.? But we presented a strong case and had the support of the CBC as well as independent producers from every region. On June 6, 1994, the Commission awarded the licence for Showcase,[9] and the service launched across Canada by the end of the year.

At the same hearings, the Commission heard a number of other applications and five other licences were granted. They included Lifestyle, another application that I had a hand in drafting although I left it to Hank Intven to organize and rehearse the presentation at the CRTC hearing.[10] (Lifestyle was later renamed the Women's Television Network and is now the W Network.) A third application I had prepared for a country music channel for Standard Radio came up against four other competing applicants for the country music genre and the CRTC awarded the licence to one of the competitors.

It remains to note that both Showcase and the W Network have turned out to be among the most successful Canadian channels ever launched. Showcase is now owned and operated by Shaw Media and W Network is owned and operated by Corus. By 2013, both programming services were subscribed to by almost 9 million households across Canada.

TELEVISION IN THE ALTERNATIVE

On June 6, 1994, the CRTC approved the licensing of ten new Canadian pay and specialty services. I was happy with the decision, since two of the winners were Showcase and W Network, for whom I had acted. However, two of the licences awarded—Bravo! and Canal D—gave rise to considerable controversy.

In licensing Bravo! to the CHUM organization, the CRTC had turned down a much more ambitious application for an arts channel, to be called Festival.

The CRTC decisions respecting Bravo! and Canal D were challenged by a coalition of groups, which petitioned the minister of Canadian heritage to set aside the decisions. After reviewing the petition, the minister announced that the government had decided to uphold the CRTC decisions. However, the minister stated that he would continue efforts to 'facilitate the development of alternative programming services.' The phrase 'alternative programming services' was found in paragraphs $3(1)(q)$ and (r) of the new Broadcasting Act, which had come into force in 1991, but no one knew what this concept really meant.

On September 11, 1994, the minister appointed a Group of Experts on Alternative Programming Services. This group consisted of twelve people with a wide range of background and experience, including representatives of unions, private broadcasters and the CBC. I ended up chairing the group and was largely responsible for drafting and organizing the report.

The Group met on numerous occasions and reviewed the available research. Eventually, the 114-page report of the Group of Experts was issued in May 1995. It was called *TELEVISION in the Alternative: The Future of Innovation and the Arts in the Canadian Broadcasting System.*

While the report focused on arts programming and its availability in Canada, it also was one of the first studies to address the importance of pricing and packaging to the success of Canadian niche programming services. A chapter on the evolution of Canadian pay and specialty services included a detailed analysis of the impact of carriage of such services by cable television systems on an 'extended tier' (i.e., a high-penetration unencrypted group of analog channels made available at a relatively low package price and secured with negative traps on drops serving non-subscribing households). This mode of distribution turned out to be critical to the success of dozens of Canadian programming services in the 1990s, and the report explains how and why. Of course, since 2000, analog distribution has been replaced with digital distribution in many Canadian households. However, the importance of pricing and packaging to the success of Canadian niche programming services remains.

HISTORY TELEVISION COMES TO CANADA

Given the success of Showcase, Robert Lantos wanted to own more specialty services. The Commission called for new applications to be filed in late 1995. However, the cable industry told the Commission that there were no more analog channels left and that any new channels would have to be content with carriage on a digital channel. This would involve the purchase or rental of one or more set-top boxes by each subscribing household so the penetration of such services was bound to be low.

Phyllis Yaffe was keen on applying for a second channel, given the efficiencies in operating two channels instead of one, and she suggested to Robert that Alliance apply for a history channel. One of the most popular new services in the United States was the History Channel, owned by the Arts & Entertainment Network (A&E). Many Canadian players trooped down to New York to see if they could form a joint venture with A&E to bring a Canadian version of the History Channel to Canada. Alliance Communications was among the many suitors but in the end A&E elected to form a joint venture with TSN, taking a minority position and licensing its content and the brand name.

Unlike everyone else, Robert Lantos did not give up. Why do you need to have a deal with A&E? he asked. Yes, you need history programming from around the world, but you could buy it directly from other suppliers. And A&E did not own the word *history*.

So I was enlisted to prepare a competing application for a history channel. Our tentative title for the channel was The History & Entertainment Network. A&E was fit to be tied when they learned of the title, since it stole words from the names of both their networks. Few people noticed that the acronym for our channel was THEN—surely a good title for a history service.

As I worked on the application, a preliminary question was: Where might we find Canadian archive material? While it would be possible to include some well-known Canadian history series—for example, Pierre Berton's *The Last Spike*, produced for the CBC in the 1970s—these were few and far between. A key element in the application would be to provide Canadian documentary producers with access to archival material. So an arrangement was made with CTV. In exchange for 12 percent of the equity in the channel, CTV agreed to make its archive of news clips dating back to 1961 available to would-be producers.

A second question was: How would we determine the economics of the channel? If we followed the cautionary instructions of the Commission, the model would be based on digital carriage. I recommended that we follow these instructions, although I realized that other applicants would probably seek analog carriage, which would provide much more revenue. I felt we could probably amend our application at the hearing if it turned out that analog carriage was still possible.

In the result, there were only two applications presented to the CRTC for a history channel—the TSN/A&E application using the name the History Channel, and the Alliance application. TSN presented an excellent application based on analog carriage, and highlighting the use of the extensive A&E library of history programming. They brought a number of Canada's best-known history gurus into the mix. They also proposed a far higher Canadian-content budget for the channel, based on a high-penetration analog tier. By contrast, Alliance had a much lower Canadian-content budget because it had proposed carriage on a digital tier. The overall betting odds going into the hearing were that TSN would win the licence hands down.

But we weren't yet down and out. It was obvious to the Commission that Canadian-content levels were tied to the mode of carriage. So to compare apples with apples, the Commission asked each applicant how its economic model would change if its channel was carried on a high-penetration analog tier. That gave us our opportunity. We immediately filed numbers that showed we would do more Canadian content production than TSN.

At the hearing, I felt I had a second card to play—namely, Robert Lantos's personal story. As an immigrant to Canada who had made good, he was in a unique position to talk about the importance of Canada to him and to the world. He could also contrast our all-Canadian application with TSN's dependence on a US library, and arguably excessive licence fees to A&E. So I wrote a very personal four-minute script for Robert to deliver as part of our twenty-minute opening presentation.

Then we got the CRTC hearing schedule. We were scheduled to make our opening presentation on a Friday afternoon, right after TSN, which was scheduled that morning.

Lantos called me.

'I can't be in Ottawa that day,' he said.

'Why not, Robert? It's crucial for you to be there.'

'But I have to be in France. That's the day of the world premiere of my production of David Cronenberg's new movie, *Crash*, at the Cannes Film Festival.'

We talked about how to solve the problem. Then Robert had an idea. 'Why don't we have a live satellite linkup so I can talk directly to the Commission panel from France.'

I thought about this for a minute. I could imagine all kinds of things going wrong. Of course technical problems can be solved. But ...

I said, 'Robert, that isn't going to work.'

'Why not?'

'I can just see it ... you standing in front of the Hotel Martinez in Cannes with girls in the swimming pool behind you. And you saying on the live satellite hookup, "Mr Chairman, I just wish I could be with you today…"'

Robert saw my point.

We decided to go a different route. Robert would tape his four-minute speech in advance and we would present it as a video at the hearing. And in order to make it more effective, we would put the script on a teleprompter so that Robert would be looking at the camera the whole time.

All of this was duly prepared. And at the CRTC hearing, when it came time for Robert's speech, everyone turned to watch the TV monitors in the hearing room. The Commissioners all watched dutifully as the video showed Robert talking to them. But as the speech went on, the camera moved closer and closer to Robert, so that his face filled more of the screen. The effect was riveting, far more so than the usual situation at a CRTC hearing where people look down at their scripts. Here Robert was looking directly at the panel throughout his speech. It was extraordinarily effective.

A week or so later, in the reply phase of the hearing, Robert made his appearance and he was his usual compelling self. TSN was extremely upset, not only with his attack on A&E, but also with the fact that we had 'amended' our application in midstream to make it competitive with that of TSN.

The CRTC decision was issued on September 4, 1996.[11] And to everyone's amazement, Alliance won the history licence. I was largely credited with one of the great upsets of all time. The new service, called History Television, launched in 1997 and was immediately successful. By 2013, it had reached close to 8 million subscribers.

For fifteen years, smarting from its defeat, A&E refused to license its own history programming to the Canadian service. But in 2012, History Television was acquired by Shaw Media. Negotiations ensued and Shaw struck a licensing deal with A&E to gain access not only to its library of history programming but also to the use of the name and logo of A&E's US history service. Accordingly, in the fall of 2012, History Television changed its name to the History Channel. But the Canadian service is still wholly owned and controlled by Shaw Media and 50 percent of its schedule must be devoted to Canadian programming.

History Television benefited from being launched by the cable television industry as part of an analog 'extended tier.' As I have noted, I had occasion to examine the economics of this mode of distribution in the 1995 report to the minister of Canadian heritage. The 'extended tier' was a group of analog channels sent unscrambled to all cable subscribers. Those who declined to subscribe to the package would have them blocked by the insertion of an inexpensive negative trap at the house drop. If the package price was kept relatively low, and the package contained attractive programming services, this approach could lead to relatively high penetration.

This method of distribution had first been invented by Larry Corke, a marketing executive at CableNet, who had experimented with it in an Oakville suburb in 1986. Over the next few years, the cable industry progressively adopted his idea and dozens of new Canadian specialty programming services were successfully launched on a first, second or third extended tier, using negative trap technology instead of the expensive set-top box used for the premium pay services.

In its 1996 decision, the Commission had issued fifteen new Canadian specialty licences. Four, including History Television, were given the right to be on a high-penetration analog tier. The rest were told that they had to wait until September 1, 1999, before they had the right to insist on analog carriage. Any cable operator who had reached a 15 percent digital threshold prior to that time had the right to deny access to analog and offer digital-only carriage instead.

By 1997, however, the cable industry was sold on the benefits of the extended-tier approach, which had already been used to launch a first and second extended tier. But the industry also realized that in order to get sufficient penetration for a third extended tier, cable companies would have to offer a much bigger package for an attractive price. After much discussion, the industry decided to offer a third extended tier of fifteen services for a package price of $5.95. The services included History Television, the Comedy Network, HGTV, the Score, Sportsnet, Space, TELETOON, Treehouse, CTV Newsnet, Canadian Learning Television (later Viva, then OWN) and Prime (later TVTropolis). To make the package even more attractive, the industry also moved Family Channel, the non-commercial Disney-based pay service licensed in 1987, to the new extended tier. Family Channel, like the Disney Channel in the United States, had initially been conceived as a premium pay TV service with a wholesale affiliation fee of $5 or more per subscriber. This relegated it to a scrambled low-penetration premium tier. But Family Channel soon realized that it could make more money with the same programming in a high-penetration tier, even if that meant drastically reducing its affiliation fee. Adding Family Channel—licensed as a pay TV service—to the third extended tier also made it possible to add WTBS, the popular Atlanta superstation, since the CRTC rules at the time only allowed such superstations in packages with pay TV services.

The new 'mother of all packages' rolled out in the beginning of 1997. A free trial was extended to three months. Cable companies delayed installing negative traps for a number of months beyond the trial period, hoping to increase penetration without incurring cost. In the end, the third extended tier reached a penetration of 65 percent within a year. All of the services turned out to be profitable.

One of the services licensed by the CRTC in 1996 was Report on Business Television (ROBTv), but it had delayed its plans for launch because of ownership issues involving its shareholders, Thomson Corporation (50 percent), WIC (26 percent) and Canadian Satellite Communications Inc. (Cancom) (24 percent). ROBTv had borrowed its name from the *Globe and Mail*'s financial section, 'Report on Business.'

In May 1999, Duncan McEwan, the president and CEO of Cancom, called me and asked for my advice. He could see no economic future for a niche service like ROBTv if it was launched only as a premium service on set-top boxes. But could it still be part of a high-penetration analog tier? If so, once up and running, the service could have an economic value of $40 million or more. Shaw Cable, which was seeking to acquire WIC and Cancom, had told everyone at the CCTA convention that month that ROBTv was dead in the water and would never launch. However, Grant Buchanan, the in-house counsel for WIC, which also owned 55 percent of Cancom, had looked at the CRTC rules and had come to a different conclusion.

I carefully looked at the CRTC public notices and agreed with Grant. By that point in the late spring of 1999 it was increasingly clear that the cable industry was not going to launch digital boxes by September 1, 1999.

And if they failed to meet the deadline, the Commission rules stipulated that they would have to launch ROBTv on an analog channel and negotiate 'equitable carriage arrangements' if ROBTv was up and running by that time. So my advice to the owners was that indeed they could qualify to be carried on an extended analog cable tier, but only if they launched the service on or prior to September 1, 1999.

To create a viable business news service out of whole cloth in three months flat involved an enormous risk. A service of this kind was far harder to create than a regular twenty-four-hour news service, since it needed to have state-of-the-art multiscreen financial reports as well as a much heavier roster of interview guests. It also needed to have its main studio in downtown Toronto to be near the business community. To get this going, the owners hired Jack Fleischman to set up the programming, and Mark Jan Vrem to organize the studio and the logistics. Working long hours, they managed to get the service up and running by the deadline, using a cramped temporary studio on Jarvis Street connected to a master control in Hamilton.

The cable industry had already launched its third tier two years earlier and were not happy with the idea of adjusting the tier to include ROBTv. Both Rogers and Shaw Cable scoffed at ROBTv's plans. One cable company argued that if we forced it to carry ROBTv on an analog channel it would scramble the signal and require subscribers to get an analog set-top box to descramble it, instead of putting it in a high-penetration tier. To nip that idea in the bud, I sought and obtained a public notice from the CRTC clarifying that a scrambled analog channel would not meet the Commission's requirement for an 'equitable carriage arrangement'; carriage would have to be on an unscrambled analog tier.[12]

Armed with this clarification, I spent all of August 1999 negotiating deals with each of the major cable companies on behalf of ROBTv. Though initially opposed, one by one the major players capitulated and agreed to add ROBTv to the third extended tier, thereby ensuring the success of the service.

Later ROBTv was acquired by CTV and changed its name to the Business News Network. By 2013, it had close to 7 million subscribers. However, had the CRTC not imposed its rules and had the cable industry not agreed to carry the service on the third extended analog tier, the service would never have been launched.

It is hard to overestimate the importance of the high-penetration analog extended tier to the success of the specialty services launched in the 1990s. Had they been relegated to a tier requiring an addressable set-top box, and sold one by one, almost all of them would have failed. We know this because when C-Channel was launched on this basis in 1983, it failed. But ten years later, Bravo! an arts channel with exactly the same kind of programming lineup, succeeded as part of an unscrambled extended tier. Now Bravo! has over 7 million subscribers.

WORK FOR ALLIANCE ATLANTIS

In 1998, Robert Lantos decided that he wanted to go back to his first love, film production. He was tired of the executive management of a large diverse publicly traded company. So he orchestrated a deal in which his company acquired the second largest player, Atlantis Communications, but control passed to the four founding shareholders of the latter company and Robert exited the company with upwards of $50 million, which he used to set up his new company, Serendipity Point Films.

I handled the application for approval from the CRTC and the company became Alliance Atlantis Communications Inc., headed by Michael MacMillan. During the years when Alliance had launched Showcase and History Television, Atlantis had launched Life Network (now Slice) and HGTV Canada. So the new company now had a stable of four specialty services.

In acquiring control of the company, MacMillan also acquired some of the senior management of Alliance, and he soon made Phyllis Yaffe president and CEO of all the broadcast services. He also turned to me for all his regulatory advice. Over the next few years, I helped Alliance Atlantis win more specialty television licences from the CRTC, including Food Network Canada, Fine Living Canada, Discovery Health Canada, BBC Canada and BBC Kids. (In the latter two cases, I also acted for the BBC to negotiate the joint venture relationship with Alliance Atlantis.) I helped to secure CRTC approval for MacMillan's acquisition of Salter Street Films, a Halifax-based production company that had launched the Independent Film Channel (IFC Canada).

Apart from Fine Living Canada, which ceased operations in 2009, all of these services became successful. Discovery Health Canada changed its name to TwistTV in 2011.

Over time, Michael MacMillan recognized that the stock analysts gave him high praise for his broadcast properties but no credit at all for his Canadian production business, which was inherently more risky and decidedly less profitable. So he gradually reduced the drama-production activities of Alliance Atlantis, although he maintained an international production and distribution business, which included a 50 percent interest in the monster US hit *CSI*.[13] Alliance Atlantis also maintained a controlling interest in a Canadian film distributor.

In late 2006, in a highly prescient move, MacMillan decided to put the company up for sale. In a complex arrangement, the broadcast properties were sold to CanWest Global, and the distribution business and the 50 percent interest in *CSI* were sold to others. McCarthy Tétrault acted for Goldman Sachs, which financed the deal. With everyone's consent, I acted for Alliance Atlantis to assist in the CRTC application.

Eventually the CRTC approved the deal. But within two years, Can-West Global faltered, hit by both the recession and the debt taken on earlier to acquire its newspaper properties. It went into receivership and the broadcast properties were acquired by Shaw Media in 2010, except for BBC Kids, which was sold to the Knowledge Network in BC.

SHOULD CABLE SYSTEMS
SUPPORT CANADIAN BROADCASTERS?

In 1988, I attended a CRTC hearing where one of the interveners suggested that cable systems should compensate Canadian broadcasters in order to support Canadian programming. I was dubious about the legality of this plan, thinking that it might amount to a 'tax' on cable. I mentioned my doubts to Michael Hind-Smith, the president of the Canadian Cable Television Association and a few days later, he called me and asked whether I could render an opinion to the CCTA to this effect.

I wandered down the hall to talk to Hank Intven. I asked him, what do you think? Hank thought about it briefly and expressed the contrary view. He thought it might be characterized as a regulatory scheme and be supportable under the Broadcasting Act. But who was right? We decided to take it up with John Robinette, who of all people would know what the courts would think. So we attended at Mr Robinette's office. I took five minutes to lay out the arguments for why such a scheme would be an illegal tax; Hank took five minutes to argue that it would be a permissible regulatory scheme.

Mr Robinette heard us both out. Then he turned to me with a bemused smile. 'Well, Peter,' he said, 'I'm afraid Hank has the better argument. I think the courts would support it.'

I called up Michael Hind-Smith and told him that we couldn't give him the opinion he wanted. Of course he asked: What happened to change your mind? I explained that John Robinette had taken a different view, after hearing arguments on both sides. And if Mr Robinette took a view, that would have to be the McCarthy view!

A few years later, in 1993, the Canadian Association of Broadcasters (CAB) filed a proposal with the CRTC seeking compensation from cable for free-to-air Canadian television signals. I was approached by the CAB to provide a legal opinion on McCarthy letterhead that this was within the Commission's jurisdiction. I was pleased to do so, and this formed part of the record in the proceeding. The CRTC did not accept the CAB proposal at the time. Instead, it accepted a proposal from certain cable companies to create a Cable Production Fund, to avoid a reduction in cable rates that would otherwise have applied. That Fund later morphed into the Canadian Television Fund (now the Canada Media Fund), which receives upwards of $220 million a year from cable and satellite distributors to support hard-to-finance Canadian production.

The television broadcasters did not give up their quest for direct compensation for their local signal, however, and they renewed their demands in the wake of the recession in 2007. The concept of imposing a 'fee for signal' was rejected by the Commission in 2007 and 2008, but a similar concept called 'value for signal' was approved by the CRTC in 2010, subject to a review of its jurisdiction to do so by the courts.[14] However, while the 'value for signal' regime managed to pass muster at the Federal Court of Appeal, it was struck down by the Supreme Court of Canada in December 2012 in a 5–4 decision.[15]

The rationale by the majority was twofold.

First, that no provision of the Broadcasting Act granted specific jurisdiction to the CRTC to create 'exclusive control rights over signals or programs,' and it was not sufficient for the CRTC to find jurisdiction by referring in isolation to the policy objectives set out in section 3 of the Act.

Second, that the proposed 'value for signal' regime would conflict with specific provisions in the Copyright Act.

That decision has engendered some tough talk from distribution undertakings who would like the court to strike down other CRTC policies that affect the direct economic relationship between distribution undertakings and broadcasters. The decision will certainly force the Commission to tread carefully in this area. But others can take comfort from the strongly argued dissent from four of the justices. And even the majority of the court felt that a measure would pass muster if it related to the 'core purposes' of the CRTC, described as relating to the cultural enrichment of Canada, the promotion of Canadian content and ensuring that programming is diverse.

SUPPORTING CANADIAN TELEVISION DRAMA

In 1993, I got a call from Allan King, who had just been elected president of the Directors Guild of Canada (DGC). As an organization, the DGC covered far more than just directors; in fact, it represented over 3,800 key creative and logistical personnel in the film and television industry covering all areas of direction, design, production and editing.

Allan was one of Canada's most distinguished film and television directors, particularly noted for his cinema-verité documentaries, like *Warrendale, A Married Couple* and *Dying at Grace*. But as president of the guild, he was now involved in advancing the interests of the film and television production sector. Up to that time, the DGC had rarely been involved in regulatory matters. But Allan correctly perceived that a key to the health of the sector was the CRTC. Without the imposition of requirements to commission Canadian drama and long-form documentaries, experience had shown that the only Canadian programs the private sector broadcasters would focus on would be news, sports and low-cost magazine or game shows. I was well aware of this, given my involvement in the 1982 CTV case in the Supreme Court of Canada (see p. 121). So Allan wanted me to help the guild prepare submissions to the CRTC and the government arguing for more money to be put into independent high-end television production.

Over the next seventeen years, I acted as regulatory counsel to the Directors Guild in numerous CRTC proceedings, always pushing for more support for Canadian drama. (At the CRTC, the term *drama* embraces any scripted fictional audiovisual entertainment, including 'soaps', situation comedies, hour-long drama, dramatic miniseries, made-for-TV movies and feature films.) In 2000, Allan King retired as president and Alan Goloboff was elected in his stead. But the Guild continued to take an active role before the CRTC. To mitigate the expense, I often prepared joint submissions for the Directors Guild of Canada, the Writers Guild of Canada, ACTRA (the actors' union) and CEP-NABET (the technicians' union). In the period from 2004 to 2008, in fact, the four organizations, joining with their French-language counterparts based in Quebec, often worked together as the Coalition of Canadian Audio-visual Unions (CCAU), and I drafted all of their submissions to the government and the CRTC.

During the late 1980s and into the 1990s, both CTV and Global had been required by licence condition to broadcast about two hours a week of new original Canadian drama. This stick, coupled with the carrot of support from a government fund and the support of the CBC, had led to the significant growth of the independent television production sector in Canada. By 1998, however, the renewals of the private over-the-air TV licences were coming up, and the Commission called for submissions on what to do next. On behalf of the DGC, I drafted a submission on Canadian drama calling for an expenditure requirement of 7 percent of ad revenue, coupled with a scheduling requirement of seven hours a week in prime time. The producers' association put in a similar submission. Both interventions were bitterly fought by the Canadian Association of Broadcasters, and in 1999 the CAB largely won. For the next renewal period, no expenditure requirement of any kind was imposed on the over-the-air broadcasters and they were saddled only with a rule requiring eight hours a week of so-called priority programming in prime time. But this latter requirement sounded more stringent than it was, since the definition of priority programming included reruns and regional magazine shows as well as Canadian drama.

The 1999 Television Policy turned out to be a disaster for the independent production community. The over-the-air private broadcasters, particularly Global, reduced their expenditures on Canadian drama. The only mitigating factor was that BCE undertook to spend money on

Canadian drama as part of its benefits package to acquire control of CTV in 2000.

In 2002, Charles Dalfen became the new chair of the CRTC and in one of his first speeches he identified the reduced amount of Canadian drama as one of the shortfalls of the broadcasting system in English Canada. The CCAU responded by commissioning me to draft a major submission on what should be done. Released at the Banff TV Festival in June 2005, the ninety-page study analyzed the problems of Canadian drama in detail. It ended up recommending that a 7 percent expenditure requirement for drama be imposed on the English-language private over-the-air TV stations.[16] It also proposed that the CRTC eliminate its licence fee top-up policy, which allowed private broadcasters to claim money coming from the Canadian Television Fund as if they had spent it themselves. But the Commission resisted both steps. Instead it initiated a complex drama incentive system. However, this failed in practice and it was abandoned in 2008.

In 2007, Konrad von Finckenstein, the former commissioner of competition, was appointed chair of the CRTC. He too initially resisted putting an expenditure rule for Canadian drama in place. However, given the consolidation of ownership in the sector, he was increasingly interested in handling the renewals of the over-the-air and specialty licences of each owner as a group. But he was concerned with how broadcasters might 'game' the system by using accounting loopholes. At his request, I gave a major speech at an industry conference in June 2009 explaining how group licensing might be used to address the accounting issues while at the same time solving the drama problem.

In 2010, the Commission announced that it would set an annual expenditure requirement for 'programs of national interest' (PNI), defined as Canadian drama, long-form documentary and selected awards shows, for the broadcast properties owned by each private broadcast group, and that it would eliminate the licence fee top-up policy. This was very similar to the approach I had recommended in 2009, and the guilds were elated. Although the percentage of revenue required to be spent on PNI is lower than that sought by the guilds, the new structural policy provides a meaningful safety net that can be enhanced in the coming years. When coupled with the PNI transfer benefits committed by Bell Media and Shaw Media on their recent acquisitions of control, the monies required to be spent by the private broadcasters with the independent production sector are expected to reach significant levels in the next few years.[17]

On April 11, 2011, at the Screenwriting Awards of the Writers Guild of Canada, I was presented with the 2011 WGC Writers Block Award, 'in recognition of a record of exceptional service to Canadian screenwriters.' Maureen Parker, the executive director of the WGC, made the following comments:

Tonight I have the honour of presenting the Writers Block Award and for the first time in fifteen years we are presenting it to a non-screenwriter...

Let me tell you about this year's recipient—Peter Grant. Peter Grant is a renowned name in our industry. He is a regulatory communications lawyer and, about ten years ago, he accepted the challenge of representing the Writers Guild and our sister guilds, ACTRA and the DGC, in presenting our position to the CRTC that the production of indigenous drama and docs—the real ones—were in freefall, and that the CRTC needed to step in and ensure that high quality programs, Canadian programs, continued to be made. And that's whether Canadian broadcasters want to make Canadian shows or not. We needed a regulatory expert, someone who was also incredibly smart and well connected, and after beating the bushes for such a superstar, along came Peter Grant. He said yes because he is a determined cultural nationalist who values as much as we do our own stories and the opportunity to tell them. He represents us not just on the front lines, but also in the back rooms. The rooms that we are not allowed into as writers and writer representatives. And I will tell you he made all of the difference. He has levelled the playing field and allowed our voices to be heard ...

Naturally I felt honoured by the award and by Maureen's effusive comments. But as it happens, I was at a communications conference in England that week and Grace accepted the award on my behalf.[18]

In October 2012, for similar reasons, I was given a Lifetime Honorary Membership in the Directors Guild of Canada. But this time I was at a conference in Singapore. The DGC filmed my acceptance speech and my son Robbie accepted the award on my behalf.

ACTING AS THE BROADCASTING ARBITRATOR

In 1992, I got a call from Chaviva Hosek, asking me if she could put my name forward to be the new broadcasting arbitrator. I had met Chaviva years earlier when I helped her set up the leaders' debate on women's issues for NAC.

What is the broadcasting arbitrator? The post was created under the Canada Elections Act, and it involves chairing meetings of all the political parties to determine the allocation of the paid time on broadcasting services that is made available to the parties under the act during a general election. It also involves arbitrating disputes between the parties and the broadcast stations during the election period.

The post had been created in the mid-1980s and the first arbitrator was Charles Dalfen, the former vice-chair of the CRTC. (He later served as chair of the CRTC from 2002 to 2006.) However, Charles had not been reappointed because of a problem that had occurred in the 1988 election (more about that below). Under the act, all the parties represented in the House of Commons were to attend a meeting to name a successor. If they couldn't agree, the arbitrator would be appointed by the chief electoral officer. Chaviva Hosek represented the Liberals and put my name forward as a non-partisan suggestion. A few other names were suggested. All the nominees were then asked to write a letter describing their approach to determining the 'public interest.' I wrote a short piece stating that I viewed the public interest in the widest possible terms. Shortly after, I got a call from the chief electoral officer. All the parties (Conservative, Liberal, NDP, Bloc and Reform) had agreed on my name. So he was now authorized to enter into a contract with me to act as the broadcasting arbitrator. However, he had a small request: Would I agree to a clause that required me to stay in Canada during the election period?

I asked him why such a clause was considered necessary. He told me that when the writ dropped for the 1988 federal election, Charles Dalfen was nowhere to be found. It turned out he was giving a lecture at a university in Tel Aviv, Israel. So for the crucial first three days of the election, when the arbitrator was supposed to issue guidelines to the political parties, his secretary acted as the de facto arbitrator! The parties were unhappy, and so they wanted the next arbitrator to be in Canada at the crucial time. I agreed to this stipulation and thus began my career as the broadcasting arbitrator for Canada.

Under the Act, six months after each federal general election, the post of broadcasting arbitrator is automatically terminated. Within ninety days of the polling day, the chief electoral officer is required to convene a meeting of the parties then represented in the House of Commons to appoint a successor. Since a unanimous vote is required, my reappointment could be vetoed by any one party. I fully expected that I was destined to be a one-term arbitrator, since at least one party would be bound to be unhappy with my allocation decisions and would blackball me. But to my great surprise, the parties all unanimously agreed on my reappointment, election after election. (On further reflection, I assume that my unanimous reappointment was driven by the theory 'Better the devil you know ...')

In the end, I acted as arbitrator during the federal general elections held in 1993, 1997, 2000, 2004, 2006, 2008 and 2011. I also acted as the arbitrator for the 1992 referendum, which voted down the Charlottetown Accord. By 2008, however, I had the clause requiring me to be in Canada for the election period amended. By that time, I was doing more international travel, and there was no need for such a clause given the availability of reliable electronic communications in all major business centres. So the requirement to stay in Canada was waived as long as I made arrangements to remain accessible by phone or e-mail.

Following my appointment in 1992, I called for a meeting of all the political parties to discuss the allocation of the paid-time entitlements under the Canada Elections Act. Under the act, all broadcasters were required to make available six and a half hours of prime time over the election period for purchase by the political parties at the lowest equivalent rate applicable. The act itself provided a formula for allocating this time among the parties. It was based on their performance in the last election: percentage of votes obtained, number of seats won, and—this last point given half weight—the number of seats contested. But the act also stipulated that this allocation could be modified by the broadcasting arbitrator if he considered that the statutory formula was 'unfair' or 'contrary to the public interest.'

Although pressed by the smaller political parties to divide the time equally, my predecessor had simply applied the statutory formula. In the

1992 meeting, however, the smaller parties renewed their pressures. One of them was the recently formed Reform Party, which had managed to garner a single seat in the House of Commons in a by-election in 1989. The smaller parties argued that the statutory formula under the Act discriminated against newly emerging parties, since it ended up giving the time to parties based on their past performance. A low allocation of paid time also presented a problem for a party *able* to buy more time, because the allocation operated as a cap on the amount of time that could be bought by the party on each station. (This aspect was struck down in 1995 by the Alberta Court of Appeal in the Reform Party case.[19]) The amount of paid time allocated also determined the free time allotted under the act, since free time (required only of certain networks, not all stations) was to be divided *pro rata* to the paid-time allocation.

I was sympathetic to the arguments of the smaller parties. But at the same time, I could see that the parties represented in the House of Commons had a strong claim for more time, since they had more members and typically more issues to attack or defend. (In fact, the smaller parties typically bought no paid time at all, because they had no money to pay for it.) So what to do? In the end, I came up with a modified formula. I took one-third of the time off the top and awarded it equally to all the parties, regardless of their size or past performance. The rest of the time I allocated on the basis of the statutory formula.[20]

This was not a perfect solution but to me it represented rough justice. So that was the formula used in the 1993 election. In the ensuing six federal general elections, I applied the same 'modified allocation formula' to the paid time. All the parties represented in the House of Commons ended up agreeing with my modified formula. Of course the smaller parties (and by mid-2013 there were eighteen political parties in all) continued to seek an equal-time approach. But I resisted any further departure from the statutory factors.

During each election, I supervised the relationship between the parties and the broadcasters in regard to paid time and free time. For example, in situations where a broadcaster claimed to be 'sold out', I was given the power to order a broadcaster to drop a regular commercial (say, for Procter & Gamble) and replace it with a political ad. But, in fact, I never had to issue such an order. By cajoling the broadcaster and interacting with the political party in question, I was always able to achieve a negotiated solution.

Over the years, my role as the broadcasting arbitrator gave me a unique catbird seat on federal elections. I was required to be non-partisan and the fact that all the parties represented in the House of Commons have agreed to my reappointment seven times probably shows that I was successful in that regard.

As well, I have witnessed the increasing use of television ads in Canadian political campaigns. With this has come a greater tendency to use negative ads. But we are far from the mindless and demagogic situation in the United States. In contrast to the United States, the Supreme Court of Canada has blessed the setting of financial limits on election spending, applicable to the parties as well as other persons.[21] In the 2011 federal general election, the total spending by all the parties on TV ads was about $25 million, while in the United States, total spending on TV ads for the 2012 federal election was about $3.5 billion. In other words, instead of spending 10 times the Canadian amount, the Americans spent 130 times the Canadian amount! And all indications are that this disparity will only grow in the future, since the US Supreme Court opened the floodgates for third-party ads in the Citizens United case.[22]

In the fall of 2011, Grace and I took a vacation in Ireland at just the time when its presidential election was going on. That gave me a chance to observe the use of television in a very different setting. Ireland, like the United Kingdom, completely bans radio and TV ads for political parties and candidates during elections. Candidates are essentially limited to mailbox stuffers, billboards and door-to-door canvassing. The use of television is limited to free time broadcasts, and appearance at debates.

Following the election in Ireland was fascinating. Every telephone or hydro pole seemed to have a poster for one or another of the seven candidates for president. But there were no paid TV ads. Television coverage by the local channels was intense and included a number of presidential debates. Seán Gallagher, a former member of the Fianna Fáil national executive, was comfortably leading the opinion polls ahead of the final televised debate. But his campaign came undone when he admitted live on air to collecting a 5,000 EUR cheque for a Fianna Fáil fundraiser event from a man he described as a 'convicted criminal and fuel smuggler'. And two days later, Michael D. Higgins was elected the ninth president of Ireland.

THE ONTARIO ACCISS STUDY

In 1993, I received a call from Elaine Todres. She was the deputy minister of culture, tourism and recreation in the Ontario government. In October 1990, the NDP had unexpectedly won the provincial election, and the new premier was Bob Rae. He selected Anne Swarbrick to be his minister of culture and she decided to initiate a study into Ontario's cultural industries. Elaine Todres told me that the government had made a lot of enquiries and wanted me to be the co-chair of the study, along with Alexandra Raffé, an Ontario filmmaker. My contribution would be done *pro bono*, but it would involve a year of meetings with senior people in all the cultural sectors.

So was born the Advisory Committee on a Cultural Industries Sectoral Strategy, which later became referred to by its acronym, ACCISS. Alex Raffé and I acted as co-chairs, and there were twenty-nine committee members; as well, dozens of other people from various cultural-industry sectors were asked to serve on working groups, focus groups, functional groups and roundtables.

I learned a lot about the cultural industries in the course of this work. By this point, Toronto was the centre of what we now refer to as a 'creative cluster,' with a critical mass of talent and infrastructure to support the creation of content. But it was also obvious that many of the components of the cluster had little connection with each other. This became clear when we set up a working group on distribution issues, with representatives of each sector. To the Canadian magazine industry, this meant the problem of getting newsstand distribution; to the Canadian film industry, it meant getting Canadian distribution rights to films in competition with the Hollywood majors; and to the Canadian recording industry, it meant negotiating deals with the four major foreign-owned labels. Each sector worked within a silo with its own unique set of problems.

In the educational book publishing sector, the province had considerable clout because of its control of the choice of course-adoption texts, particularly for the elementary and high school markets. But this was handled by the provincial department of education, which had little or no interest in helping the Canadian-owned book publishers. The field was dominated by foreign publishers who would simply Canadianize their texts by hiring a Canadian academic to rewrite an existing text designed for the US market. Wouldn't the system be healthier if we could support a viable group of Canadian-owned publishing firms who would create educational texts entirely within Canada? But I rapidly learned that trying to change the system was almost impossible given the lack of interest of educators in the Canadian-owned book publishing sector.

The 124-page report of the advisory committee was published in August 1994. It was called *The Business of Culture*, and included a vision statement, performance objectives applicable to the Canadian-owned, Ontario-based cultural industries, a set of goals and thirty-one recommendations.

Unfortunately, the Rae government fell in the Ontario provincial election of June 1995 and was replaced by a Conservative government led by Mike Harris. The ACCISS report was promptly put on the shelf, where it has remained ever since.

LAW SOCIETY CONFERENCES
AND THE BROADCAST HANDBOOKS

In 1973, I had chaired a symposium on communications law convened by the Law Society of Upper Canada in Toronto, and the Law Society had published a two-volume handbook of mine on broadcast law and regulation. My work with the Commission precluded any further conferences for a few years. In 1980, however, I was approached by the students at the University of Ottawa Faculty of Law to help them organize a two-day national symposium in Ottawa. This was co-sponsored by the Law Society and the Canadian Bar Association and was quite successful.

Two years later, in 1982, I co-chaired another national conference on communications law and policy, under the auspices of the Law Society. This time it was held in Toronto, and my co-chair was Robert J. Buchan of the Johnston & Buchan law firm in Ottawa. Thus began a series of conferences on communications law and policy held every two years, sponsored by the Law Society of Upper Canada. The biennial conferences were widely attended by up to three hundred communications lawyers, executives and government officials.

Through the 1980s these conferences were held in Toronto. In 1986 and 1988, I convened a dinner for all the speakers in my home on the Friday evening of the conference. These were very agreeable events, bringing together the key people from the broadcast and telecom sectors in a non-partisan environment. Grace and I would put tables with flowers and candles in the basement and the upstairs bedrooms and as many as sixty-five people would have dinner in our home.

For the 1988 conference, I also prepared a hardcover book, *Canadian Communications Law and Policy: Statutes, Treaties and Judicial Decisions*. This was intended to be the first volume of a multivolume treatise on communications law and policy. The Law Society provided a copy of the book to all registrants to the 1988 conference and this was very well received.

Starting in the 1990s, however, Bob Buchan and I decided to move the conferences to Ottawa, primarily because the CRTC had very little money for travel and this facilitated attendance by Commission staff. For the 1990 conference, Bob Buchan hosted the speakers' dinner at his home. However, for all subsequent conferences, he moved the speakers' dinner to the Rideau Club, of which he was a member. This made the event somewhat more formal, but undoubtedly lessened the wear and tear on Bob and his wife!

In 1991, the government enacted a new Broadcasting Act and I decided to prepare an annotated version of the Act, comparing it to its predecessor legislation. The Canadian Cable Television Association was keen to provide such an annotation to its members so I negotiated a deal: in exchange for funding, I would have it privately printed and a free copy would be given to each CCTA member. It was published in October 1991, only four months after the legislation came into force.

Looking more closely at the annotation, I suddenly realized that this could constitute the opening section of a regulatory handbook that would include CRTC regulations, exemption orders and policy statements on broadcasting. So over the next year or so, I prepared the larger work and it was published by McCarthys in 1993.

Given the fast pace of regulatory developments, it was clear that a new edition would be necessary every two years or so. So I conceived the idea of issuing the new edition of the handbook at the biennial Law Society communications law conference. The Law Society would purchase them from McCarthy Tétrault at a discounted price and each registrant would get a 'free' copy. McCarthys would then sell extra copies to the trade and (at a heavy discount) to the CRTC itself.

This was approved and the second edition of what became the *Canadian Broadcasting Regulatory Handbook* was published in 1994. The handbook quickly became the standard reference in the broadcast industry. A new edition was published every two years. By 2012, it had reached its eleventh edition. After the first six editions, I settled on a red cover for the handbook. Since then, it has been commonly referred to as the Red Book.

In 2002, I developed a companion handbook, *Regulatory Guide to Canadian Television* (the Yellow Book), providing regulatory information on all the television services licensed by the CRTC. And in 2006, I developed a third handbook, called *Regulatory Guide to Canadian Radio* (the Green Book), dealing with radio policy. Like the Red Book, the Yellow and Green Books have now gone through multiple editions.

Finally, in 2009, I decided to update the summaries of judicial decisions on communications law contained in my 1988 book. To do this, I had the 340 summaries of decisions in the 1988 book scanned into the computer. I enlisted twelve summer students at McCarthy Tétrault to prepare initial summaries of the 170 judicial decisions rendered from 1988 to 2009 that related to communications law. I edited all of this material, developed a comprehensive subject index, and the book was published at the Law Society biennial conference in 2010. It is entitled *Communications Law and the Courts in Canada,* and is now referred to as the Blue Book.

In 2012, new editions of the broadcast handbooks were published. These were supplemented by a new book, *Canadian Telecommunications Regulatory Handbook*, created by my colleague Hank Intven. Called the Black Book, it covered both CRTC telecom regulation and Industry Canada spectrum regulation, and effectively completed what amounts to a five-volume McCarthy Tétrault communications law library, a truly remarkable achievement.

THE CRAIG BROADCAST STORY

In 1993, I had worked on the Lifestyle application for a women's channel, which succeeded in getting a licence from the CRTC in 1994. The two entrepreneurs who had conceived of the channel needed additional investors and we decided to approach some regional television operators. One that came to mind was Stuart Craig, who owned a CBC affiliate in Brandon, Manitoba, and an independent TV station in Winnipeg.

In the end, Stuart Craig turned me down, and the investment was taken up by Randy Moffat, who owned CKY-TV, the CTV affiliate in Winnipeg. (This turned out to be Moffat's shrewdest investment. In 2001 he sold the successful W Network service to Corus for $200 million!)

Stuart Craig's reason for turning us down in 1993 was that he needed all his financial resources to apply for new television stations to serve Calgary and Edmonton. CanWest Global, controlled by Israel (Izzy) Asper, had triggered a call for such applications and Craig felt he had a chance of beating Asper.

Craig asked if I would help him with his applications in Alberta. I responded enthusiastically, and this led to a series of retainers from the Craig family over the next ten years as they tried to expand their scope beyond Manitoba.

The Craig family was one of the few third-generation broadcasters operating in Canada. Stuart's father had started a radio station in Brandon in the 1940s. In the 1950s, the Craigs had launched CKX-TV, a CBC affiliate in Brandon. The torch was passed to Stuart and in the 1980s he managed to get an independent TV licence based in Portage la Prairie that covered Winnipeg. This station competed with the CTV station (controlled by the Moffat family) and the CanWest station (controlled by Asper) so it ran programming acquired from CITY-TV Toronto and other sources. There was no love lost between the Craigs and Asper.

In the lucrative markets of Calgary and Edmonton, a third private TV service had not yet been licensed. So when CanWest applied for the third service, Stuart decided to throw his hat into the ring. By this time, his three sons—Drew, Boyd and Miles—were part of the broadcasting operation. For the application, Stuart was unable to come up with all the financing he required, so he brought in a minority investor named David Mackenzie. Mackenzie knew nothing about broadcasting but had struck it rich with Wayne Fipke and his diamond finds in the Northwest Territories. The Craig application proposed TV stations in Calgary and Edmonton to be called the A-Channel.

The hearing took place in January 1994, and was strongly opposed by the incumbent broadcasters. It did not help that the industry had just experienced a recession. And the arguments for turning down the applications were pressed vigorously by the in-house counsel for Western International Communications (which had acquired Dr Allard's TV operations in Edmonton), a young lawyer named Grant Buchanan. (In a curious irony, I lured Grant Buchanan to McCarthys six years later and, as I note on p. 192, he ended up acting for the Craigs in winning a TV licence for Toronto in 2002.) In the end the Commission turned down both the Asper and Craig applications for Alberta in June 1994.

Izzy Asper was undaunted and he reapplied two years later. The CRTC called for competing applications for Alberta in February 1996 and Stuart decided to reapply. By this time, he had found alternative financing. As before, I helped draft the application and rehearsed the team ahead of the hearing, which took place in Calgary in July 1996. Izzy Asper pushed heavily on the notion that he needed Alberta to complete his national grid of TV stations. But the Craig application was clearly superior. It promised more local programming, more Canadian drama expenditures and many other elements. The betting back east was on Izzy, but to the surprise of many, the Craig application was given the nod on November 1, 1996.[23]

But that was just the first skirmish. Izzy Asper promptly appealed the decision to the Federal Cabinet, again singing the praises of a coherent national grid of TV stations, and asking that the decision be set aside and referred back to the CRTC. I drafted a detailed counter-petition to the cabinet for the Craigs. But we needed more. So I prepared a full-page ad that ran in the national edition of the *Globe and Mail*, with a chart listing all the comparisons between the Craig and Asper applications and showing why the CRTC was right, and why the government should not upset the decision of the independent regulator. This turned the tide. Izzy's cabinet appeal was turned down on January 29, 1997.

But Stuart Craig's battle was not over. As soon as his entitlement to the new TV licences was secure, he received a letter from David Mackenzie's lawyer. After having sat on the side during the whole process, aware that the Craigs had new financing and were proceeding without him, supporting the new application with a letter to the CRTC and consenting to the use of the A-Channel name, Mackenzie now asserted a right to own a third of the shares of the new company!

This threw us into the Alberta courts and I turned to my litigation partners in the Calgary office for advice. Mendy Chernos took up the challenge and recommended that we be proactive and seek a declaration that Mackenzie's claim was improper. This allowed us to accelerate the process and eventually we won at trial, later sustained on appeal.[24]

While the Alberta skirmish was going on, in March 1996 the Commission had called for applications for a third private TV station in Vancouver. So the Craigs put an application together for this market as well. The hearing took place in Vancouver at a time when the CRTC already knew of its impending decision for the Craigs in Alberta. In the end, the third private TV licence in Vancouver went to Baton, the owner of the CTV station in Toronto.[25]

Meanwhile, the Craigs had their hands full—launching their new TV stations in Calgary and Edmonton. The Craig boys, led by Drew, the eldest, were now running the stations. Within a year, however, they decided to get into the specialty television field and they applied to the CRTC for broadcast licences to operate digital specialty services in a number of genres. One of these was for a service in the teenage lifestyle genre; it would be called Connect. I tell the story of this application in the next section (see p. 193).

However, the Craig ambitions to start up new independent TV stations in other markets in Canada were not over. The CRTC called for more applications for Vancouver or Victoria and the Craigs decided to apply for a station in Victoria that would also reach Vancouver. It would be called A-Channel on the Island. The application was heard in early 2000, but the CRTC decided to give the licence to CHUM Limited, the licensee of CITY-TV, Toronto, instead.[26]

Sadly, all of this came too late for Stuart. He had been diagnosed with cancer the previous year and he died on October 30, 1999.

In the fall of 2000, I had been approached by Torstar Corporation, which was preparing to file an application for a new TV station for Toronto. Could I act for them? I told them no, because I knew the Craigs would want to file an application as well. Eventually, Torstar went ahead with other counsel. Upon receiving the application, the CRTC issued a public notice, inviting competing applications. Within minutes, I received a call from Michael MacMillan, the chair of Alliance Atlantis. They too wanted to apply for a Toronto TV licence. Could I act for them? Here I was apologetic. After all, I had been acting for Alliance Atlantis on specialty television matters since 1993. But again I declined, knowing that the Craigs would want me to act for them. And in fact they did.

Ultimately, the race for the Toronto TV licence came down to three applicants: Torstar, Alliance Atlantis and the Craigs. Torstar was viewed by most outside observers as having the inside track. After all, the *Globe and Mail* was owned by Bell Globemedia, which owned CFTO-TV, Toronto; and the *National Post* was owned by CanWest Global, which operated the Global station in Toronto. Shouldn't the *Toronto Star* have its TV station too?

The CRTC hearing took place in Hamilton in December 2001. I had helped rehearse the Craig team, but I left the work of assisting at the hearing and drafting the reply to my colleague Grant Buchanan, who had joined our firm the previous year. The CRTC issued its decision in April 2002.[27] The panel of five commissioners was split: two voted for Torstar but three voted for Craig. So we won the Toronto TV licence, a stunning upset.

This turned out to be a bittersweet victory for the Craigs, however. They launched the station in 2003 but within a year ran into major financial problems. The only solution was for Craig to sell its Winnipeg and Alberta TV assets and CHUM was the logical buyer. So the stations were sold to CHUM.[28] The Toronto station could not be acquired by CHUM, since it already operated CITY-TV in Toronto. So the Toronto station was sold to Quebecor, which renamed it SUN-TV.[29] (Later, in 2011, Quebecor used the station to launch the Sun News service, and handed in its Toronto TV licence.)

By the end of 2004, the Craigs no longer operated any radio or TV stations in Canada. And so ended their quest to be an independent national television player in English Canada.

Ironically, CHUM itself—which now had the Craig stations in Winnipeg, Calgary and Edmonton to add to its CITY-TV stations in Toronto and Vancouver—was unable to hold on. After the death of its founder, Allan Waters, Allan's two sons decided to sell the CHUM empire to CTV in 2007. However, CTV was not permitted to keep the five CITY-TV stations since it already had stations in those markets. The five CITY-TV stations (including the three stations bought from Craig) were resold to Rogers, which now operates them. CTV kept all the other CHUM assets, which included a number of small-market stations, CKX-TV Brandon among them, as well as numerous profitable specialty services. Since it now owned the name A-Channel, CTV transferred that name to the smaller-market stations it had also acquired from CHUM. But in 2012,

CTV decided to drop the A-Channel designation and rebrand those stations as CTV Two.

Before leaving the Craig saga, I should add that they became involved in MDS distribution technology, in which tall transmission towers are used to distribute encrypted TV channels in competition with the cable industry. They won the first MDS licence in Canada for Manitoba in 1995, calling it Skycable.[30] They added other MDS licences in the West, although their bid for an Ontario MDS licence was unsuccessful. However, the limited-spectrum allocation given to MDS precluded full competition with the cable or satellite companies. In the end, the Craig boys wound down their Canadian MDS operations, selling their rights to the Canadian spectrum, for $80 million, to Inukshuk Wireless Inc. As for Craig Wireless, it went public and continues to utilize valuable spectrum in California, Greece and Norway. In spite of all this, the Craig boys no longer have operations in Canada. Their first TV station, CKX-TV, Brandon, did not survive the recession of 2008–09 and CTV (which had acquired it from CHUM in 2007) let it go off the air in October 2009.

HOW MTV CAME TO CANADA

In the course of my work for the Craig family, I helped to draft a number of applications by them in 2000 to get licences to operate digital specialty channels in various genres. The launch of one of these channels involved a fascinating story in dealing with the arcane world of CRTC policy.

Since the introduction of pay and specialty services in Canada in 1982, the Commission has had a policy of keeping out non-Canadian pay or specialty services in genres that could be considered either totally or partially competitive with Canadian services. So HBO has never been permitted to operate in Canada; instead its programming is included in the services of the Canadian-owned services TMN and Movie Central, both of which have significant Canadian programming obligations. Similarly, the ESPN service cannot be seen in Canada, but much of its programming is on TSN. And I have recounted my role in winning the History Television licence for Alliance, which depended on keeping the History Channel (US) out of Canada (see p. 167).

The CRTC policy has not been without controversy, particularly when the CRTC kicked the US Country Music Channel off the Eligible List upon licensing a Canadian service in the same genre in 1994. This led to a trade law complaint from the United States, which was only resolved by negotiation with the injured party (see p. 201).

However, the policy has been remarkably successful. It has enabled over 150 Canadian broadcast services to succeed, each of them providing a balance of Canadian and foreign programming in various genres. All of these services are owned and controlled by Canadians, although a number of them have foreign companies as minority investors, who supply their programming and occasionally their branding, through carefully drafted licence agreements.

One of the non-Canadian services that always wanted to enter Canada was MTV. Owned by Viacom, the music video service was started in 1981. Offered on basic cable throughout the United States, MTV has also launched its service around the world. It currently owns and operates MTV services in dozens of countries, including versions in many languages. But MTV has never been permitted to operate in Canada. Instead, its chosen niche, music videos, has been occupied by MuchMusic, a Canadian specialty service launched by CHUM in 1984. There was no love lost between MTV and MuchMusic, since the existence of the latter effectively stopped MTV from coming into Canada.

In 2000, I was asked by the Craigs to help them apply for a number of digital specialty services in various genres. One of the applications, mentioned earlier, was for a teenage lifestyle service to be called Connect. A second was for a service devoted to TV classics to be called Retro, which would be modelled after a US service owned by Viacom that was called TV Land. A third application was for up to five music video specialty services called Music 5, focusing on pop, dance, urban R&B and Hot Hits.

All of these applications won a CRTC licence. Connect even won a highly coveted Category 1 digital licence (only thirteen such licences were granted), which required all cable and satellite companies to carry the service.

Shortly after winning the licence, Drew Craig visited the Viacom offices in New York. He was there to negotiate the potential basis for bringing Viacom's TV Land service to Canada by using his Retro service. But after hearing about the Connect licence, Viacom suddenly became very interested in another idea. Would it be possible to bring MTV into

Canada through the Connect licence? Viacom also noted that the Craig music video service focusing on pop music could be launched as MTV2.

I looked closely at the conditions of licence for Connect. The service was described as 'dedicated to the concerns and aspirations of Canada's youth aged twelve to twenty-four. It will provide entertainment and education for teens. Programs will include informal education, human interest, sitcoms, animation, and video clips.' The use of video clips was limited to 10 percent of the schedule.

When it launched in 1981, MTV had focused on music videos. But now in 2000, it was a much different service. Music videos were a minor part of the service and MTV had evolved into a lifestyle channel. So I saw no impediment to a deal with Viacom, provided music videos were kept to only 10 percent of the schedule and Craig had ownership and control of the channel.

Armed with this advice, Craig negotiated a joint venture agreement with Viacom under which Connect was renamed MTV Canada, Music 5—Pop was renamed MTV 2, and Retro was renamed TV Land. All three digital services launched across Canada in October 2001. Through this manoeuvre, MTV had finally arrived in Canada.

It did not take long for MuchMusic to wake up. In January 2002, it fired off a lengthy complaint to the CRTC. Arguments flew back and forth between CHUM and Craig. Grant Buchanan and I had great fun helping Craig rebut CHUM's arguments. And in the end, the CRTC ruled in Craig's favour. Given its relatively limited use of music videos, MTV Canada was not deemed to be competitive with MuchMusic. As for MTV2, Craig was asked to clarify its definition of pop music and this too was approved by the Commission.

Fast forward to 2004. In that year, faced with financial problems, Craig ended up selling its Western television stations and its specialty services to CHUM. But there was an obvious problem. How could the services branded with the MTV name be owned by MTV's archrival? CHUM quickly terminated the Craig deal with Viacom and renamed the three services. MTV Canada became Razer; MTV2 became PunchMuch and TV Land became Comedy Gold.

Viacom was down but not out. It promptly went across the street to CTV, which operated a digital specialty service called Talk TV. That service had been licensed back in 1996 to be 'devoted to talk programs.' But most of the content was also consistent with what was on MTV. So a deal was quickly hammered out between CTV and Viacom and Talk TV changed its name to MTV. MTV was back in town.

Now we fast forward again, to 2007. Following the death of CHUM's founder, Allan Waters, Allan's two sons decided to sell the CHUM empire to CTV. Since CTV was already in bed with Viacom, it decided to rename some of the CHUM services. The service formerly known as MTV Canada but now called Razer changed its name again, to MTV2. As for the old MTV2, which CHUM had renamed PunchMuch, it changed its name to Juicebox.

Many observers looking at this bewildering change of names and alliances will question the Commission's policy of 'niche protection'. Does it really work when program niches overlap so much? There is some merit to this criticism. In 2009, in fact, the Commission decided to eliminate niche protection for mainstream sports and mainstream national news services. And in 2012 it proposed to do the same for popular music specialty services.

In the meantime, however, note the incredible success that we have had with Canadian specialty services covering a wide diversity of program genres. Yes, the MTV brand has come to Canada. But it operates within the constraints of a Canadian-owned-and-controlled service such that the program choices are in the hands of Canadians and a significant amount of programming must be Canadian.

8. Branching Out

TRADE LAW AND CULTURAL POLICY

In 1985, the Royal Commission on Canada's Economic Prospects, headed by former Liberal cabinet minister Donald Macdonald, issued its report. It called for a free trade agreement between the United States and Canada. The royal commission had been launched by the Trudeau government in 1981 but its final report was handed to Brian Mulroney, the new prime minister in the Tory government that had won office in the federal election of 1984. The new government accepted the report and so began the negotiations that eventually led to the Canada-US Free Trade Agreement in 1988.

Shortly after the government announced its intent to pursue such an agreement, I got a call from Pierre Juneau, who by this time was the president of the CBC. He was concerned with the implications of free trade for Canada's cultural policies, and asked if I could help him set up a high-level committee of communications executives to lobby to keep culture 'off the table.' He suggested that we contact people like Donald Campbell, the chairman of Maclean Hunter Limited, and John W. Bassett, the chairman of Baton Broadcasting, the owner of the largest CTV affiliate, CFTO-TV, Toronto. I did so, and within a few weeks, we had assembled a blue-ribbon committee for the cultural industries. Apart from Campbell and Bassett, it included Harold Greenberg, the president of Astral; Philippe de Gaspé Beaubien, the chairman of Telemedia; William Carradine, senior VP of Southam Inc.; and Stephen Roth, the president of Alliance Entertainment. These were all heavy hitters with profitable businesses in the cultural sector. To be more inclusive, however, I also added Malcolm Lester, president of Lester & Orpen Dennys, to represent the Canadian-owned book sector; Andrew Hermant, president of Manta Sound, to represent the Canadian-owned recording industry; and Claude Fournier, president of the Quebec Film Institute. I was appointed counsel to this committee. Don Campbell acted as chair of the committee since Pierre Juneau felt that it would be inappropriate for himself to take a leading role. Don enlisted one of his senior executives, Harvey Botting, to act as secretary to the committee, and Harvey and I became friends.

At the first meeting, it was decided to call the group the Canadian Culture/Communications Industries Committee. I was asked to assemble an inventory of Canadian protection and assistance measures for its cultural industries. The private sector heavy hitters on the committee passed the hat and quickly found $100,000 to fund this study. I completed the 143-page study in September 1986. It was the very first study to provide a detailed overview of ten sectors of the cultural industries in Canada with current statistics, and it outlined the key issues arising from the Canada-US free trade negotiations. A confidential copy was provided to the government.

At the same time, I drafted a glossy lobbying document for the committee, including supportive quotes from everyone and signed by all ten members of the committee. Its title was 'Free Trade & Cultural Identity: Will We Have Access to Our Own Markets?' This was widely circulated to the government and the media.

The following year, the federal Department of Communications issued its own defence of cultural policies, 'Vital Links: Canadian Cultural Industries'; it included many of the same arguments that I had worked up for the committee.

The Canada-US Free Trade Agreement was signed in 1988 and it included a 'cultural exemption' clause, a clause that specifically excepts measures respecting cultural industries from obligations otherwise imposed by the agreement. But in fact the clause did not entirely exclude cultural measures. Canada agreed to zero-rate its customs tariffs on imported cultural goods (copies of books, magazines, films and tapes). It also agreed to require cable and other television distributors to pay copyright royalties for the retransmission of distant signals, and it agreed to certain investment disciplines in regard to its book publishing policy. In a more controversial trade-off, Canada also agreed that if it took any measure that would, in the absence of the 'exception,' breach other terms of the treaty, the US would have a limited right of retaliation. (When the agreement was expanded to include Mexico in 1994 with the North American Free Trade Agreement [NAFTA], Canada maintained its cultural exemption.)

The actual drafting of the cultural exemption clause in 1988 did not become an issue until the last twenty-four hours, when it became apparent that a deal would be reached. Given the contentiousness of the matter, no attempt had been made to define or draft a clause. However, once a deal was in sight, the clause was drafted on the fly. It was done by a senior lawyer from the Department of Justice who had been seconded to the trade negotiator's team. He later told me that his instructions from the trade negotiator were to make the clause 'as opaque and ambiguous as possible so that it would not serve as a rallying point for or against the treaty.' The lawyer, whose name was Konrad von Finckenstein, later became the commissioner of competition in 1997–2003 and then the CRTC chair in 2007–2012.

By the 1990s, Canada was heavily involved in the Uruguay Round of multilateral trade negotiations, which culminated in a series of trade agreements reached in 1995. The agreements entered into created the World Trade Organization (WTO), set up a binding dispute-resolution process, reconfirmed the terms of the General Agreement on Tariffs and Trade (GATT) and added a new General Agreement on Trade in Services (GATS). In the latter agreement, a number of European countries led by France had pressed for a 'cultural exception.' The United States, intent on rolling back the television broadcast quotas in Europe, refused to countenance this approach. In the end, the GATS was silent on the matter of cultural services. However, the national-treatment provisions in the GATS only applied to those service sectors for which each country made affirmative commitments. To the dismay of the Motion Picture Association of America, the United States agreed to go forward with the agreement even though almost all countries refrained from making national-treatment commitments in regard to audiovisual services. As a result, Canada benefited from the GATS negotiation because it too was able to avoid having its cultural services affected by trade disciplines. However, the GATS also called for future negotiating rounds in which further trade liberalization would be expected.

THE SPLIT-RUN CASE

Within a year of the completion of the Uruguay Round in 1995, Canada found itself on the receiving end of one of the first trade disputes brought before the WTO. It was brought by the United States, which attacked Canada's protection and assistance measures supporting the Canadian-owned magazine sector. This had been triggered by the infamous *Sports*

Illustrated case, where Time Warner had sought to introduce a split-run edition of its sports magazine into Canada but Canada had repelled it with a punitive tax.

For decades, Canada had protected Canadian magazines from the competition of foreign split-run magazines by prohibiting their importation. (A split-run magazine would be a Canadian edition of a foreign magazine, using editorial matter that had already been amortized in the foreign market, and stripping in Canadian ads. Canada freely allowed foreign periodicals into the country provided they did not try to 'cream-skim' the Canadian ad market with split-run editions. There were only two magazines that were permitted to have Canadian split-run editions: *Time* magazine and *Reader's Digest*, both of which were grandfathered exceptions.) In 1993, Time Warner had proposed to avoid the customs tariff on a new split-run edition of *Sports Illustrated* by sending the page proofs by satellite to a printing firm in Canada. After Canada introduced legislation to tax away any profits from such activities, the United States brought its complaint.

The Canadian Magazine Publishers Association (CMPA), representing the Canadian-owned sector, retained McCarthy Tétrault to help it, and that propelled me into the split-run case.

Cases brought before the World Trade Organization were argued behind closed doors in Geneva by government lawyers. However, I was able to work behind the scenes with the federal government advocates, assisted by a talented junior at McCarthy Tétrault, Eileen Clarke. (Eileen later became a lawyer with the Ministry of the Attorney General in Ontario.) On behalf of the CMPA, we also worked with trade-law experts to help devise alternative measures that would pass scrutiny under the WTO rules.

In the end, the WTO sided with the United States, ruling that a number of Canada's measures breached the provisions of the GATT. Canadian arguments that US magazines were not 'like products' (similar) to Canadian magazines fell on deaf ears. Following its defeat, Canada introduced a new services-oriented measure that it felt would pass scrutiny at the WTO, since it would fall under GATS not GATT. However, the United States threatened immediate trade retaliation. Eventually the two countries settled their differences in mid-1999, with Canada agreeing to allow split-run editions of foreign magazines with up to 18 percent Canadian ads.

This settlement gave the US what appeared to be a partial victory although it turned out that its terms did not facilitate the entry of split-run magazines after all. In order for the split-run edition to be economic, the US publisher had to convince generic US advertisers to pay extra for inclusion in the Canadian edition, and such ads would need to take up at least 82 percent of the ad space. But the US advertisers generally declined to pay extra for inclusion in the Canadian edition, having benefited for so many years from the free overflow of their ads into Canada. So very few split-run editions emerged and they all eventually ceased publication. Even *Time Canada*, which had been grandfathered, ceased publication in the face of the recession of 2008–09. Aided by direct subsidies, which were permitted by the WTO ruling, however, the Canadian magazine sector not only survived but prospered. The CMPA changed its name to Magazines Canada in 2003.

THE COUNTRY MUSIC CASE

In 1994, I had filed an application for a CRTC licence to operate a country music video specialty channel. At that time, Canadian cable companies had long been carrying Country Music Television (CMT), a US music video channel operated by a partnership of Gaylord Entertainment and Westinghouse. CMT had been added to the so-called Eligible List back in 1984, but the CRTC had made it clear that if a Canadian service were licensed in the future in a format competitive with an authorized non-Canadian service, the latter could be dropped from the list, terminating its authority to be carried on cable.

Ten years later, the moment the CRTC had foreseen finally came. Five Canadian companies applied to the CRTC for a licence to operate a Canadian country music video service. My application was on behalf of Standard Radio and Allan Gregg, and the team made an excellent presentation to the CRTC. But the winning nod went to the Country Network, a partnership of Rawlco and Maclean Hunter, which had proposed the highest Canadian-content level and the lowest wholesale charge to cable carriers of any of the five applicants. Following its policy, the CRTC also deleted CMT from the Eligible List, effective on the launch date of the new service.

But CMT was not about to hang up its Stetson that easily. Gaylord Entertainment saddled up a posse of lawyers and lobbyists to press its case before Congress and the US administration. CMT argued that the United States had the right to retaliate under the cultural exemption clause of NAFTA. Its argument was flawed, but US trade law tends to ignore such niceties. This time, the US government did not bother pursuing a remedy through the WTO. It simply threatened retaliation for what it alleged was an unjustified confiscation.

During the height of the dispute, I was invited to debate the US trade lawyer acting for CMT at a conference in Montreal. The US advocate— who later acted for the American lumber industry to oppose softwood lumber imports from Canada—scoffed at the notion that the CRTC policy could be said to support 'Canadian' music. 'Country music is American and comes from Nashville', he argued. How could Canada suggest it had its own country music?

Having just been involved in applying for a country music channel, I was well prepared to argue with him. For he had revealed a deep ignorance of musical history. Country music has roots in Canada at least as deep as those in the Appalachians. Irish, Gaelic and Breton folk tunes— all among the antecedents of modern country music—go back more than two centuries in Canada. George Wade and His Cornhuskers were first broadcast over the predecessor of the CBC in 1933. Don Messer first appeared on radio the following year. Wilf Carter first recorded in 1932, Hank Snow in 1936. Over the next six decades, many hundreds of country artists have emerged and become successful in Canada. They include the Rhythm Pals, Tommy Hunter, Gary Buck, the Mercey Brothers, Family Brown, Carroll Baker, Patricia Conroy, Stompin' Tom Connors, Michelle Wright, George Fox and many others.

The US trade lawyer knew none of this. But why would he? There is not much of an opportunity to experience Canadian country music in Washington.

Of course, some Canadian country artists become popular in the United States and worldwide: think of Hank Snow, Anne Murray and more recently Shania Twain. But many more are known only to Canadians. Their most potent form of advertising is to be heard on Canadian country music radio stations, where there is a 35 percent Canadian-music quota, and to have their music videos watched on the Country Network, where 40 percent of the music videos presented would be required to be

Canadian. From there on, they must depend on their own talent to reach and resonate with Canadian audiences.

Under pressure, the owners of the newly licensed Canadian country music channel negotiated a compromise. Prior to its country channel being licensed, Maclean Hunter had been sold to Rogers and in that transaction, no value had been assigned to the potential new channel. So Rogers felt free to give a piece of the new channel to the US owners. In the result, CMT received a 20 percent interest in the Canadian channel, which was branded Country Music Television Canada. Washington backed off. Canadian nationalists criticized the outcome as another instance of Canada caving in to American pressure. But rather than undermining Canadian cultural policy, the negotiated 'compromise' strongly supported it.

The new channel prospered, rising from fewer than 2 million subscribers in 1994 to almost 11 million by 2013, helped by the fact that since it was a Canadian service all Canadian cable and satellite distributors were required to carry it. CMT Canada's ownership went through a number of changes, ending with 90 percent of the voting shares being held by Corus Entertainment. Country Music Television Inc., the US company, ended up with a 10 percent voting interest—but in a service that was much more profitable than it had been before. True, the service carried the US brand. But it was originated and controlled entirely in Canada. Licence conditions required at least 40 percent of the music videos it broadcast to be Canadian and at least 22 percent of its gross revenue to be invested in Canadian video and program production. The content and spending requirements offer crucial support to Canada's musical talent in this genre.

My experience with the CMT case, as well as with the MTV case I described earlier (see p. 193), underlined the importance of Canada's broadcast policy in ensuring that the keeper at the gate to programming services is a Canadian broadcaster, interested in a Canadian audience—not a foreign interest serving a predominantly foreign audience. But the CMT dispute made it clear that these policies could be subject to attack by US trade lawyers.

THE UNESCO CULTURAL DIVERSITY CONVENTION

By 1998, when the Periodicals case was coming to a head at the WTO, it was the central topic at the meetings of the cultural industries Sectoral Advisory Group on International Trade (SAGIT), a trade advisory group set up by the government of Canada to advise its minister of international trade. This was a panel of representatives of the cultural sector created by the government to advise it on trade issues. There were over a dozen other SAGITs for other sectors of the economy but this one was probably the most active.

I had been added to the cultural industries SAGIT in the early 1990s. Because of my involvement in the cultural exemption of the 1988 Canada-US FTA, I was now seen as something of an expert in how trade agreements could affect cultural policy. But my membership in the cultural industries SAGIT propelled me into the complex area of international trade law.

By 1998, the SAGIT meetings had a more urgent tenor. In the Canada-US FTA, and in the Uruguay Round in Geneva, Canada had dodged some bullets. But now it had been blindsided by the US complaint to the WTO about Canada's policies to protect and assist its magazine sector.

As we discussed the case with our government trade negotiators, the mood became increasingly dispirited. The Periodicals case brought us face to face with a troubling reality. The WTO structure seemed to be biased against the kind of analyzis that distinguished cultural products from other trade products. For example, in a dispute-resolution process, who would be the impartial judges? Judges were picked from a roster of former WTO trade officials or trade-law academics. All of them had an institutional bias towards liberalizing trade. All of them wanted the WTO treaties to 'work' and they wanted to minimize any perceived loopholes. None of them seemed to have any acquaintance with the curious economics of cultural products. While they might attend symphony concerts and profess to be sensitive to 'culture,' they would have little inkling of the forces that affect trade in popular cultural products or in distinguishing one form of expression from another.

It was also clear that the WTO itself would not be sympathetic to a 'protocol' that exempted cultural policies from trade retaliation. The delegates to WTO meetings were trade ministers, not culture ministers. They generally came from hard-nosed economic ministries and had clout. Culture ministers were all too often seen as lightweight dispensers of subsidies to the arts community. They would have no impact on the WTO.

The staff of both the culture and trade ministries attended these SAGIT meetings, and from time to time the Canadian heritage minister, Sheila Copps, would also attend. Miss Copps was very supportive. But she wanted ammunition. Her cabinet colleagues were not all convinced. Give me some arguments besides just 'cultural protection,' she would say.

It was clear to all of us that it would be pointless to tackle the WTO head-on. First, we needed to educate the world. But what to do? As we kicked ideas around the table, André Bureau, now the chair of Astral Communications Inc., suggested having the government create the position of cultural ambassador, to be held by someone who could travel the globe proselytizing the concept of cultural sovereignty.

Then I suddenly had an idea: How about pushing for an international treaty specifically dealing with culture and trade? The room quieted as I talked further. Instead of focusing on the concept of a 'cultural exemption,' why don't we talk about the need to protect 'cultural diversity'? And if we can't win inside the WTO, maybe we can influence public opinion outside it. After all, the land mines treaty was done without any involvement of a UN organization at all. The real issue was how to mobilize world opinion behind our goals.

There was quite a lot of discussion as to how such a treaty might be negotiated. There was broad agreement that it would be best to do it outside the aegis of the WTO. The obvious agency to tackle it would be UNESCO, although there were reservations about that agency's clout or effectiveness.

By the end of the meeting, the group had coalesced around my idea. And it was decided to prepare a report—ostensibly to the minister, but also for public dissemination—outlining the idea in more detail. A writer was hired to aid in putting the report together. I helped draft the key portions. The report was published in February 1999 and was the first to propose a legally binding cultural-diversity convention that would address the interface between cultural policies and trade obligations. In the end, it was left open as to where such a treaty might be negotiated.

As to content, the report recommended the following:

Canada could initiate a new international instrument, which would lay out the ground rules for cultural policies and trade, and allow Canada and other countries to maintain policies that promote their cultural industries.

A new cultural instrument would seek to develop an international consensus on the responsibility to encourage indigenous cultural expression and on the need for regulatory and other measures to promote cultural and linguistic diversity. The instrument would not compel any country to take measures to promote culture, but it would give countries the right to determine the measures they will use (within the limits of the agreement) to safeguard their cultural diversity.

A kind of blueprint for cultural diversity and the role of culture in a global world, the instrument would clearly define what was covered, and stress the importance of cultural sovereignty.

The new instrument would identify the measures that would be covered and those that would not, and indicate clearly where trade disciplines would or would not apply. It would also state explicitly when domestic cultural measures would be permitted and not subject to trade retaliation.

Later that year, the Canadian government endorsed this idea. And over the next five years, an incredible head of steam built around the concept of an international convention on cultural diversity. During that period, I spoke at conferences in Rabat, Lucerne and Cape Town to garner support. But spearheading the exercise was Canada's heritage minister, Sheila Copps. With her leading the fray, ministers of culture, cultural professional associations and representatives of civil society from around the world all became involved.

One of the early milestones occurred in May 2000, when the European Commission and UNESCO sponsored an event called the Forum on Globalization and Cultural Diversity, held in Valencia, Spain. Delegates from the audiovisual sector in countries from six continents attended. I attended the forum and was chosen to be the rapporteur. No one there was aware of the Canadian idea before I described it to them, but there was immediate agreement with the concept and the final communiqué included a statement that 'there is an urgent need for the negotiation of a new international instrument on cultural diversity to address issues related to cultural products.' This was the first international recognition of the concept of a new cultural trade instrument.

In the fall of 2000, the International Network of Cultural Policy (INCP) met on the Greek island of Santorini. Following a UNESCO conference on cultural diversity held in Stockholm in 1998, the INCP had been created in 1998 with the strong support of Sheila Copps, to bring culture ministers from around the world together in annual meetings. (Having no culture minister, the United States was not included in the INCP.) In Santorini, a working group led by Canadian officials presented a discussion paper and an illustrative list of principles to be used as a starting point for the development of an international instrument on cultural diversity. In the ensuing annual meetings of the INCP, the membership of which grew to include seventy-two countries, the culture ministers exchanged ideas, advanced the discussion and built support.

At the Santorini meeting, a group of private non-governmental organizations (NGOs) representing artists' and cultural groups in twenty-one countries decided to create an International Network on Cultural Diversity (INCD). This organization timed its meetings to coincide with the ministerial meetings of the INCP. Over time, the INCD grew to include five hundred individuals from seventy countries. By lending the voice of civil society to the pressures for a new international instrument, the INCD played a significant role in garnering further support.

Also in 2000, the Coalition for Cultural Diversity (CCD)—a group of Canadian cultural professional associations that had been established in Quebec in 1998—decided to embrace the concept of a new instrument for cultural diversity. It then focused its attention on helping to create sister organizations in other countries, so that professionals in the cultural field in those countries would have a focal point to lobby their governments to support the proposed convention. Robert Pilon, the CCD's executive director, spent most of the next few years on a plane travelling to conferences and meetings in countries on six continents. Eventually, through his efforts and many others', coalitions for cultural diversity were set up in forty-two different countries.

In June 2001, culture ministers of La Francophonie, an international organization of fifty French-speaking countries, meeting in Benin, added their backing to 'the principle of a universal international regulatory instrument that supported the promotion of cultural diversity.' La Francophonie proved to be a key player in supporting the new instrument.

As I recount in the opening paragraphs of this book, the matter finally came to a head in October 2005 with the adoption of the UNESCO Convention on the Protection and Promotion of the Diversity of Cultural Expressions, despite frantic efforts by the United States to oppose it.

The debate took place at the UNESCO headquarters in Paris, the same place I had attended back in 1974 as rapporteur for a group of experts on a different convention (see p. 85). However, I was not present for the 2005 deliberations. Over the days of debate, the dialogue was emotional and heartfelt. The final vote came on October 20, 2005, and the convention was approved by a vote of 148 in favour, 2 opposed (the United States and Israel) and 4 abstaining (Australia, Nicaragua, Honduras and Liberia). The US delegation did not help matters by ending the session with an angry and bitter closing speech.

My role in the effort to convince governments and cultural organizations—first in Canada, and then around the world—to develop and adopt the convention was relatively minor. But I do claim credit for originating the idea for such a convention. Like the other members of the cultural industries SAGIT, however, I had no idea the concept would catch fire the way it did.

Two of the government officials at the Department of Canadian Heritage who worked diligently on the UNESCO file during this period were Jean-Pierre Blais and Barbara Motzney. Seven years later, in 2012, Jean-Pierre became the chair of the CRTC, and Barbara was named chief consumer officer at the CRTC.

DIRECT-TO-HOME SATELLITE SERVICES

The concept of television delivered by satellite started back in 1976, when HBO launched a national pay-television service using a geostationary satellite to deliver its signal to cable television head ends across the US. Within a few years, dozens of cable channels emerged based on this new technology. At the cable head end, you needed a relatively large (6-foot diameter) dish to receive the signal. But that did not deter people in rural America, who bought large satellite dishes to receive the signals directly.

In Canada, it was soon recognized that this new technology could be used to deliver a package of Canadian television signals to rural and remote areas. For the hundreds of communities across Canada too remote to have cable service, the solution was to have a national satellite service feeding a package of Canadian signals to cable systems serving as few as two hundred households. After a competitive hearing, the CRTC licensed Canadian Satellite Communications Inc. (referred to as Cancom) in 1981 to carry out this function.[1] Two years later, the CRTC allowed Cancom to add a package of US signals (all originating from Detroit) to its offering.[2] Cancom was the first satellite service of its type in the world, and proved highly successful in the 1980s.

I did not take part in any of the CRTC hearings to license Cancom or its affiliated cable systems across Canada, although I did become directly involved in three later developments that affected the evolution of satellite services in Canada.

The first was spawned by the decision of the satellite services in the United States to encrypt their signals, to prevent unauthorized persons from receiving those signals. This was supported by provisions in the US Communications Act penalizing those who tried to crack the encryption system. But Canada had no equivalent provisions. A thriving industry of satellite 'pirates' quickly sprang up.

At the behest of the pay TV services (First Choice and Allarcom) I was asked to lobby for a statutory amendment that would not only achieve the same goal, but also make it possible for the affected companies to bring a private civil action to enforce the statute and get damages. The federal government was dubious. Weren't property and civil rights provincial matters under the constitution? To address this issue, I enlisted the aid of John Robinette, and he rendered a legal opinion for our clients that supported federal jurisdiction.

On June 4, 1991, a new Broadcasting Act was enacted. And as part of the legislative package, the government enacted sections 9 and 18 of the Radiocommunication Act, which made it a penal offence to decrypt a radio signal without authorization, and which created a private cause of action against those doing so. In the next few years, these provisions spawned dozens of court cases, but the legality of the provisions was ultimately upheld in the Supreme Court of Canada in 2002.[3]

My second involvement in the satellite-services field occurred in 1992, when I got a call from Gary Kain, the president of Regional

Cablesystems Inc., a company that was a 1986 spinoff from Cancom. Regional operated a number of small cable operations in the Atlantic provinces receiving the Cancom satellite signals. Gary was concerned that the Canadian Cable Television Association was dominated by the bigger cable operators like Rogers, Shaw and Videotron. So he created the Canadian Association of Small Cable Operators (CASCO), and asked me to draft their submissions to the CRTC. I was happy to do so and for a number of years I helped CASCO in this regard.

By 1992, the impending launch of the American service DirecTV as a direct broadcast satellite (DBS) service was creating concern because the footprint of the DBS satellite signals would reach most of Canada. DirecTV, which launched its service in 1994, was dubbed the 'death star' by many observers because of its perceived impact on the Canadian broadcasting system. (In 1995 a second American DBS service now called the Dish Network launched.) People were wringing their hands because they saw no way for a domestic regulator in Canada to regulate these US services if they sought Canadian subscribers.

Gary Kain asked me to draft a submission for CASCO on this issue. Surely there was something the CRTC could do. Based on my legal research, I had always felt that there were measures that could be taken to assert and enforce jurisdiction over these satellite services if they targeted Canadian subscribers, even if they had no assets in Canada.

Accordingly, I prepared a hard-hitting brief to the Commission and defended it at a hearing in early 1993. Three months later, the Commission adopted all my arguments and asserted jurisdiction over foreign-based satellite services. Its decision contained these passages, all based on my analysis:[4]

With respect to foreign DBS service providers that may wish to enter the Canadian market, the Commission has determined that it would in certain circumstances have jurisdiction over them under subsection 4(2) of the *[Broadcasting] Act*. A DBS service provider whose signal is receivable in Canada could be found to be carrying on a broadcasting undertaking in Canada in whole or in part where, for example, it has some or all of the following characteristics:

- it acquires program rights for Canada
- it solicits subscribers in Canada
- it solicits advertising in Canada
- it activates and deactivates the decoders of Canadian subscribers.

The Commission will apply the appropriate enforcement tools to assert its jurisdiction over these undertakings should they enter the Canadian market without making contributions to the Canadian system as required of all broadcasting undertakings under the Act ...

In addition, the Commission has decided, as suggested by the Canadian Association of Small Cable Operators (CASCO), that where a non-Canadian satellite service is distributed by a DBS operator not authorized by the Commission, the service may be removed from the lists of Eligible Satellite Services. Furthermore, where a non-Canadian satellite service not currently on the lists of Eligible Satellite Services is distributed in Canada by a DBS operator not authorized by the Commission, that service will not be considered for inclusion on the lists.

With this announcement, the Commission made it clear that any direct broadcast satellite operation (what we now refer to as a direct-to-home or DTH operation) that wanted to serve Canadian subscribers would need CRTC approval.

This brought about my third involvement in the satellite sector. In 1994, I was retained by a company called ExpressVu to apply for a CRTC licence to offer a direct-to-home (DTH) satellite service. At the time, ExpressVu was one-third owned by Tee-Comm Electronics Inc., one-third by a combination of WIC and Cancom and one-third by BCE Inc. In 1994, in a controversial order, the CRTC had exempted DTH satellite undertakings from the need to get a licence provided such undertakings met certain standards, one of which was that they use Canadian satellite facilities to distribute all of their programming services. But behind the scenes, DirecTV had the support of a high-powered Canadian executive, Joel Bell,[5] who wanted to bring DirecTV into Canada through a joint venture controlled by Power Corporation of Canada. Bell's concept was to use satellite dishes that would receive signals from both the US and Canadian satellites. To do so, he would need a CRTC licence, whereas all-Canadian operations would not. In the fall of 1994, the government established a three-member panel to review DTH policy and it issued a report to the Federal Cabinet in April 1995 recommending that the Commission's exemption order be revoked and that the licensing of all DTH distribution undertakings be required.

The government followed the recommendations of the panel and duly called for DTH licence applications, issuing policy directions calling for DTH competition and specifically permitting DTH operations utilizing both Canadian and US satellites.

As I was acting on behalf of ExpressVu, my aim was to get a licence for its all-Canadian DTH operation. But I also sought to put roadblocks in the way of the Power DirecTV application fronted by Joel Bell. It was obvious that Power DirecTV would qualify for a CRTC licence, given the terms of the cabinet direction. However, the Power DirecTV application was vulnerable in one aspect. It had proposed that all costs incurred to uplink and transmit Canadian programming services be borne by the specialty- and pay-programming undertakings and be recovered through a uniform affiliation fee charged to all distribution undertakings, including cable. There was a logic to this proposal in that it would level the playing ground between DTH and cable. But there were good arguments against it as well and I marshalled them on behalf of ExpressVu.

In the end, the CRTC gave both Power DirecTV and ExpressVu a DTH licence but declined to make the cost-recovery order sought by Power DirecTV.[6] In the face of this, Joel Bell reassessed the economics of his proposal and decided to abandon the field. In the end, ExpressVu's only DTH competitor was a Shaw operation called Star Choice (formerly HomeStar), which used the same technological format to receive signals as that used by cable and thus was able to avoid most satellite transponder costs. The two DTH operations have continued in operation to this day. BCE later bought out its partners and became the sole owner of ExpressVu, now called Bell TV. Star Choice is now called Shaw Direct.

In the end, those who had called DirecTV the 'death star' turned out to be wildly inaccurate. As of the time of writing, Bell TV and Shaw Direct between them had close to 2.9 million subscribers, a higher penetration of households in Canada than DirecTV and the Dish Network have on a combined basis in the United States. While there continue to be Canadian residents willing to act illegally that receive US DBS signals, their numbers were never higher than 5 percent of households and that percentage has declined significantly in the face of enforcement efforts. Canadian DTH services licensed by the CRTC and contributing to the creation of Canadian programming now occupy the field.

The issue of how to assert jurisdiction over foreign broadcasters has recently resurfaced in the context of the arrival of Netflix and other over-the-top (OTT) services that are delivered through the Internet. Can

Canada regulate these services if they have no physical assets in Canada and operate entirely from file servers located outside the country? My answer is an unequivocal yes, and I have rendered a number of opinions to this effect.[7] People who argue otherwise have not studied the jurisprudence. In short, the question of regulation in this area is a political one not a legal one.

CABLE TELEVISION IN THE BAHAMAS

One of the members of CASCO, and a close friend of Gary Kain, was Philip Keeping, the owner of Cable 2000, which operated a number of small cable systems in New Brunswick. The Commonwealth of the Bahamas had called for bids to operate cable systems in the islands and Phil had put in a tender, arguing that his unique experience in Canada in serving multiple tiny cable systems was perfectly suited to the problems of the Bahamas, where they wanted service on many remote islands, not just the larger, more populated ones. Phil managed to win the franchise in 1994, beating a number of other contenders. But now it was necessary to negotiate the terms of a franchise agreement with the Bahamian government. And revisions to their copyright legislation were necessary to legalize the reception and redistribution of TV signals received from the United States.

I was retained to carry out this task and Stephen Stohn and I went down to Nassau on a number of occasions to help draft the franchise agreement and copyright rules governing what later became Cable Bahamas. This turned out to be a fascinating exercise. The Bahamian copyright law was based on the UK copyright law of 1956 and made no provision for the compulsory licensing of the retransmission of free-to-air signals. (The US had made such provision in 1976 and Canada had dealt with it in 1989.) Cable Bahamas needed to include the US free-to-air signals received from Miami in addition to other broadcast services that it was prepared to pay for but for which negotiations were compromised by the lack of rights. Stephen and I came up with amendments to the Bahamian copyright legislation that solved these problems. Among them was a provision that the royalty amount to be paid should be based on the Canadian model, i.e., a flat rate of so many cents per subscriber to be paid into trust for the benefit of possible claimants. We also drafted a comprehensive fifteen-year franchise agreement.

To finance the Bahamas operation, Phil Keeping sold off Cable 2000 to Fundy Cable. Meantime, Regional Cablesystems began expanding its operation by acquiring other small non-metropolitan cable systems in Canada, notably Northern Cable in 1998, which gave the company two larger markets, Sudbury and Timmins. In 2001, the company changed its corporate name to Persona Inc. and I was asked to join its board of directors as it became a publicly listed company on the Toronto Stock Exchange. However, this only lasted until 2004, when the company was bought by venture-capital companies and taken private. In 2007, the company was acquired by EastLink.

BROADCASTING CONSULTING IN SRI LANKA

Throughout the mid-to-late 1990s, Hank Intven was active in international consulting in telecom regulation in dozens of countries all over the world; in this, he was often financed by the World Bank. I was happy to have him focus on telecom work, freeing me to spend almost all my time on broadcasting work, almost entirely for clients appearing in front of the CRTC.

Spurred by the Basic Telecommunications Accord in the 1995 WTO General Agreement on Trade in Services, the telecom sector was liberalizing around the world. Developing countries needed to create regulatory agencies, award spectrum, and licence wireless companies and other telecom competitors. So there was a lot of international telecom consulting work to be done. But this was not the case in broadcasting. Unlike the telecom sector, there was relatively little international consulting work in the broadcasting field. The trade disciplines in the WTO agreements did not apply to broadcasting, so countries could evolve their broadcasting systems at their own pace and typically with their own unique rules.

I did express interest to Hank in doing some international consulting work in the broadcasting field, and one opportunity presented itself. Sri Lanka had retained Hank to do some telecom work for its newly formed Telecommunications Regulatory Commission and they had been favourably impressed. As it happened, the government of Sri Lanka also wanted to carry out a review of its broadcasting policies. So in 1998 I was retained by the Sri Lanka Ministry of Posts, Telecommunications and the Media to prepare a report recommending new broadcast legislation.

To do the research, I travelled to Sri Lanka in mid-January 1999. For ten days, based in Colombo, I visited all the local broadcasters and spoke to government officials and other interested observers. At one point, I travelled 'up-country' to the Kandy area, to attend the launch of a community radio station. I then returned home and prepared my report, which was submitted in March 1999.

Arriving in Sri Lanka plunged me into an environment that was quite alien to me. While I had travelled to Sydney, Australia, in 1987 to give a speech on broadcasting policy, I had never been to India or any other points in Asia before. So Sri Lanka proved to be something of a revelation.

The time of my visit occurred during a lull in the violence between the Tamils (led by the LTTE) in the northeastern part of the island and the Sinhalese-dominated government, although there was tight security in all the sites I visited. I spent the first part of my visit just trying to understand the Sri Lankan broadcasting environment and comparing it with the systems I was familiar with. The language spoken by 74 percent of the population was Sinhala, a language spoken nowhere else except in the tiny Maldive Islands. However, Tamil was a second official language and was spoken both by ethnic Tamils and by the small Muslim population, the two groups together amounting to about 14 percent of the population. (English is also fluently spoken by approximately 10 percent of the population, and is widely used for education, scientific and commercial purposes, so I had no difficulty in communicating with the key people.) There were local TV stations devoted to each language.

A breakthrough came when I learned that local Sinhala TV drama was thriving but local Tamil TV drama was practically nonexistent. Of course, the reason was obvious. Right next door to Sri Lanka was Tamil Nadu, a large province in the southeastern quadrant of India. The capital city of Tamil Nadu was Madras (which changed its name to Chennai in 1996). Just as Hollywood dominates English-language TV drama, so the city of Madras dominated the production of Tamil-language drama. In fact, just as Hindi-language programming was produced from Bollywood, based in Bombay (which changed its name to Mumbai in 1995),

Tamil-language programming was dominated by production in Madras, which was sometimes called Kollywood.

So why would a Tamil-language TV station in Sri Lanka commission local drama when it could acquire popular drama much more cheaply from next door? It was in the same situation as a TV station in English Canada considering whether to commission local drama, when they could get English-language drama cheaply from Hollywood. On the other hand, the Sinhala-language TV stations in Sri Lanka were more like TV stations in Quebec, which made room for popular local TV *teleromans* in French. So the Sri Lankan broadcasting system actually had similarities to the Canadian experience!

Apart from my work in analyzing the broadcasting environment, I was intrigued to be exploring a cultural setting quite different from Canada. It was refreshing to be in a setting where McDonald's was unknown, and where people ate with their hands. The Sri Lankans were a handsome people, and, as in India, Western dress mingled with Eastern. But probably nothing showed the cultural divide more than the classified ads I read in the English-language Sunday newspapers published in Colombo.

Here is a typical ad taken from the Sri Lanka *Sunday Observer*:

B/G professional father seeks well-mannered partner for his 29, 5'5" fair slim pretty Business Management (Col) CIMA (passed finalist) daughter working as Senior Executive in a International Company. Brought-up with Sri Lankan values. Owns assets worth millions. Reply with horoscope.

Email: [address]@gmail.com

This was only one of over fifty such ads placed by parents seeking a match for their daughter. A similar number of ads each week placed by parents sought a bride for their son. The financial assets on offer were always prominent, as was the horoscope reference. And what did 'B/G' refer to? Upon enquiry, I learned that this was an abbreviation for Buddhist Govi. The Govi (short for Govigama) caste is the most influential and dominant caste in Sri Lanka. The phrase 'Sri Lankan values' is also interesting. No one could tell me quite what it meant, but clearly it evidenced a concern over the potentially adverse influence of Western culture. This despite the fact that the country continued to show a respect for the legal system inherited from the period of British rule. (One of the top constitutional lawyers told me how much he enjoyed the Canadian dramatic TV series *Street Legal*.)

Recently, Miranda Kennedy, an American writer who had moved to India, commented on the phenomenon of arranged marriages in that country. As she noted:[8]

In the months after I first moved to Delhi, I spent more time than I'd like to admit trawling through the marriage classifieds in the Sunday newspapers with horrified fascination. I couldn't help but feel a westerner's resistance to arranged marriage. The ads seemed unabashed, brazen; boiling marriage down to its core: a tying-together of families based on convenience, caste, religion and status.

Reading them—'Brahmin girl, 23, from well-educated, traditional family. Pure-veg household. Girl is homely, slim and fair-skinned'—I tried to imagine the partnership that would result. After one or two chaperoned meetings, the young couple would find themselves seated beside one another on ceremonial cushions, eyes lowered, knees carefully not touching, while their fathers negotiated the terms of the alliance, and a Hindu priest, or pujari, offered a prayer to the gods. It seemed to me to be leaving an awful lot to the gods. I tried to imagine the kind of man my mother would pick for me. It didn't seem fair not to be able to make my own mistakes.

I had much the same reaction. The marriage situation also pointed to a not-unrelated issue, the conflict between the Sinhalese and the Tamils. To a Western observer, there was no way to distinguish the two groups—they both came from the same ethnic stock and looked identical. (Even the Sri Lankans told me that the only way they could tell if someone was a Tamil was to look at his or her name.) Yet it was considered quite unacceptable by both sides for a Tamil and a Sinhalese to marry. To do so would result in ostracism by one's own family. So this was one of the less attractive features of Sri Lankan society.

I proceeded to write my report. The most obvious problem with the Sri Lankan system was that broadcast licences were issued directly by the minister of Posts, Telecommunications and the Media, and not by an independent regulator. The potential for political interference in the broadcasting system was obvious. I recommended a diverse broadcasting system subject to regulation by an independent body, with protections for freedom of expression, and with broadcasters given an obligation to support and promote local programming.

Shortly after my report was tabled, the government changed and the internal violence increased between the government and the LTTE. My report ended up being shelved. A few years later, the government commissioned a second report, this time by Daniel Sandelson, a lawyer with the UK firm of Clifford Chance. But his report was also shelved. The reasons for inaction on both reports are probably convoluted, but one possible factor may be particularly noted: in comparisons of corruption in various countries around the world, Sri Lanka does not do well. In such an environment, to the extent that broadcast licences are valuable franchises, it's clear that ministerial control over licensing might be seen as preferable to giving it to an independent regulator.

A SUCCESSOR: GRANT BUCHANAN

By the year 2000, I began to think about retirement. I would turn sixty-five in six years. But who would replace me at the firm? In the telecom sector, of course, I could rely on Hank Intven to keep the firm humming. But we needed a senior person to do broadcast work, and perhaps some telecom work as well. The junior associates we had hired over the years had been useful but many of them left to join other firms or to enter the industry. This included people like Stephen Zolf, Graham Henderson, Heather Howe, Monique Lafontaine and Sherry Kerr. Jeremy Oliver, who had been a brilliant rising star in the telecom area, had died prematurely of cancer. I felt we needed someone with both experience and *gravitas.*

I surveyed the industry and decided that the best choice was Grant Buchanan. After a few years at the Bank of Nova Scotia and then at Johnston & Buchan, he had joined Dr Charles Allard's broadcast operation in Edmonton. When Allarcom was bought out by Western International Communications (WIC), Grant became WIC's senior in-house counsel. (As such, he prepared a vigorous intervention that delayed new TV in Alberta for over two years.) Then Izzy Asper bought the WIC stations and Grant became free. I pursued him and he joined our team at McCarthy's on September 1, 2000.

In the thirteen years since, Grant Buchanan has proven to be a wonderful colleague: imaginative, responsive, hard-working and detail oriented. In addition to developing his own busy practice, he was happy to pick up our major broadcast files and run with them. His background as a banking lawyer came in handy in analyzing complex financing arrangements.

Over the years, Grant Buchanan and I have been involved in a number of high-profile broadcasting transactions. One of these was the acquisition of the broadcast assets of Alliance Atlantis Communications by CanWest Global, with the financing help of Goldman Sachs. I ended up doing the regulatory work for Alliance Atlantis, and Grant Buchanan was involved for Goldman Sachs. Grant also did most of the regulatory work for the successful application of the Craigs for a Toronto TV station (see p. 192).

One of our most interesting files involved the application of Sirius Canada for a national satellite radio licence. Grant was largely responsible for drafting the shareholder and licensing agreements and we worked closely together on the successful CRTC application. This was followed by close teamwork between us on the Copyright Board tariffs applicable to satellite radio, assisted by Sherry Kerr, who had left McCarthys to become the general counsel of Sirius Canada. Later Grant became heavily involved in the merger of Sirius Canada with its rival, XM, which was approved in 2011.

Grant also helped me on an application for a pay-television licence to compete with The Movie Network and Movie Central, on behalf of a company called Spotlight, controlled by George Burger, a former Alliance executive. Ultimately, the Spotlight application did not win a licence. Instead, the CRTC granted a licence to a competing application brought by Chuck Allard, the son of the late Dr Allard. This may have been a blessing in disguise because the Allard operation has encountered severe financial problems in trying to compete with the incumbents.

BRINGING RAI INTERNATIONAL TO CANADA

In 2002, I became involved with another foreign broadcaster. This time it was Radiotelevisione Italiana (RAI), the national public broadcaster in Italy. Since 1985, Canadians had had access to RAI programming through a Canadian ethnic specialty service called Telelatino, which broadcast in Italian, Spanish and English, and which was required to broadcast 15 percent Canadian content.

In 1995, RAI introduced a twenty-four-hour service to North America called RAI International. It was carried by the Dish Network in the United States and Italian-Canadians pressed RAI to bring its service directly into Canada as well. CRTC approval would be required before RAI could be added to the Eligible List. Pending that approval, however, many interested Italian-Canadian viewers purchased satellite dishes to receive the signal illegally from the Dish Network.

At one point in 1997, Telelatino had agreed to sponsor the addition of RAI International to the Eligible List. But this was never done and in 2000, RAI was persuaded to sign a term sheet with Telelatino to create an all-Italian service to be called RAI Canada. It would be controlled by Telelatino and would have 15 percent Canadian content but 85 percent of the content would come from RAI. The CRTC issued RAI Canada a broadcast licence in 2000 but the term sheet was never finalized and the RAI Canada service was never launched. In the meantime RAI became increasingly concerned with Telelatino's actions, including its alleged misuse of RAI programming.

Of course, RAI had a real problem in achieving its goal to come directly into Canada. CRTC policy prohibited the entry of non-Canadian programming services if they were 'totally or partially competitive' with a Canadian programming service. Back in 1998, for example, Telelatino had been successful in convincing the CRTC not to add Euronews to the Eligible Lists. In denying the application, the Commission noted that news and information accounted for 19.2 percent of Telelatino's audience and therefore Euronews would be 'partially competitive' with Telelatino. Telelatino was also highly dependent on RAI programming—particularly Italian soccer—for its ratings. It was clear that Telelatino would oppose adding RAI International to the Eligible List.

Although we knew this would provoke an uphill battle, the decision was taken by RAI to terminate its programming deal with Telelatino, to repudiate the RAI Canada initiative and to apply to come directly into Canada. Rogers Cable was keen to sponsor RAI's application, but RAI needed Canadian counsel of its own. Phil Lind at Rogers may have been no fan of mine, but he was good enough to refer RAI to me.

I enlisted one of my juniors, Monique Lafontaine, to assist in the effort, and off and on for the next three years, we helped RAI to seek and ultimately obtain the right to bring its service directly into Canada. The effort was not an easy one, because we were opposed at every step by

Telelatino. Neither Monique nor I spoke Italian but we were able to work through RAI's outside counsel in Rome, a delightful and very savvy woman named Francesca Lodigiani, who had a wonderful understanding of the Byzantine politics of Italian broadcasting.

My first step was to serve a formal notice of program termination on Telelatino, to be effective nine months later, in September 2003. This put real pressure on Telelatino, and they retained my old friend Chris Johnston to try to negotiate a way out of the impasse. Had it been left to the two of us, I am sure we would have worked out a deal. But our respective clients were intransigent.

In the end, Rogers Cable sponsored RAI's application to come directly into Canada and this was filed in the spring of 2003. As expected, Telelatino filed a detailed intervention opposing it. But RAI pulled out all the stops and enlisted the support of Italian-Canadians across the country. We helped in drafting the request for support. In addition to getting hundreds of individual intervention letters of support, RAI organized a petition drive that ended up with over 100,000 signatures. Buses filled with Italian-Canadians from Toronto and Montreal pulled up at the CRTC offices in Gatineau in August 2003 to file the petition and to demonstrate in favour of RAI. I was somewhat nervous about the heavy-handedness of this approach but the Italian-Canadians who supported RAI were irrepressible.

While the CRTC considered the interventions and the Rogers reply (which we helped to draft), the matter became very political. A federal general election had been called for June 28, 2004, and the CRTC decided to delay its decision until after the election. Paul Martin, who had succeeded Jean Chrétien as prime minister while this matter was bubbling, was pressed to support RAI. His Montreal candidates were faced with signs reading RAI YES, LIBERALS NO. In the end, Paul Martin managed to win office in the election but only with a Liberal minority.

The Commission's decision was issued on July 15, 2004.[9] As I expected, the CRTC denied the RAI application on the basis of its then-existing policies. But recognizing the direction of the political winds, the Commission also invited comments on amending the policy. This gave us a new opening and we drafted an extensive brief on what the Commission should do. Before the end of the year, the CRTC issued a new policy.[10] It would now allow general interest foreign-language services to come directly into Canada. However, if there was an existing Canadian programming service in that language, the subscriber would have to receive the Canadian service as well. So Telelatino's subscriber base would be protected.

Within a month, Rogers Cable filed a new application to bring RAI International to Canada. We assisted Pamela Dinsmore at Rogers in drafting it and the Commission approved the application on May 13, 2005.[11]

RAI launched its RAI International service as a subscription service across Canada that summer, and Monique Lafontaine and I were invited to a televised launch party in Toronto that featured some of Italy's best-known singers. It was a wonderful and emotional event. I have to say that acting for RAI was engaging but also a little frustrating as we tried to meld the emotional demands of Italian-Canadians with Canadian broadcasting policy.

BLOCKBUSTERS AND TRADE WARS

By 2002, with Grant Buchanan and Monique Lafontaine backing up my broadcast practice, and Hank Intven and Lorne Salzman handling the telecom side, I thought this was a good time to take a break. In that year, the firm gave me a five-month sabbatical. Together with my four weeks of vacation time, this gave me a six-month opportunity to do something different.

Building upon my experience as a member of the cultural industries SAGIT, I decided to put together a book that would support the idea of an international convention on cultural diversity. To do this, however, I felt I had to go back to first principles.

Too often I had seen the arguments for cultural policies like content quotas or subsidies based entirely on emotional grounds. Given the background of the arts community, and its desire to have its voices heard, this was understandable. But it seemed to me that a strong case could be made for cultural policies on purely economic grounds. It was clear to me that the domination of popular culture by Hollywood and by the multinational publishers and record companies was not driven by normal market forces but by structural factors in many ways unique to the cultural industries.

In looking at the literature, however, I realized that the economics profession had not studied this area very well. The economics of the performing arts had been looked at by William Baumol and William G. Bowen in the 1960s. But apart from recent groundbreaking work by Harvard professor Richard Caves, there had been little attempt to study the area of popular culture—film, TV shows, books, magazines and sound recordings.

I drew up a fifty-page outline. The book would examine three areas—first, the world of cultural economics and why cultural products like books, films and TV shows did not behave like ordinary commodities; second, the 'tool kit' of measures employed by governments around the world to provide space and choice for local cultural products, in the face of competition from international bestsellers and blockbusters; and third, the efforts to develop an international treaty to exempt such measures from trade retaliation. This last portion would be an unabashed argument for the passage of such a treaty by UNESCO, the idea I had pushed back in 1998 in meetings of the cultural industries SAGIT.

Scott McIntyre, the head of Douglas & McIntyre, was keen to publish such a book, but I quickly realized I could not do it alone. I therefore approached Chris Wood, a professional writer formerly with *Maclean's*, to be my co-writer. (Chris had done an excellent job writing the biography of the Craig family, which I had persuaded the Craig boys to commission when their father was diagnosed with cancer. That book, *Live to Air: The Craig Broadcast Story*, came out in early 2000, a few months after his death.)

Even with the help of Chris Wood, my book took much longer than six months of my time. In the end, I worked part-time on it for a further year. Once we had completed our research (reading the literature, setting up interviews), Chris and I divvied up the chapters, with each of us doing a first draft of half of the chapters, and then reviewing and editing each other's draft. The manuscript was largely completed in the spring of 2003. At that point, I circulated the draft to Pascal Assathiany, the head of Éditions du Boréal, Quebec's most prestigious publisher. Pascal agreed to publish it in French, provided his edition came out simultaneously with the English edition, and that I added some material on the Quebec situation. I was pleased to do so. The time taken for translation delayed the English publication by six months and the two books came out simultaneously in February 2004.[12]

In the fall of 2003, however, the English edition was ready and Scott McIntyre gave me a few dozen advance copies. I sent them to a number of people, seeking appropriate blurbs for the back cover of the book. To my astonishment and delight, I got blurbs from a number of people I had never met who loved the book. These included Richard Caves, the Harvard economist; Robert McChesney, the US media scholar; and Lord David Puttnam, the UK producer of the international hit film *Chariots of Fire*.

When the book was finally published, in February 2004, it received flattering reviews in the *Globe and Mail,* the *Toronto Star,* the *Winnipeg Free Press* and *Le Devoir* (Montreal). Matthew Fraser, the then-editor of the *National Post,* wrote a personal review for that paper that disagreed with my thesis but credited me with rendering 'a great service to cultural nationalists by articulating their mantras in the cold, dispassionate language of economics and public policy.'[13] Elsewhere in his review, he paid me the back-handed compliment that, 'If Canadian Culture Inc. has an in-house corporate counsel, it is Peter Grant.'

Blockbusters and Trade Wars: Popular Culture in a Globalized World ended up being shortlisted for the Donner Prize, awarded annually to the best Canadian book on public policy. Chris and I split an award of $5,000 fifty-fifty.

The book has had an interesting afterlife. A paperback edition emerged a year later and the book was course-adopted by a number of communications policy courses in universities across Canada. It eventually sold over 5,000 copies, which is quite positive for a public policy work of this kind.

More important, however, the book played a small role in advancing the arguments for an international treaty on cultural diversity. I have outlined earlier in this memoir my role in pushing this idea forward in Canada. Eventually, UNESCO took up the challenge and organized a committee of experts to draft such a convention. My book was circulated to the committee and to interested ambassadors to UNESCO. As I have noted earlier, the UNESCO Convention on the Protection and Promotion of the Diversity of Cultural Expressions was overwhelmingly approved on October 20, 2005. The convention went into force on March 18, 2007, and by the middle of 2013, it had been ratified by 128 countries, representing over two-thirds of the world's population.

CHAPTERS/INDIGO

Chapters Inc. was originally formed in 1995, following the merger of Coles and SmithBooks. Under CEO Larry Stevenson, the company aggressively expanded, opening superstores across Canada. With the expiry of a three-year freeze in the terms of trade imposed by the Competition Bureau, however, Chapters began squeezing publishers. In 2000, to assist this exercise, it created a captive wholesaler to extract higher discounts.

A year earlier, I had helped Douglas & McIntyre Ltd. cope with the demise of General Publishing, a book distributor. But the Chapters pressures affected a significant number of Canadian-owned publishers, all of whom were members of the Association of Canadian Publishers (ACP), which I had incorporated back in 1975. In June 2000, faced with increased problems with receivables and returns from Chapters, the ACP set up a working group to address the issue, with representatives of sixteen ACP members.

In the meantime, Heather Reisman created Indigo Books in 1996 and by 2000 had expanded the company to fourteen locations. In late November 2000, Reisman made a bid to purchase control of Chapters. Chapters was already the largest book retailer in Canada. Combining its stores with the Indigo stores would create a retail behemoth, with over 65 percent of the Canadian English-language book market. Given this level of concentration, Reisman needed approval from the Competition Bureau, which would normally oppose such a merger. The key was for her to get the support of publishers. And since the bureau would look to Canadian publishers for advice on the form of any consent order to be filed with the Competition Tribunal, the ACP actually had some bargaining power. (None of the individual ACP members were large enough to have such power. Even when you combined all 140 ACP members, their market share would have been less than 25 percent.)

I was retained by the ACP to act for it in this matter. Over the next few weeks, I helped the ACP Working Group develop a wish list, which went through six drafts before it was finalized. The wish list was then sent to Heather Reisman and I handled the subsequent negotiations with Ms Reisman and her lawyers. (In this, I was assisted by Lorne Salzman at

McCarthy Tétrault, who had developed an expertise in competition law in addition to his telecom work.)

A key element in the wish list was to enshrine Terms of Trade in the consent order, covering such matters as the discount from the retail price to be kept by the store, the allowable returns, the timeline for payments and payment for advertising. The purpose of this was to preclude Chapters/Indigo from using its market power to force individual publishers to agree to unfair terms in order to have access to the stores. The Competition Bureau preferred structural approaches such as divestment, so it was an uphill battle to convince it to adopt a behavioural approach like a code of conduct.

The Competition Bureau was not knowledgeable in the book publishing sector so all of these terms had to be developed by the ACP. I drafted the Terms of Trade based on extensive discussions with the ACP working group and a review of the terms of trade of several ACP members. Thinking of the financial constraints on small publishers, I also realized that if Chapters/Indigo did not comply with the consent order, it would need to be enforceable at low cost. So my solution was to add an arbitration annex to the consent order.

The ACP was particularly concerned about the fate of Canadian-authored books, so it sought a commitment from Reisman that at least 15 percent of Chapters/Indigo shelf space (and windows and tables) be devoted to books by Canadian authors. She agreed to this but it was not possible to include this in any consent order. After all, neither the bureau nor the tribunal would care about 'Canadian authors' or other 'cultural matters,' since these have nothing to do with competition policy. The solution was to put this and other 'cultural' points in a binding side letter with ACP, enforceable on its own terms.

The consent-order approach was satisfactory for five years, but at that point, it would expire. There was little the ACP could do about that. However, in the binding side letter with ACP, Reisman agreed to provide for a collective bargaining obligation to ACP members after it expired, provided such an obligation did not contravene the Competition Act.

The Competition Bureau worked closely with me and based its draft consent order on our proposed Terms of Trade. In the end, Chapters/Indigo became subject not only to the consent order approved by the Competition Tribunal but also to a separate side letter of agreement with the ACP, which included the shelf space requirement for Canadian-authored books, the collective bargaining obligation after the consent order expired and other clauses of obvious benefit to Canadian-owned publishers.

The work involved in drafting and negotiating all of this with Heather Reisman's lawyers (she ended up using two different law firms) was not small, taking up over $100,000 of my time, if billed at commercial rates, in addition to the time contributed by others in the firm. Of course, ACP could not afford it. So I treated the matter as *pro bono*. A year later, the ACP was kind enough to honour me at their annual dinner. But I have to say that my real payment for the work was the satisfaction of helping out the small publishers when they needed it.

The Chapters/Indigo merger was not, however, a success story from the point of view of the Competition Bureau. They had insisted on having a number of bookstores divested as part of the deal. Although these stores were put in trust, no purchaser was found that was prepared to pay the reserve price and also continue them as bookstores. So in the end all the stores reverted to Ms Reisman's control.

Accordingly the only consolation to the book industry was the behavioural restrictions in the consent order, which precluded Chapters/Indigo from varying the terms of trade. However, the consent order expired on June 8, 2006. So did the side agreement with ACP, except for the collective bargaining clause. But this too eventually became impossible to utilize. Under the agreement, the clause did not apply if Ms Reisman reasonably determined, 'based on advice from legal counsel, that such collective negotiation would not be in compliance with any applicable law.' At the time I drafted the clause in 2001, collective action by ACP members in regard to its terms of trade with Chapters/Indigo would not have constituted a breach of section 45 of the Competition Act, because the market share of ACP members was less than 25 percent, not enough to be considered 'undue'. In 2009, section 45 of the Competition Act was amended to remove the 'undue' defence. Accordingly, even the obligation of Chapters/Indigo to negotiate in good faith with ACP or its members disappeared.

Since 2009, life for both small book publishers and for bricks-and-mortar bookstores has gotten much tougher. Chapters/Indigo has tightened its terms of trade, but it has also been faced with competition from the arrival of the e-book. In 2012, Douglas & McIntyre Publishers, faced with increased returns and higher costs, was pushed into bankruptcy by its bank. Its imprints were sold to Canadian buyers in 2013 but the scale of its operations will undoubtedly diminish in the face of the grim reality of Canadian publishing.

In the wake of these events, the importance of government subsidy of the Canadian book publishing sector through the Canada Book Fund and other means has only intensified.

MY CHANGING RELATIONSHIP WITH BELL CANADA

In 2002, Bell Canada's management changed dramatically. After having been run by telephone executives, including Jean de Grandpré and Jean Monty, BCE decided to appoint Michael Sabia, a former senior civil servant and executive with CN Railways, who had joined Bell in 1999, to run the company. The following year, Sabia appointed Lawson Hunter to be the executive vice-president and chief corporate officer of Bell Canada and BCE Inc. So from 2003 to 2008, Lawson was responsible for overseeing regulatory, governmental relations and corporate affairs for the Bell group.

To say that this was a surprise is an understatement. Lawson Hunter had been the director of investigation and research under the Combines Investigation Act in the early 1980s, where he had been a gadfly seeking more competition in the telecom sector. If anything, Lawson was probably more reviled by the Bell Canada executives than I was. But with Michael Sabia now in the driver's seat, and with Bell forced to embrace a competitive environment, times had changed. And Lawson was now a highly regarded competition lawyer at the Stikeman Elliot law firm.

In July 2003, I got a call from Lawson. He was well aware that I had been Bell's nemesis. But he wondered if I could provide an outsider's perspective on the regulatory issues confronting Bell and what it should be doing. I was flabbergasted. 'But Lawson,' I replied, 'they hate me over there at Bell.' Lawson laughed. 'Oh, that's all changed,' he said. He asked me to prepare a report on what Bell should be doing on the regulatory front.

I had fun writing the twenty-five-page report and it was duly submitted to Bell's senior management. Lawson promptly called me up and asked me to participate in a discussion of the report with Bell's in-house regulatory people, by that time headed up by Sheridan Scott, a lawyer who had formerly been with the CRTC and then with the CBC. (Sheridan left shortly after to become the new commissioner of competition and she was replaced by Mirko Bibic, who had been a competition lawyer, from Lawson's law firm, Stikeman Elliot.)

Among other matters, my report proposed that Bell become much more aggressive in seeking telecom deregulation and in fighting the cable industry. This approach fit well with Lawson's views and over the next few years, Bell put considerable resources into this battle. However, Bell encountered resistance at the CRTC, then chaired by Charles Dalfen, who had previously acted for a number of Bell's telecom competitors, including Call-Net. Lawson felt that the only way to break the logjam was to take the case for deregulation outside the Commission. He convinced the Liberal government to appoint a telecommunications policy review panel to look at the matter. The panel consisted of Dr Gerri Sinclair, André Tremblay and my partner Hank Intven. Of the three, Hank was by far the most knowledgeable about the field of telecom regulation, having advised governments and regulators around the world. After a year of intensive work, the final report of the review panel was released on March 22, 2006. It was a remarkable report, with well-balanced and practical recommendations, many of which pointed to a more market-driven deregulatory approach. Hank's influence on the shape and content of the report was also very evident. To put it mildly, the report could not have been done within the allotted time frame and to that standard of quality without his involvement.

By the time the report was released the government had changed. The report was handed to the new Conservative government under Stephen Harper and its newly appointed minister of industry, Maxime Bernier. Bernier knew relatively little about the telecom industry but he latched on to the report as if it were manna from heaven. The government moved quickly and on December 18, 2006, issued an unprecedented telecom policy direction to the CRTC to require it to take a more deregulatory approach.

The TPR Report had also recommended legislative changes but this was clearly going to take much longer to implement. So to speed the process, Bell Canada and Telus, the two largest telecom carriers in Canada, jointly retained Hank Intven and Mary Dawson, a highly regarded legislative draftsperson formerly with the Department of

Justice, to draft a model act to implement the recommendations of the report. This was published at a major telecom conference in June 2007. In a minority government situation, however, the government shied away from major legislative change and no comprehensive bill had been introduced by 2013. The CRTC did respond to the 2006 policy direction, and Lawson Hunter felt that his initiative to push for the telecommunications policy review panel report had paid off. To his credit, Lawson generally supported the report, although some recommendations were inconsistent with Bell's interests. These recommendations were also adopted by the government.

Over the next few years, Bell became more friendly to McCarthy Tétrault and it began referring corporate and litigation work to the firm. From time to time, we also assisted them with a few regulatory matters. In 2006, for example, we helped Bell orchestrate a reduction of its interest in CTV without triggering a requirement to pay 'benefits.'

The real change occurred in August 2010, when McCarthy Tétrault was retained to help Bell reacquire control over the CTV network and all its broadcast properties. (Bell had originally gained control of CTV back in 2000 but it later dropped its interest to a minority position in 2006.) This was doubly ironic. Three decades earlier, I had cut my teeth in the broadcast arena by fighting CTV and in the telecom arena by fighting Bell. Now I was part of the team helping Bell acquire CTV!

RETIREMENT?

I turned sixty-five on November 26, 2006. Normally that would have meant retirement from the firm effective January 1, 2007. However, I suggested to the firm that my relationship be continued for three years. This was enthusiastically supported by Hank Intven and Grant Buchanan so the firm was happy to agree. In fact, the arrangement was later extended to nine years. Under the new arrangement, I got a nice office and a nice piece of change, plus a travel budget. But I didn't have to bill any hours to clients. Instead I was expected to write speeches, attend conferences, edit the handbooks and provide 'strategic advice,' with the heavy lifting given to my colleagues.

I was delighted with the new arrangement, and it worked out well for the firm, since a number of major matters came in where I was able to make a useful contribution.

Other matters also took up some time. I continued my work as the broadcasting arbitrator. I also became an adjunct professor at the Faculty of Law, University of Toronto (where I taught Broadcasting Law and Policy), and at the Schulich School of Business at York University (where I taught Communications Policy). In 2010, I co-chaired the Law Society of Upper Canada biennial Communications Law and Policy Conference for the last time. Bob Buchan and I passed the torch to Grant Buchanan and Laurie Dunbar.

With my new-found freedom, I took the opportunity to do some thinking and writing about communications and cultural policy. In 2006, I wrote a piece for the *Literary Review of Canada* on the implications of the 'long tail' for Canadian book publishers.[14] In 2008, I did a sixty-five-page study for the International Affiliation of Writers Guilds entitled 'Stories Under Stress: The Challenge for Indigenous Television Drama in English-Language Broadcast Markets.'[15] The following year, I co-authored a study for Telefilm Canada: 'Broadcaster Support for Canadian Feature Film: Expanding the Audience with Television Platforms'.[16] In 2010, I wrote an essay on the evolution of the UNESCO Convention on Cultural Diversity.[17] And in 2013, I co-authored a study for the Directors Guild of Canada on the financial implications of the CRTC policy on 'programs of national interest.'[18] In addition, I gave occasional lectures on current issues in cultural policy.

The firm did not discourage any of this, although sometimes my views caused problems for its potential clients. The best example of this was undoubtedly my foray into the issues raised by broadcasting on the Internet.

SHOULD INTERNET SERVICE PROVIDERS CONTRIBUTE TO CANADIAN CONTENT?

This started when I received an invitation from the CRTC to give a speech at an invitational forum in Ottawa on October 2007. The forum was to discuss new media (e.g., Internet and mobile services) in a lead-up to a planned CRTC hearing in 2009 to discuss the Commission's 1999 exemption order, which had exempted the Internet from broadcast regulation.

I showed up at the CRTC forum and decided to shake things up by arguing that perhaps it was time to require Internet service providers (ISPs) to contribute to the creation of Canadian content. After all, I pointed out, cable and satellite distribution undertakings were required by the CRTC to contribute 5 percent of their revenue to the funding of Canadian content, with most of that going to support the Canada Media Fund. Over 50 percent of the content distributed by ISPs constituted 'broadcasting' within the definition in the Broadcasting Act, I added. Since paragraph 3(1)(e) of the Act states that 'each element of the Canadian broadcasting system shall contribute in an appropriate manner to the creation and presentation of Canadian programming,' wasn't it time to consider imposing a levy on ISPs to support Canadian content?

The words were scarcely out of my mouth when Mike Hennessy, the lobbyist for Telus, sitting in the front row, cried out, '*No!*' And so began a lively debate in which the key ISPs (owned by Rogers, Bell, Telus and Shaw) decried my idea, while the guilds and producers applauded it. In February 2008, I was invited to give a keynote address on the subject to the annual convention of the Canadian Film and Television Production Association and I developed my idea somewhat further. I proposed imposing a levy on ISPs of 2.5 percent of residential broadband revenue, which might go to the Canada Media Fund and which would generate more than $70 million a year to the support of Canadian content.[19]

This became a major rallying cry by producers and others at the CRTC hearings the following year, with the producers supporting it and the ISPs vigorously opposing it, arguing among other matters that as a legal matter they were not 'broadcasting undertakings' under the Act. (I had acknowledged that there was a legal question in my speech to the CFTPA, but argued that the better view was that ISPs were subject to the Broadcasting Act.) In the end, the CRTC decided against my levy idea. 'The Commission considers,' it said, 'that no evidence was presented to establish that additional funding to support the creation and presentation of Canadian new media broadcasting content would further the objectives of the Act.'[20] This statement was somewhat astonishing, given the acknowledged benefits of the Canada Media Fund (supported by levies on cable and satellite companies), and the chronic lack of funding for high-value Canadian content.

However, the real issue was one of jurisdiction, and the CRTC decided to refer that question to the Federal Court of Appeal. In that proceeding, the ISPs argued successfully that the terms 'broadcasting' and 'broadcasting undertaking' in the Broadcasting Act were not meant to capture entities that merely provide the mode of transmission and that have no measure of control over programming. That decision was upheld by the Supreme Court of Canada in 2012.[21] The result is that ISPs will not be required to contribute to Canadian content unless the Broadcasting Act is amended to bring them into the system.

It is important to realize that this decision does not preclude the Commission from regulating Internet-based programming services like Netflix, YouTube or Hulu. As I have noted earlier, these so-called over-the-top programming services clearly constitute broadcasting undertakings under the Broadcasting Act if they target viewers or subscribers in Canada, and this is true even if they have no physical assets in this country.

At this point in time, the Commission has chosen to exempt over-the-top services from licensing requirements under the Act. As OTT services expand their operations in Canada, however, pressures will increase to review and perhaps revise that exemption order, so as to require OTT services that reach a significant size to contribute to Canadian programming.

The communications law team at McCarthy Tétrault, reunited in 2013.
Back row, from left: Lorne Salzman, Monique Lafontaine, Tony Keenleyside,
Bram Abramson. Front row, from left: Hank Intven, Peter Grant, Grant Buchanan.

9. Changing Channels

THE EVOLUTION OF COMMUNICATIONS
AND CULTURAL POLICY

This may be an opportune time to offer a few thoughts on how communications and cultural policy has evolved over the years in Canada.

As I noted in the introduction, I was an active player in two major transformations in Canada. The first was the move from monopoly to competition in the telecommunications sector. The second was the significant growth of Canada's cultural industries and the expansion and consolidation of the Canadian broadcasting system during the same period.

I had a unique platform from which to observe these changes. Since I had what is commonly referred to as a 'transactional' practice, I acted over the years for a large number of different clients before the federal communications regulator. Like many litigators, I generally limited my retainer to the specific application before the CRTC for consideration. So quite frequently someone I had successfully opposed would retain me on a different matter a few years later. Over the years I ended up acting for (and often against) virtually all the major players in the broadcast and telecom industry.

In the cultural industries, my client base was limited (by choice) to the Canadian-owned sector, although much of my work here was done *pro bono*, because of the limited financing available to these players. But I ended up acting for clients in the book publishing industry, the magazine sector, the music industry and the film and television production sector.

Before making more general comments, I should note my delight in practising in this field. The lawyers who ended up practising communications law in Canada have all been generous, bright, courteous and honourable. This applies not only to my colleagues at McCarthy Tétrault over the years—Lorne Salzman, Hank Intven, Stephen Stohn, Tony Keenleyside, Michel Racicot, Grant Buchanan, Stephen Zolf, Monique Lafontaine and Bram Abramson—but also to my sometime adversaries.

They included Gordon Henderson, Bob Buchan, Chris Johnston, John Hylton, Greg Kane, Kathy Robinson, Ernie Saunders, Bernard Courtois, Michael Ryan, Gary Maavara, Laurie Dunbar, David Elder, Willie Grieve, Janet Yale, Yves Mayrand, Ken Engelhart, Pam Dinsmore, Dennis Henry, Mirko Bibic, David Kidd, Jon Blakey, Jay Kerr-Wilson, Doug Barrett, Susan Wheeler, Lori Assheton-Smith, Aidan O'Neil, Steve Whitehead, Joel Fortune, Chris Taylor, Chris Weafer, Margot Patterson and many others. The CRTC was well served by its in-house counsel as well, including John Lawrence, Avrum Cohen, Sheridan Scott, John Keogh, Allan Rosenzveig and Christianne Laizner. We were a unique fraternity and I think we all felt lucky to be practising in an area that was at the cutting edge of new technology, with constantly changing clients and issues.

It is also worth noting that my role was quite different in broadcast hearings than it was in telecom or Copyright Board proceedings. In the latter case, I appeared as an advocate and cross-examined witnesses. In broadcast proceedings, however, cross-examination by the parties was generally not permitted and the Commission used a presentational approach, where the commissioners would question the principals, not the lawyers. In that scenario, my role was more like that of a director or scriptwriter. Apart from preparing the written application or intervention, my job was to draft the oral presentation and rehearse the people appearing before the Commission, anticipating any likely questions. I made an extra effort to personalize each presentation so that it would be in the voice of the person making the speech.

In the wake of consolidation, it is clear that I was prescient to become involved in both carriage and content from the beginning of my career. Most lawyers in the communications law field focused only on broadcasting or only on telecommunications. Few of them combined this with an involvement in entertainment law, including copyright law and policy. I was fortunate to be heavily involved in all of these sectors.

My involvement in Canada's cultural industries was also fortuitous. Given my background in music, it is probably not surprising that I enjoyed working with people in the book and magazine publishing industries, the sound recording sector and the film and television production sector. These sectors tend to operate as silos, with relatively little communication among them. But they face similar problems in terms of cultural and trade policy and I have been in a unique position to help them in times of crisis.

CONSOLIDATION

Over the years, the types of matters that require the help of communications lawyers have changed significantly. The days of winning lucrative radio or TV licences in competitive hearings are largely over. There are fewer situations where the regulator can award 'beachfront property', in the form of lucrative pay or specialty television licences. Most of the broadcast licences I helped to win have now gone into the portfolios of four major private players—Bell Media, Shaw Media, Rogers Media and Corus Entertainment. The original owners and entrepreneurs who conceived of and financed those applications have for the most part left the scene.

This doesn't mean that communications law has stalled. If anything, it has become more challenging and complex. With the rise of new media—the Internet and mobile phones—the nature and content of regulation has changed. As a result communications law is far more technical.

The consolidation of the Canadian communications sector is probably the most noticeable phenomenon in the past few years but it is a process that has been going on for decades. Back in the 1950s and 1960s when first and second television services were introduced across Canada, the private TV licences all went to local families resident in each community. For a time, there was a regulatory policy that no person could control more than one station that was a CTV affiliate.

Kapuskasing, my old hometown, for example, was served with a repeater of CFCL-TV, Timmins, which was owned by J. Conrad Lavigne, a suave local entrepreneur raised in Cochrane, Ontario. CFCL-TV was a dual affiliate of CBC's English and French television networks, and Lavigne extended his reach by adding rebroadcast transmitters throughout northeastern Ontario. At one point, he owned the largest private microwave transmission network in the world. Like other local stations across Canada, CFCL-TV had a studio for local news and talent, and I remember appearing on the station in the late 1950s accompanying my vocal group, the Unknowns.

But this was not to last. Gradually, almost all of the families given broadcast licences across Canada sold their stations and ownership consolidated. A few lasted into the second generation (e.g., the Moffats, the Bassetts, the Aspers, the Waters) and even into the third generation (the Craigs), but eventually they all sold out to larger companies seeking to achieve the benefits of size and scope. Conrad Lavigne expanded his reach by launching CBC-affiliated stations in North Bay, Sudbury and Pembroke, to try to offset the competition from CTV service licensed in those markets. But even he could not hold on in the face of the financial pressures. In 1980, he sold his broadcast holdings to Mid-Canada Television, which operated both the CBC and CTV stations in these markets as a twin-stick operation. Baton Broadcasting, the owner of CFTO-TV Toronto, acquired the Mid-Canada operations in 1990. (Later Baton acquired control of the CTV network, until Baton/CTV was purchased by BCE in 2000.) The CBC affiliates in Northern Ontario originally owned by Conrad Lavigne were all sold by CTV to the CBC in 2002.

The same scenario applied to the cable television industry. The original cable licences for each Canadian city were granted to local entrepreneurs. The CRTC encouraged local ownership, thinking this would lead to more responsive community programming as well as ownership diversity. So for a time, during the 1970s and 1980s, there were dozens of local owners of cable systems in markets across Canada.

But again this did not last. Led by the irrepressible Ted Rogers, the cable industry began to consolidate. There was a flurry of acquisitions and by the mid-1990s most of the cable subscribers in Canada were in systems owned by Rogers, Shaw, Videotron or Cogeco. The consolidation of cable was also driven by technology, as cable television systems rebuilt their systems to carry more channels, and then discovered they could also offer retail Internet services over the coaxial cable infrastructure. However, the CRTC still frowned on cross-ownership between cable systems and television programming undertakings. When Rogers acquired Maclean Hunter in 1994, for example, it had to divest CFCN-TV Calgary, a CTV affiliate.

This all changed with the entry of Bell Canada into the broadcasting field in 1995, when it took a minority stake in the ExpressVu satellite operation, which launched its service in 1997. Bell acquired the rest of the ownership of what became Bell ExpressVu (now Bell TV) in 2000. And in the same year, it decided to acquire CTV, propelling it into the ownership of TV stations and specialty services.

The impact of these steps by Bell Canada on the future structure of the broadcasting industry in Canada cannot be overemphasized. Seeing their prime competitor in the BDU business acquire programming services, the cable industry, led by Rogers, sought and obtained a reversal of the CRTC policy keeping cable BDUs and programming services apart.[1] And since then, most of the major TV programming services, other than the CBC, have been acquired by companies operating satellite or cable distribution businesses—Bell, Rogers, Quebecor and Shaw.

Many may decry the increase in consolidation. One of the key regulatory issues is how unaffiliated independently owned programming services will be treated by the large broadcast distribution undertakings, and this issue has been canvassed in a number of CRTC proceedings. In a decision issued in the fall of 2011, the Commission announced a new regulatory framework to deal with vertical integration between programming and distribution services. It indicated that the best way to address this issue was to apply the concept of 'undue preference' within a code of conduct, so that broadcasting distributors would not be permitted to discriminate unfairly against independently owned programmers.[2] Whether this approach will succeed remains to be seen. But note that, in doing so, the CRTC is working with a telecom concept first applied in the Challenge case in 1977.

The increase in consolidation is also dismaying to those who value the innovation that comes from new players. The entrepreneurs who conceived the programming services for whom I helped to win CRTC licences have all sold their assets and left the scene. Will the remaining owners be as exciting and creative? Or will they be more risk-averse, driven by executives who are bottom-line oriented and who value predictability over change?

That said, there are undoubtedly some potential benefits to consolidation. One of the key benefits is that the players are of sufficient size and scope to be able to produce or commission Canadian programming that would otherwise be uneconomic. The two categories that especially need help are costly Canadian drama at a national level and local news in smaller centres.

When Conrad Lavigne owned CFCL-TV, Timmins, he was able to produce a local news program and a local talent hour (that one on which my high school vocal group performed). But he could not afford to commission anything more expensive. Any big-ticket Canadian drama or variety programs came only from his affiliation with the CBC.

And CTV commissioned no regular Canadian television drama before the 1980s.

By 2013, this had all changed. English-language Canadian television drama could now be commissioned by five different national players—CBC, Bell Media, Shaw Media, Rogers Media and Corus Entertainment. The first four had both over-the-air and specialty television platforms across Canada on which to exhibit their programs. As for Corus, in addition to its national specialty services like W Network and YTV, it also operated the regional Movie Central pay service in Western Canada. With Bell Media having acquired the Eastern Canada TMN service from Astral in 2013, Bell could work together with Corus to commission drama for what amounts to a national pay window. And a few other smaller players like TV Ontario were also entering the Canadian drama game, albeit on a more limited basis.

Of course, experience has shown that none of the privately owned players will support Canadian drama or long-form documentary without specific regulatory requirements. These forms of programming are inherently uneconomic for private players in Canada given the availability of popular US entertainment programming at licence fees that are a fraction of the cost of new homegrown productions. But each of the private players named above is now required to expend a percentage of its advertising and subscription revenue on Canadian drama, long-form documentary and selected award shows (collectively called 'programs of national interest' [PNI] by the CRTC). I have recently had occasion to calculate the implications of the PNI policy in English Canada, and it is expected to give rise to drama and documentary television production amounting to $1 billion or more per year.[3]

The move from scheduling rules (so many hours a week of Canadian drama) to expenditure rules (a minimum percentage of advertising and subscription revenue to be spent on Canadian drama) has many advantages. A key benefit is that it gives the licensee complete flexibility in regard to the kind of drama to be financed. The licensee can opt for a larger volume of cheaper drama. Or it can elect to support fewer higher-cost dramas. The licensee can make the quality vs. quantity trade-off, but in the end it must still spend the dollar amount required. The result is that the focus for the licensee will turn away from the accountant's question, 'How can I get away with spending less?' and towards the programmer's question, 'Since I have to spend the money anyway, which

Canadian drama will get me more viewers?' This is a profound change in attitude and I see it as one of the benefits of imposing an expenditure requirement for drama.

As for local newscasts, these may make economic sense in larger urban centres in Canada. But they need financial support to exist in smaller cities, including markets like Timmins, which serves my old hometown of Kapuskasing.

To address this issue, the Commission has specifically required Bell Media and Shaw Media, the two largest private television group owners in English Canada, to maintain local newscasts in their smaller markets, as part of their conditions of licence renewal. For a few years, the Commission also required broadcasting distribution undertakings to contribute to a Local Programming Improvement Fund to support local newscasts by independently owned television broadcasters in even smaller markets. But in July 2012, the CRTC, to the surprise of many, decided to cut back and eventually eliminate that fund by 2014. Six months later, the Supreme Court of Canada ruled that the CRTC lacks the jurisdiction to allow private local television stations to negotiate direct compensation for the retransmission of their signals by cable and satellite companies. The result of these two decisions is that the private television broadcasters in smaller markets will continue to be financially challenged in delivering local programming. Accordingly, one can expect them to seek further relief from the Commission.

THE FUTURE OF CULTURAL POLICY

As a lawyer confronting issues of this kind, I have been struck by a few key points. The first is the importance of maintaining a distinctive Canadian rights marketplace. In the audiovisual space, it is crucial in my view that the CRTC continue to be able to determine which foreign broadcast services a cable or satellite distribution company can carry, how and in which packages they may be carried, and the application of the simultaneous substitution rules to such services. That gives our Canadian broadcasters the ability to use copyright licensing to maintain a Canadian rights marketplace, which is absolutely essential for our broadcasting system to survive and thrive.

In this respect, our interests are entirely congruent with those of Hollywood. In the copyright area, our cultural industries share the same concern over piracy and national boundaries that animate the multinational companies in the business of content creation and distribution.

A second observation I would make derives from a conversation I had with Jim Farley, a highly respected judge in the Ontario commercial court who returned to McCarthy Tétrault upon his retirement from the bench. I noted that some reviewers of my 2004 book had commended me on my nuanced analysis. 'Nuance!' cried Farley. 'I hate nuance! What I want is a bright line!'

Undoubtedly, lawyers find it much easier to practice in an area where there are clear boundaries. But bright lines are quite difficult to achieve in regard to communications and cultural policy. Examples abound. What should be the essential attributes of a 'Canadian' film or TV show? How do you determine when an undertaking is 'controlled' by non-Canadians? When is self-dealing by a distributor 'undue'? All of these questions admit of differing answers depending on the circumstances. And there is room for a healthy difference of opinion as to where the actual line should be drawn.

To me, that is what makes cultural policy interesting.

Having acted for so many players in the Canadian communications field (and often against the same players in subsequent unrelated transactions), I have a healthy cynicism about the commitment of the private sector to Canadian cultural expression. There have been a number of players who have distinguished themselves in this regard but there is also a long history of players who will only support Canadian content to the extent that it is required by regulation, and who will seek to minimize or avoid the rules.

The increase in consolidation has not been a positive development in this regard. As the companies have increased in size, there is a great risk that the innovation and commitment of the original founders and entrepreneurs will be replaced by a focus on short-term bottom-line considerations. In addition, as I have noted elsewhere, with bigger players and larger sums at stake, the role of industry associations in bridging differences between the players diminishes.[4] The positions of the parties become more adversarial. And when a regulator makes decisions that may affect profit levels, there is a greater propensity to challenge these actions in the courts.

All of this makes the role of the government and the communications regulator in supporting diverse Canadian cultural expression ever more important. CRTC members have occasionally seen their role as one of seeking a 'consensus' in the industry or working in 'partnership' with the private sector. That is a misperception. The Commission's proper role is to seek to achieve the objects of the legislation, even if the private players disagree.

GOING DIGITAL

As I reminisce about my checkered career, I often wonder what it would have been like to work as a professional composer and arranger. To this day, I cannot watch a movie or a television show without analyzing the background music. When it comes to Canadian composers, I am a particularly big fan of Howard Shore, the composer for most of David Cronenberg's films and more recently for the Lord of the Rings trilogy. I also enjoy Jim McGrath's work for the Degrassi TV series. I could give many more examples, for Canada has been blessed with some very gifted composers and arrangers over the years.

Of course, the job of composing music for film and television has changed dramatically since I studied arranging in the mid-sixties. Now there are sophisticated software programs like Sibelius and Finale that allow you to compose at the computer, and print out all the individual parts for the orchestra. I would have loved to have had that feature when I was at the Eastman School of Music, where I spent long hours copying out all the parts for my orchestral arrangements since I couldn't afford to hire a copyist.

Now every self-respecting composer must have a digital audio workstation and know how to use it. The Berklee College of Music in Boston offers an online course in film composing, where a prerequisite is 'intermediate/advanced experience with MIDI sequencing and digital audio software for producing and finalizing musical mock ups (MP3) via sample library,' as well as 'the ability to import video (QuickTime) and create an offset start point in your digital audio workstation (DAW application) for scoring purposes.' So times have definitely changed!

The fact that composing and arranging have entered the digital world would be no surprise to anyone working in the cultural industries. Popular culture in all its forms has gone digital.

This has been a mixed blessing. Yes, production costs have been reduced in some areas (think about the demise of the linotype machine). Film and television production has greatly benefited from the advent of editing and budgeting software. The rise of digital aggregators has arguably helped in making less popular titles (the 'long tail') available to consumers. But in the area of distribution, the easy access to content on the Internet has spawned a host of problems for creators that are still being worked out. Since these problems arise at the intersection of communications law with copyright law, I am fascinated with the policy implications.

In *Blockbusters and Trade Wars* I outlined a number of measures that could be said to comprise a 'cultural tool kit' to be used by governments to sustain or develop a broader range of cultural expression. I identified six types of measures in particular: public broadcasting, scheduling requirements on private broadcasters, expenditure requirements on privately owned cultural gatekeepers, national ownership rules, competition policy measures, and subsidies and tax incentives.[5] When properly applied, measures of this kind could be quite effective in maintaining a level of pluralism in cultural expression. However, most of the measures have weaknesses as well as strengths and they need to be carefully drafted and implemented in order to be fair and effective.[6]

With the digitization of media, the fragmentation of audience and the increased availability of cultural products on the Internet, the cultural tool kit needs to be constantly reinvented. In an on-demand world, for example, scheduling requirements become less relevant and greater emphasis needs to be placed on measures such as public broadcasting, expenditure requirements on private sector players, and subsidies.

This is not just a problem for Canada. The globalization of popular culture has given rise to similar issues in other countries. And as new trade treaties are negotiated, the United States is continuing to bring pressure for countries to remove any protection and assistance measures that they may have put in place to increase space and choice for local cultural expression.

As evidenced by the overwhelming support around the world for the UNESCO Convention on Cultural Diversity, many other countries share Canada's concerns in this area. On May 23, 2013, for example, the

European Parliament by a wide margin adopted a resolution 'calling for the exclusion of cultural and audiovisual services, including those provided online' from the ambit of the free trade agreement expected to be negotiated between the European Union and the United States. The European Coalitions for Cultural Diversity welcomed the resolution and issued a press release stating that 'the exclusion of the audiovisual and cultural sectors from the EU-US trade mandate is the one and only way to guarantee that Member States retain their sovereign right to adopt and implement cultural policies, in accordance with the 2005 UNESCO Convention.'

In the past year or so, Canada has embarked on a number of trade negotiations, and I have been happy to assist the Canadian Coalition on Cultural Diversity on a *pro bono* basis in understanding the issues. In the upcoming Comprehensive Economic and Trade Agreement (CETA) with the European Union, the EU has been quite sympathetic to Canada's concerns in this regard and I expect the wording of the treaty, if adopted, will make specific reference to the principles of the UNESCO Convention on Cultural Diversity.

Given its proximity to the United States, Canada has had more direct experience in trade disputes in the cultural area than any other country. So it is not surprising that other countries look to Canada for ideas and inspiration. Given the broad global recognition of the importance of cultural diversity, we have a wonderful opportunity to be a trailblazer. And few things could be more heartening or inspiring.

End Notes

1. KAPUSKASING

1 'He's coming here ... for the sun!' *Toronto Daily Star*, September 1, 1965, p. 1.

2 Gary Lautens, 'Singing the Icicle Blues', *Toronto Daily Star*, September 3, 1965, p. 3.

3 Margaret Grant, *Your Child and the Piano: How to Enrich and Share in Your Child's Musical Experience* (Toronto: Marseg, 1976; released in paperback by Beaufort Books, 1980).

2. UNIVERSITY

1 Harold A. Innis, *The Fur Trade in Canada* (Toronto: University of Toronto Press, 1930).

2 Hap Wilson, *Missinaibi: Journey to the Northern Sky* (Erin: Boston Mills Press, 1994), p. 107.

3 These included *Empire and Communications* (1950; reprinted Toronto: Dundurn, 2007) and *The Bias of Communication* (Toronto: University of Toronto Press, 1951).

4 Robert E. Babe, *Canadian Communications Thought: The Foundational Writers* (Toronto: University of Toronto Press, 2000), p. 56.

5 Later, Dennis Lee wrote the lyrics for a song I wrote for my brother's wedding. It is reproduced in *Acta Victoriana*, vol. 88, no. 1 (1963), pp. 13–15.

6 André Previn, *No Minor Chords: My Days in Hollywood* (New York: Doubleday, 1991), p. 14.

7 Sally Ness, 'A Nite of Inconsistencies', *The Varsity*, November 20, 1963, p. 3.

8 See William Whitworth, 'Profile: On the Tide of the Times', *The New Yorker*, September 24, 1966, p. 67.

9 See, for example, 'King of the World Run Off Campus', *Toronto Daily Star*, October 14, 1961.

10 Warren Mueller became a litigation lawyer at the Toronto firm of Goodman & Carr. Steve Goudge, who had been in the Bob Revue with me at Victoria

College, became a litigation lawyer at the Gowlings firm in Toronto and was appointed to the Ontario Court of Appeal in 1996.

11 See, for example, www.law.indiana.edu/instruction/lrw/common/Ojibway.pdf.

3. BECOMING A COMMUNICATIONS LAWYER

1 Robert Fowler was the president of the Canadian Pulp and Paper Association (later the Forest Products Association of Canada) at the time of his two reports. As such, he may well have met my father, who often attended the annual technical meetings of the association in Montreal.

2 See Peter S. Grant, 'The Regulation of Program Content in Canadian Television: An Introduction', 11 *Canadian Public Administration* 322–391 (Fall 1968).

3 Since then, there have been a number of books published on the early days of telephone regulation. See *Monopoly's Moment: The Organization and Regulation of Canadian Utilities 1830–1930* (1988), by H.V. Nelles and Christopher Armstrong; *Telecommunications in Canada: Technology, Industry and Government* (1990), by Robert E. Babe; and *Telecom Nation: Telecommunications, Computers, and Governments in Canada* (2001), by Laurence B. Mussio. These books were not available when I started my research in the early 1970s.

4 Martin Gardner exposed Uri Geller as a fraud in his book *Science: Good, Bad and Bogus* but declined to disclose how the trick was performed. In reviewing that book, Stephen Jay Gould complained about this: 'Although I don't blame Gardner for obeying the unwritten rules of his magicians' guild, it is frustrating to be told that somebody fooled a bunch of eminent scientists with a simple trick known to all professionals, and to be put off by a gentle reminder that magicians never tell.' Stephen Jay Gould, *An Urchin in the Storm: Essays About Books and Ideas* (New York: W.W. Norton, 1987), p. 214.

5 The fin-syn rules (short for financial/syndication rules) were implemented by the FCC in the early 1970s and required the US broadcasting networks to obtain all their prime-time dramas and sitcoms from independent producers. The rules also prohibited the networks from financing or syndicating those programs to other stations. The rules were rescinded in 1993. For a discussion, see *Blockbusters and Trade Wars*, pp. 276–277.

6 See *Capital Cities Communications Inc. v. CRTC et al*, [1978] 2 S.C.R. 141.

4. WORKING FOR THE CRTC

1 For the text of the decision, see *Bell Canada, Increase in Rates*, Telecom Decision CRTC 77-7, June 1, 1977, 3 C.R.T. 87.

2 For the text of the decision, see *Bell Canada, Tariff for the Use of Support Structures by Cable Television Licensees*, Telecom Decision CRTC 77-5, May 27, 1977, 3 C.R.T. 68.

3 For the text of the CRTC decision, see *Telesat Canada, Proposed Agreement with Trans-Canada Telephone System*, Telecom Decision CRTC 77-10, August 24, 1977, 3 C.R.T. 265.

4 *Telesat Canada, Rates for Space Segment Services and Phase III Costing Manual*, Telecom Decision CRTC 92-17, September 28, 1992.

5 For the CRTC decision, see *Challenge Communications Ltd. v. Bell Canada*, (1977) 3 C.R.T. 489 (Telecom Decision CRTC 77-16, December 3, 1977).

6 See *Re Bell Canada and Challenge Communications Ltd.*, (1978) 86 D.L.R. (3d) 351, [1979] 1 F.C. 857.

7 See *CNCP Telecommunications, Interconnection with Bell Canada*, Telecom Decision CRTC 79-11, May 17, 1979.

8 T. Murray Rankin, *Freedom of Information in Canada: Will the Doors Stay Shut?* A research study prepared for the Canadian Bar Association (Ottawa: Canadian Bar Association, 1977).

5. RETURN TO MCCARTHYS

1 See *Bell Canada—Interim Requirements Regarding the Attachment of Subscriber-Provided Terminal Equipment*, Telecom Decision CRTC 80-13, August 5, 1980, 6 C.R.T. 203.

2 See *Bell Canada, Increase in Rates*, 7 C.R.T. 851 at 860 (Telecom Decision 81-15, September 28, 1981).

3 Richard Posner, 'Natural Monopoly and Its Regulation,' 21 *Stanford Law Review* 548 (1969).

4 See *Interexchange Competition and Related Issues*, Telecom Decision CRTC 85-19, August 29, 1985.

5 See *Competition in the Provision of Public Long Distance Voice Telephone Services and Related Resale and Sharing Issues*, Telecom Decision CRTC 92-12, June 12, 1992.

6 See *B.C. Tel, Increase in Rates*, Telecom Decision CRTC 85-29, December 23, 1985.

7 See *Bell Canada, Review of Revenue Requirements for the Years 1985, 1986 and 1987*, Telecom Decision CRTC 86-17, October 14, 1986.

8 See *Accessibility of Telecommunications and Broadcasting Services*, Broadcasting and Telecom Regulatory Policy CRTC 2009-430, July 21, 2009.

9 See Decision CRTC 90-1060, October 16, 1990.

10 *CRTC v. CTV Television Network*, [1982] 1 S.C.R. 530.

11 *Re Association for Public Broadcasting in British Columbia and CRTC* (1980), 115 D.L.R. (3d) 73, [1981] 1 F.C. 524.

12 See Decision CRTC 82-240, March 18, 1982.

13 Jack Miller, 'First Choice Pleads for "Urgent" Lifeline', *Toronto Daily Star*, November 11, 1983, p. F1.

14 See Decision CRTC 83-959, November 16, 1983.

15 See Decision CRTC 84-654, August 16, 1984.

16 See Decision CRTC 86-812, September 2, 1986.

7. COMMUNICATIONS LAW IN ACTION

1 See *Intercity Broadcasting Network Inc.*, Broadcasting Decision CRTC 2011-369, June 9, 2011.

2 See Decision CRTC 86-768, August 14, 1986.

3 See Decision CRTC 87-343, May 7, 1987.

4 See Decision CRTC 87-905, December 1, 1987 (Family Channel); and Decision CRTC 87-903, December 1, 1987 (YTV).

5 *Black v. Law Society of Alberta*, [1989] 1 S.C.R. 591.

6 Some years later, Gary created the National Songwriting Contest and the Canadian Radio Music Awards. In 2006, he was inducted into the Canadian Music Industry Hall of Fame.

7 Decision CRTC 88-512, August 25, 1988.

8 The following year, in order to remove my legal defence, the Commission amended its standard FM conditions of licence to require substantial compliance by FM stations with *each* of the four requirements. However, in 1997, the Commission dropped the hits requirements entirely for almost all markets.

9 Decision CRTC 94-280, June 6, 1994.

10 Decision CRTC 94-282, June 6, 1994.

11 Decision CRTC 96-599, September 4, 1996.

12 *Distribution of Specialty Services*, Public Notice CRTC 1999-126, August 3, 1999.

13 CSI had been a project green-lit by CBS with the expectation that Disney would handle international distribution and come in for 50 percent of the cost. But as Disney owned a competing network (ABC), it ultimately decided to back out of the deal. To mitigate the inherent risk in all prime-time dramatic series, CBS asked Alliance Atlantis to take up Disney's position at the last minute. Alliance Atlantis did so and ended up becoming a 50 percent owner of one of the most successful television series in history. In mid-2007, the 50 percent interest held by Alliance Atlantis in the CSI franchise (*CSI*, *CSI New York* and *CSI Miami*) was sold to investors for C$900 million.

14 See *A Group-Based Approach to the Licensing of Private Television Services*, Broadcasting Regulatory Policy CRTC 2010-167, March 22, 2010, paragraphs 141–168.

15 *Reference re Broadcasting Regulatory Policy CRTC 2010-167 and Broadcasting Order CRTC 2010-168*, 2012 SCC 68 (CanLII), reversing 2011 FCA 64 (CanLII). The case for striking down the 'value for signal' regime was argued by Neil Finkelstein, Steve Mason and Dan Glover of McCarthy Tétrault, acting for Cogeco Cable. Neil had acted for both Cogeco and Bell Canada at the Federal Court of Appeal but after Bell acquired CTV in 2011, Bell decided to switch sides and support the Commission's jurisdiction.

16 See *The Need for a Regulatory Safety Net: Broadcasting Policy and Canadian Television Drama in English Canada in the Next Five Years*, a report by the Coalition of Canadian Audio-visual Unions, June 13, 2005.

17 For a full analysis, see Peter S. Grant et al, *Cornerstone: An Analysis of the Impact of the CRTC Policy on 'Programs of National Interest' on English-Language Television Production in Canada* (Directors Guild of Canada, June 2013).

18 For a full description of the event, see *Canadian Screenwriter*, vol. 13, no. 3 (Summer 2011), p. 35.

19 See *Reform Party of Canada v. Canada (Attorney General)*, [1995] 4 W.W.R. 609.

20 For the text of my thirty-one-page decision, dated December 31, 1992, see the Elections Canada website at www.elections.ca/abo/bra/all/1992.pdf.

21 See *Libman v. Quebec (Attorney General)*, [1997] 3 S.C.R. 569; and *Harper v. Canada (Attorney General)*, [2004] 1 S.C.R. 827.

22 *Citizens United v. Federal Elections Commission* (2010), 130 S.Ct. 876.

23 Decision CRTC 96-731, November 1, 1996.

24 See *Mackenzie v. Craig*, 1997 CanLII 14875 (AB Q.B.), [1998] 2 W.W.R. 106.

25 Decision CRTC 97-39, January 31, 1997.

26 Decision CRTC 2000-219, July 6, 2000.

27 Decision CRTC 2002-81, April 8, 2002.

28 Decision CRTC 2004-502, November 19, 2004.

29 Decision CRTC 2004-503, November 19, 2004. In 2011, the station morphed into the Sun News channel.

30 Decision CRTC 95-910, December 20, 1995.

8. BRANCHING OUT

1   Decision CRTC 1981-252, April 14, 1981, 7 C.R.T. (Part 1) 20.

2   Decision CRTC 1983-126, March 8, 1983, 8 C.R.T. (Part 1) 749.

3   See *Bell ExpressVu Limited Partnership v. Rex*, [2002] 2 S.C.R.559.

4   *Structural Public Hearing*, Public Notice CRTC 1993–74, June 3, 1993.

5   Joel Bell had served as principal economic adviser to Prime Minister Trudeau and he was a founder of Petro-Canada and the first president and CEO of the Canada Development Investment Corporation. But he was fired from CDIC a month after Brian Mulroney came to power in 1984, later winning a $3.4 million lawsuit for wrongful dismissal. He was famously engaged to classical guitarist Liona Boyd for eight years, although she married John B. Simon in 1992.

6   *Introductory Statement—Licensing of New Direct-to-Home (DTH) Satellite Distribution Undertakings, and New DTH Pay-Per-View (PPV) Television Programming Undertakings*, Public Notice CRTC 1995-217, December 20, 1995.

7   For a recent discussion, see Peter S. Grant et al, 'Enforcement Tools Relating to OTT Services', chapter 10 in *Cornerstone: An Analysis of the Impact of the CRTC Policy on 'Programs of National Interest' on English-Language Television Production in Canada* (Directors Guild of Canada, June 2013).

8   See Miranda Kennedy, 'Husband, by Arrangement', *The Guardian*, March 19, 2011.

9   Broadcasting Public Notice CRTC 2004-50, July 15, 2004.

10 Broadcasting Public Notice CRTC 2004-96, December 16, 2004.

11 Broadcasting Public Notice CRTC 2005-51, May 13, 2005.

12 *Blockbusters and Trade Wars: Popular Culture in a Globalized World* (Vancouver: Douglas & McIntyre, 2004); *Le Marché des étoiles: Culture populaire et mondialisation* (Montreal: Les Éditions du Boréal, 2004).

13 Matthew Fraser, 'An Insider's Guide to Culture Inc.', *National Post*, April 24, 2004.

14 See Peter Grant, 'Is Small Beautiful?' *Literary Review of Canada*, November 2006.

15 A copy of this study, dated December 2008, is available on the IAWG website at

http://iawg.org/iawg/News/Entries/2009/1/1_Drama_Study_files/ Stories%20Under%20Stress.pdf and also at http://www.mccarthy.ca/pubs/IAWG_DRAMA_REPORT_FINAL.pdf.

16 This study, dated February 2009, and co-authored by Peter Grant and Michel Houle, is available on the Telefilm Canada website at http://www.telefilm.ca/document/en/01/17/eng-crtc-houle-grant-final.pdf.

17 Peter S. Grant, 'The UNESCO Convention on Cultural Diversity: Cultural Policy and International Trade in Cultural Products', chapter 21 in *The Handbook of Global Media and Communications Policy* (New York: Blackwell, 2011).

18 Peter S. Grant et al., *Cornerstone: An Analysis of the Impact of the CRTC Policy on 'Programs of National Interest' on English-Language Television Production in Canada* (Directors Guild of Canada, June 2013). The study can be found at http://www.dgc.ca/images/cms/DGC13_PNI_Report_FINAL.pdf.

19 Peter S. Grant, 'Reinventing the Tool Kit: Canadian Content on New Media'. Presentation to the CFTPA 'Prime Time in Ottawa' conference, February 22, 2008. The paper is available on the McCarthy Tétrault website at www.mccarthy.ca/pubs/CFTPA_Reinventing_Tool_Kit.pdf.

20 *Review of Broadcasting in New Media*, Broadcasting Regulatory Policy CRTC 2009-329, June 4, 2009, paragraph 40.

21 *Reference re Broadcasting Act,* 2012 SCC 4, affirming 2010 FCA 178. Tom Heintzman of McCarthy Tétrault, assisted by Bram Abramson, argued the matter on behalf of the Canadian producers and guilds.

9. CHANGING CHANNELS

1 Public Notice CRTC 2001-66-1, August 24, 2001.

2 Broadcasting Regulatory Policy CRTC 2011-601, September 21, 2011.

3 See Peter S. Grant et al, *Cornerstone: An Analysis of the Impact of the CRTC Policy on 'Programs of National Interest' on English-Language Television Production in Canada* (Directors Guild of Canada, June 2013).

4 Peter S. Grant, 'Canadian Communications Law in the 21st Century', in *Communications Law and the Courts in Canada* (Toronto: McCarthy Tétrault, 2010), p. 14.

5 Peter S. Grant and Chris Wood, *Blockbusters and Trade Wars: Popular Culture in a Globalized World* (Vancouver: Douglas & McIntyre, 2004), pp. 168–314.

6 *Ibid.,* p. 316.

Index of Names

Index of Subjects

Acknowledgements

'The Garage Band' © Grace A. Westcott, 2007, reproduced with permission.

All photographs are from Peter S. Grant's private collection.

Certain of the description of the development of the UNESCO Convention is taken from Peter S. Grant, 'The UNESCO Convention on Cultural Diversity: Cultural Policy and International Trade in Cultural Products,' chapter 21 in *The Handbook of Global Media and Communications Policy*, first edition, edited by Robin Mansell and Marc Raboy, © Blackwell Publishing Ltd., 2011; used by permission.

The logos and/or service marks of the broadcast services shown in the frontispiece are included with the permission of the relevant owners or licensees of those services, which is gratefully acknowledged. HISTORY and the 'H' History logo are the registered trademarks of A&E Television Networks, LLC. © 2012 A&E Television Networks, LLC and is used under license. All rights reserved. BBC CANADA is a Shaw Media Network.

The quotation on p. 217 by Miranda Kennedy originally appeared in *The Guardian* on March 19, 2011, and is reprinted with its permission.

Thanks

Given my long career as a Canadian lawyer working in the trenches of cultural and communications policy, I have many people to thank. First and foremost are my colleagues at McCarthy Tétrault, a firm I have been with for some forty-five years. The current managing partner of the firm, Marc-André Blanchard, strongly supported the publication of this memoir. So too have my colleagues at the firm, many of whom figure in some of the stories I tell.

Malcolm Mercer, the general counsel of the firm, reviewed an earlier version of the manuscript, and I also provided copies of relevant excerpts to my clients or former clients, all of whom consented to the disclosure of the portions of the narrative relating to my work for them. These included Mirko Bibic, Carol Cooper, Drew Craig, Stephen Ellis, Ian Greenberg, Sturla Gunnarson, Gary Kain, Robert Lantos, Michael MacMillan, Marc Mayrand, Duncan McEwen, Maureen Parker, Gary Slaight, Konrad von Finckenstein, Bob Wood, Carolyn Wood and Phyllis Yaffe.

As this narrative indicates, I ended up acting for many of the key players in Canada's cultural industries and they included some very creative people. I owe a debt of gratitude to all of them for their ideas, their support and their friendship.

In telling stories about my career, there is a risk that there may be too much inside baseball for a general reader. However, I am hopeful that the stories may provide some insight into the evolution of Canada's cultural industries and the policies that sustain them.

To my publishers, Tim and Elke Inkster, and my editor, Chandra Wohleber, a special thanks for bearing with me through the process of writing and research.

Finally, I want to thank Grace and my four children. They have provided constant encouragement and support and this book is dedicated to them.